ENGAGING DIALOGUE

Traditions in American Cinema
Series Editors Linda Badley and R. Barton Palmer

Titles in the series include:

The 'War on Terror' and American Film: 9/11 Frames Per Second
Terence McSweeney

American Postfeminist Cinema: Women, Romance and Contemporary Culture
Michele Schreiber

Film Noir
Homer B. Pettey and R. Barton Palmer (eds)

In Secrecy's Shadow: The OSS and CIA in Hollywood Cinema 1941–1979
Simon Willmetts

Indie Reframed: Women's Filmmaking and Contemporary American Independent Cinema
Linda Badley, Claire Perkins and Michele Schreiber (eds)

Vampires, Race and Transnational Hollywoods
Dale Hudson

Who's in the Money? The Great Depression Musicals and Hollywood's New Deal
Harvey G. Cohen

Engaging Dialogue: Cinematic Verbalism in American Independent Cinema
Jennifer O'Meara

edinburghuniversitypress.com/series/tiac

ENGAGING DIALOGUE
Cinematic Verbalism in American Independent Cinema

Jennifer O'Meara

EDINBURGH
University Press

Edinburgh University Press is one of the leading university presses in the UK. We publish academic books and journals in our selected subject areas across the humanities and social sciences, combining cutting-edge scholarship with high editorial and production values to produce academic works of lasting importance. For more information visit our website: edinburghuniversitypress.com

Edinburgh University Press Ltd
The Tun – Holyrood Road
12 (2f) Jackson's Entry
Edinburgh EH8 8PJ

First published in hardback by Edinburgh University Press 2018

Typeset in 10/12.5pt Sabon by
Servis Filmsetting Ltd, Stockport, Cheshire,
and printed and bound by CPI Group (UK) Ltd, Croydon, CR0 4YY

A CIP record for this book is available from the British Library

ISBN 978 1 4744 2062 4 (hardback)
ISBN 978 1 4744 3176 7 (paperback)
ISBN 978 1 4744 2063 1 (webready PDF)
ISBN 978 1 4744 2064 8 (epub)

CONTENTS

FIGURES

ACKNOWLEDGEMENTS

First, I would like to thank Edinburgh University Press for enthusiastically supporting this project – particularly Gillian Leslie, for her expertise and making the process flow so smoothly. Thank you to the series editors, R. Barton Palmer and Linda Badley, for their helpful input on the manuscript, as well as to the anonymous reviewers whose feedback and encouragement were much appreciated. Many thanks also to Soda Pictures for granting the permission to use an image from Jim Jarmusch's *Night on Earth* on the cover.

This book builds on my doctoral research at Trinity College Dublin from 2011 to 2014, and so I extend my gratitude to the university for funding my PhD with an Ussher Fellowship. The first two years of my research were also supported by a Non-Foundation Scholarship. Within the Department of Film Studies, I am particularly grateful for Paula Quigley's thorough supervision, as well as for the input of my external examiner, Donna Peberdy. At Trinity, my research also benefited from sharing ideas (and lots of caffeine) with Ciara Barrett, Jennie Rothwell and Heather Browning.

The concepts in this book developed in tandem with presenting research at a variety of conferences. Thank you to the organisers of the European Network for Cinema and Media Studies (NECS) (Università Cattolica del Sacro Cuore, 2014); the British Association of Film, Television and Screen Studies (BAFTSS) (Birkbeck, University of London, 2014); Cinematic Reflections on Stardom and the 'Stardom Film' (King's College London, 2013); Revisiting Star Studies (Newcastle University, 2013); Cinesonika 3 (University of Ulster, 2013); Marginalised Mainstream: Fading and Emerging (University of London,

2013); Contemporary Gendered Performance & Practice (Queen's University Belfast, 2013); Language/Cinema (University of Leeds, 2012), and Genres in Transit (Trinity College Dublin, 2012). Equally, I am grateful to the various journals and book editors who published aspects of my research related to dialogue in American independent cinema as it emerged – meaning that in most cases I have not needed to repeat such analysis here. Some parts of Chapter 3 were previously published, however, in *Verse, Voice, and Vision: Poetry and the Cinema* (ed. Santos 2013), *The Films of Wes Anderson: Critical Essays on an Indiewood Icon* (ed. Kunze 2014), and *The New Soundtrack* (5.2 2015).

Since 2015, I'm fortunate to have had the opportunity to teach or present material related to this book while working at the University of St Andrews; the National University of Ireland, Maynooth, County Kildare, Ireland; and the National University of Ireland Galway. I'm grateful for the support of my colleagues at each of these institutions, particularly to Maria Pramaggiore, Katie Stone and Lucy Fife Donaldson for graciously providing advice on any numbers of issues.

Lastly, I must thank my friends and family, especially Shane and Catriona, as well as Liz in Los Angeles, whose proximity to the film industry has long evoked envy in my celluloid consciousness (and well before I learned to throw such terms about). Most importantly, thank you to my parents, Ann and Tom, for supporting me in every path I choose to take: academic, geographic and other.

INTRODUCTION

This book examines the centrality of dialogue to American independent cinema, arguing that it is impossible to separate small budgets from the old adage that 'talk is cheap'. Yet, as the creativity of the resulting indie dialogue reveals, this is no bad thing. With a focus on the verbally creative works of Wes Anderson, Noah Baumbach, Hal Hartley, Jim Jarmusch, Richard Linklater and Whit Stillman, the book aims to demonstrate the ability of dialogue to engage audiences and bind together the narrative, aesthetic and performative elements of selected independent cinema, from the 1980s until the present day.

While it may come as a surprise to anyone who has ever quoted a favourite line of film dialogue, cinema is still considered a visual rather than a verbal medium. But what makes certain dialogue pleasurable for an audience, and should we only praise speech that is easily extracted and repeated? Furthermore, do certain filmmakers have an identifiable verbal rather than visual style? By examining the design and execution of dialogue from multiple perspectives (sound and image, characterisation, performance, gender, adaptation and authorship), I develop an integrated framework for understanding how dialogue functions, at the level of an individual or group of filmmaker(s). When compared to the dialogue norms of more mainstream cinema, the verbal styles of these independent writer-directors are found to be marked by alternations between various extremes, particularly those of naturalism and hyper-stylisation, and between the poles of efficiency and excess. More broadly, these writer-directors are used as case studies that allow for an understanding of how dialogue functions in verbally experimental cinema, which, this book contends, is more often found in 'independent' or 'art' cinema. A reception-focused approach is taken to the design and execution of their dialogue, in order to analyse how they craft speech that engages audiences in rewarding ways.

In order to capture the centrality of dialogue to the work of these writer-directors, I coin the term *cinematic verbalism*, and the related label of *cinematic verbalists*, to refer to their work. The label takes as its basis the standard definition of a 'verbalist' as someone who is skilled with words, but, since it is partly the ways that dialogue is embodied and integrated that gives their speech a medium-specific quality, the 'cinematic' component is crucial. The term thus captures the six filmmakers' shared interest in verbal style, but it will also allow for attention to be paid to how these words are rehearsed, performed, filmed and treated in post-production.

It is difficult to pinpoint precisely what constitutes a 'literary' as opposed to a 'cinematic' film, with C. Paul Sellors (2010: 19) noting that '[a]lthough treated as a property of a film, the term "cinematic" is really a term of critical appreciation'. Generally, 'literary' cinema is considered to be that in which meaning is communicated predominantly through words, while 'cinematic' productions instead require the images and their order to bear most of the narrative weight. By focusing on how dialogue in this independent cinema is designed and executed, we will question the association of dialogue-centred films with the 'literary' or 'un-cinematic'. In contrast to the oppositional relationship between the terms 'cinematic' and 'literary', the concept of cinematic verbalism thus aims to raise awareness of (and appreciation for) dialogue that channels both media. As such, the term 'cinematic verbalism' can also be used to describe other dialogue that is incorporated in such a way that the speech gains impact through the specifics of the medium.

The intention of this book is not to argue that dialogue is used uniformly across the six filmmakers' work, or even within their individual bodies of work, but that each of them uses dialogue to enhance their auteurial signature and as a fulcrum on which the other elements of their films turn. Considerable overlaps in the forms and functions of their speech do, however, allow for a broader, synthesised analysis. For instance, their dialogue often substitutes for action due to a narrative focus on communication problems. That is, their cinema not only includes creative dialogue techniques, but the narratives are often *about* verbal miscommunication. Given the collective size of the cinematic verbalists' body of work, and in order not to overshadow Stillman's more limited output, this book focus on a selection of their films that exemplify their approach to dialogue more generally. The films covered span just over three decades from Jarmusch's *Stranger Than Paradise* (1984) to more recent releases, such as Baumbach's *Frances Ha* (2012) and Stillman's fifth film, *Love & Friendship* (2016).

One explanation for why these six writer-directors share a creative approach to dialogue is that they also share a background in literary pursuits. Prior to their debut features – with release dates spanning from Jarmusch in 1980 to Anderson in 1996 – Baumbach, Jarmusch, Linklater and Stillman all majored in English Literature at university, while Anderson wrote plays that were performed at The University of Texas at Austin where he studied Philosophy. Only Jarmusch and Hartley enrolled in film school, with Jarmusch attending New York University as a post-grad and Hartley attending State University of New York at Purchase (where he studied Literature as well as Filmmaking). Jarmusch initially pursued a career in poetry, while Baumbach and Stillman worked on prose and journalism, respectively. As a result, many of their initial creative experiences were related to writing. Excluding Hartley and Jarmusch, this group likely had less technical skills than other first-time directors emerging in the same period since, by 1992, 72 per cent of first-time directors were graduates of film schools (Levy 1999: 34). Indeed, by way of explaining the small number of all film-school students who go on to direct a feature film, Emanuel Levy argues that agents are as keen to see finished scripts as student films (37). So, although Levy explains that most aspiring directors end up working as producers or executives (36), the emphasis on scripts as a differentiation device partly explains how Anderson, Baumbach, Linklater and Stillman could establish careers despite being in the minority of directors emerging in the 1990s with no production training.

For the most part, the filmmakers are geographically based and produce films outside of Hollywood and the studio system. Anderson and Linklater have worked from their home state of Texas, with Baumbach, Hartley, Jarmusch and Stillman generally based in New York.[1] Between them, they have directed approximately seventy-five feature-length productions, with an additional thirty short films. Although not necessarily the sole writer on every film, they have roughly eighty writing credits in total (including some collaborations between Anderson and Baumbach), making it reasonable to categorise them as writer-directors.[2] In contrast to screenplays drafted and rewritten by multiple writers (often before a director is even attached to the project), reports also suggest that the six exercise a rare control over all stages of the process, from casting to sound design, post-production and marketing. This makes it easier to discuss how their dialogue reflects a personal 'vision' – much more so than would be the case with a director realising a screenplay that they did not write. Equally, it would be remiss to give a screenwriter (who does not direct) credit for dialogue that gains its impact due to choices made at the production and post-production stages. As will be demonstrated in the chapters to follow, the cinematic verbalists' control over each stage of the dialogue process is central to its overall effect.

Existing literature on the six filmmakers grants their dialogue a certain amount of attention. In *Cinema of Outsiders: The Rise of American Independent Film*, Levy describes Stillman's 'relentless verbal characters' and the 'unnatural cadence' of their speech (1999: 198), while J. J. Murphy's (2007) study of independent screenplays identifies how Hartley's stylised, musical and colloquial speech avoids naturalistic conventions and 'emphasize[s] verbal dialogue over narrative action' (89; 103). Murphy further indicates the value of a more thorough consideration of Hartley's verbal style when he notes that the filmmaker 'enjoys playing with language' (103). Writing on Anderson, Cynthia Felando comments on Anderson's 'carefully crafted dialogue', and notes that he gives 'delectable lines' to major and minor characters (2012: 72). The distinctiveness of Baumbach's dialogue is instead implied by The Criterion Collection edition of his debut, *Kicking and Screaming* (1995), since the DVD cover eschews an image to instead market the film using a series of printed quotations.

Aside from their literary backgrounds, the work of the six writer-directors bears the influence of both 'New Hollywood' (especially the dialogue of Woody Allen, Robert Altman and John Cassavetes) and European 'art' cinema, particularly the French New Wave. Michel Marie summarises the importance of dialogue to filmmakers of the *Nouvelle Vague* period:

> Three decades after the coming of sound, [the French New Wave] allowed directors to exploit all the possibilities in the soundtrack, and especially speech. It offered a cinema that was not ashamed to speak, helping dismiss the out-of-date myth, imposed by theorists in the 1920s, that located the primacy of the cinema in the image. (Marie 2003: 80)

In tracing the influence of the *Nouvelle Vague* on the cinematic verbalists, I predominantly make comparisons between the six writer-directors and their clearest inspirations (Jean-Luc Godard, Louis Malle, Éric Rohmer and François Truffaut),[3] while identifying differences in the way that dialogue functions for the two groups. The full range of verbal influences is hard to pinpoint, particularly since one period's dialogue conventions can subtly influence those of the next. Because although a line can be traced between verbally experimental 'Hollywood Renaissance' figures such as Altman and Allen and American independent cinema at the end of the twentieth century, the former were partly inspired by European auteurs of the 1950s and 1960s, who were, in turn, influenced by classical Hollywood. Indeed, Christopher Beach rather accurately positions Stillman's comedies of manners as successors to those by Woody Allen *and* Ernst Lubitsch (2002: 196). The cinematic verbalists' work can also be considered as part of the trend in low-budget, dialogue-driven films, which took off after the success of films like *My Dinner with André* (Malle 1981) and later *sex, lies and videotape* (Soderbergh 1989). But their dialogue has equally been influential, and its impact can be seen (and heard) in more recent indie cinema, particularly the so-called 'Mumblecore' films of the 2000s that are notably marked by wordy and often inarticulate speech.

This book contributes to the small but growing body of literature that focuses unapologetically on cinema's verbal properties. Historically, when dialogue is singled out for attention in film studies the same few examples tend to be repeated: the speed of the exchanges in *His Girl Friday* (Hawks 1940),[4] the centrality of 'Rosebud' to *Citizen Kane* (Welles 1941)[5] and the misheard line of dialogue that forces a reassessment of the narrative in *The Conversation* (Coppola 1974).[6] Alternatively, references to dialogue are made in passing. Dialogue is often paraphrased in summaries of plot or character, disregarding the narrative or aesthetic significance of the wording or delivery. When lines are quoted, they tend to be incorporated as though independent components of a scene or character, thus 'freeing' the critic to focus on other elements of cinema deemed more creative or meaningful. It was not until Sarah Kozloff's *Overhearing Film Dialogue* (2000) that a more concerted effort was made to theorise dialogue's many forms and functions. Kozloff divides her study into theory determining dialogue's various functions (including the anchorage of characters and the diegesis, the communication of narrative causality and adherence to the code of realism)[7] and an application of these functions to various genres (Westerns, screwball comedies, melodrama and the gangster film). Her approach is illuminating and allows certain common dialogue impressions to be substantiated and others disproved. When applied to Hollywood cinema, Kozloff's argument that genre is the most powerful force shaping dialogue is convincing. Yet her argument fits poorly with much of the dialogue in non-mainstream, including that of the cinematic verbalists. In fact, Kozloff notes that dialogue in low-budget independent cinema is the 'most adventuresome', and she rightly identifies the financial impetus for such speech:[8]

> Partly this stems from independent filmmakers' genuine desire to break new ground, but novel approaches to dialogue have also moved to the fore because they are cheaper and more easily accomplished than extensive special effects or lush production value. (Kozloff 2000: 24)

By exploring these novel approaches, this book extends on this point and the historical connections between adventurous dialogue and 'independent' and 'art' cinema will be considered in more detail in Chapter 1.

Since the publication of Kozloff's monograph, dialogue research has predominantly moved towards studies of the verbal style of individual filmmakers. Preceding Kozloff's study by a year was Todd Berliner's (1999) analysis of the experimental verbal style of John Cassavetes. Although Berliner is the only other scholar to isolate mainstream dialogue norms (which he identifies in order to demonstrate how Cassavetes subverts them),[9] Paul Coughlin (2005) subsequently considered the 'language aesthetics' of Joel and Ethan Coen, while studies of writer-directors from the classical Hollywood period have also emerged. Joe McElhaney (2006) situates Preston Sturges's speedy speech in terms of modernity and François Thomas demonstrates overlapping speech to be an Orson Welles' trademark (2013). In a study that aligns somewhat unexpectedly with some of the findings in this study, Brian Wilson (2013) identifies Howard Hawks's use of both naturalistic and highly stylised speech. Also connecting the verbal style of classical Hollywood to that of contemporary indie cinema is Jeff Jaeckle's (2013a) comparison of the dialogue of Wes Anderson to that of Sturges. Jaeckle serves as editor of *Film Dialogue* (2013b), the first collection of essays on the subject, one that is grouped into sections on genre, cultural representation and auteur studies – including those by Thomas and Wilson. The collection expands on Kozloff's genre approach and further establishes the trend for the verbal style of individual filmmakers to be analysed.[10]

Despite this small trend – since 1999 – for analysing the dialogue of specific writer-directors, to date no attempts have been made to compare or unite a group of filmmakers on the basis of verbal style. Berliner (2010) comes closest in *Hollywood Incoherent: Narration in Seventies Cinema*, when he provides a brief analysis of the dialogue of Robert Altman, Martin Scorsese and Woody Allen, as part of his broader consideration of 1970s narrative conventions. One may question the suitability of auteur studies of any kind, let alone those focused on verbal style, and on this matter I side with Adrian Martin (2004: 95–9) who explains that 'the author question' posed in 1960s film studies is no longer relevant, given that audiences are trained to be 'auteurists' by a contemporary culture that classifies, markets and analyses films based on the director's name. In other words, regardless of whether auteur theory was initially warranted in a medium as collaborative as cinema, *audiences* have come to receive films from such a perspective. Timothy Corrigan (1990) and Catherine Grant (2000) have similarly highlighted how filmmakers themselves can internalise auteurial approaches to such an extent that they design, produce and market films (and their own personae) to encourage audiences to receive their body of work as cohesive. As will become clear in later chapters, dialogue design and execution can be a key way in which a writer-director can increase the sense of cohesion across their work, particularly when working independently and with a small budget. In certain ways, identifying personal approaches to verbal style fits well with existing conceptions of auteurism as based partly on a distinctive aesthetic style. Like with previous labels such as *Nouvelle Vague* or the 'Hollywood Renaissance', I argue that Wes Anderson, Noah Baumbach, Hal Hartley, Jim Jarmusch, Richard Linklater and Whit Stillman can be grouped together on the basis of their experimentation with conventions – verbally driven conventions.

Dialogue Integration and an Integrated Book Structure

Kozloff dedicates a chapter of *Overhearing Film Dialogue* to the integration of dialogue through performance, shot content and scale, editing, and sound design. Her insights are rich and motivated by the rightful claim that 'words in a script become transfigured when they are spoken by an actor, filmed by the camera, edited together, underscored with music' (2000: 90). But she concludes that the range of dialogue integration in cinema is so complex that her attempt to demonstrate its importance is 'woefully inadequate' (122).[11] This book considers an integrative approach to dialogue fundamental to a proper understanding of verbal style in cinema, particularly in the work of the filmmakers under discussion, and so it is structured accordingly.

Chapter 1 considers the long-standing relationship between audiences and dialogue, particularly those of non-mainstream cinema, in order to determine a reception-based methodology for examining engaging dialogue. The next two chapters address dialogue's relationship with the formal style, in terms of how it is integrated with the image and soundtracks. Chapter 2 examines whether the filmmakers blend visual and verbal styles in complementary or jarring ways, and thus identifies the creative possibilities available to writer-directors who have control over both the words and the images. For example, we will compare the foregrounding of words in the mise en scène to their use of spoken words. The chapter also examines how their use of voice-over aligns with and departs from those in more mainstream cinema.

In Chapter 3, dialogue is considered from the perspective of the integrated soundtrack, particularly how music and sound effects are arranged to impact our perception of speech. Instead of assuming that verbally rich films automatically downgrade sound effects and music by foregrounding speech, the analysis explores how their dialogue works with (rather than against) these other elements of the sound mix. Attention will be paid to their use of foreign accents and non-English language, as well as to the rhythmic qualities of their dialogue. It is argued that through the use of verbal techniques that rely on the musicality of dialogue, American independent cinema draws audiences' attention to the artificial nature of scripted speech, as well as to speech's aesthetic qualities. This chapter is partially based on material published previously in *Verse, Voice, and Vision: Poetry and the Cinema* (ed. Santos 2013), *The Films of Wes Anderson: Critical Essays on an Indiewood Icon* (ed. Kunze 2014), and *The New Soundtrack* (5.2 2015).[12]

Moving from the stylistic to the narrative functions of dialogue, Chapter 4 consider how audiences' understanding of characterisation is entwined with their speech. Typically, the cinematic verbalists' films are constructed around character rather than plot, with my analysis considering how dialogue that is scripted to reveal nuances of personality can contribute to the impression that certain characters are more complex and 'realistic' than others. Here we will consider how independent film dialogue can serve as action through the development of verbal 'games', as well as how speech can create the illusion of a character having a life beyond the diegesis.

Chapter 5 outlines the impact of performance on the cinematic verbalists' dialogue, including their habits in terms of casting, rehearsing and filming, as well as evident preferences for a certain delivery style. Drawing on performance literature, particularly the growing body of work on the voice in cinema, we will consider the physical, verbal and vocal skills required to effectively perform this kind of speech, including the physical shaping of words through gesticulation. It is argued that their dialogue is often embodied in ways that suggest spontaneity and create the impression that characters are thinking 'out loud'.

Building on the two preceding chapters, Chapter 6 examines the relationship that this independent cinema presents between dialogue and gender. The analysis reveals how, in something of departure from Hollywood conventions, women in their films displays characteristics like profanity and aggression typically associated with male dialogue, while men voice their deepest feelings, thus verbally aligning themselves with alternate forms of masculinity.

In light of findings from Chapters 2 through 6, Chapter 7 contends that although the cinematic verbalists have strong literary influences, they channel these in complex and 'cinematic' ways. By considering the relative lack of analysis of dialogue in adaptation studies, and the applicability of the literary concept of 'double voicing' to the six writer-directors' verbal auteurial style, the chapter demonstrates a more nuanced dynamic between film dialogue and its tendency to be described as a 'literary' device.

Although each chapter has a distinct focus, some flexibility is maintained across categories in order to highlight dialogue's role as a binding device. Furthermore, since each of these sections deals with dialogue in tandem with another area of film studies, a certain amount of sub-field specific literature will be introduced with each chapter. Indeed, since discussion of film dialogue is often 'submerged' in literature on a broad range of subjects, references to dialogue are unearthed from a wide range of sources.

Unless indicated otherwise, all dialogue quotations are transcribed from the finished films. Although I limit my focus on cinematic verbalism in American independent cinema to six filmmakers, I contend that *elements* of their dialogue style also apply to various other non-mainstream writer-directors, such as Harmony Korine, David Lynch and Terrence Malick. For the most part, discussion of overlaps between the cinematic verbalists' dialogue style and that of other writer-directors is limited to the conclusion, where the broader implications of this research are discussed.

Notes

1. There are certain exceptions, particularly in relation to funding: many of Hartley's and Jarmusch's films have received European and/or Japanese funding, with some of these partly filmed outside the United States. Stillman's most recent film, *Love & Friendship*, was also notably transnational; it was filmed in Ireland, and it received funding from Irish, French and Dutch production companies.
2. Anderson has co-written nearly all of his features (either with Noah Baumbach, Roman Coppola, Owen Wilson or Jason Schwartzman), while Linklater has served as a 'director for hire' on several films he has not written, including *School of Rock* (2003) and *Bad News Bears* (2005).
3. The cinematic verbalists are regularly compared to individual *Nouvelle Vague* film-makers. For example, Derek Hill (2008: 40) refers to Linklater as 'the cautiously optimistic Truffaut from Austin', while Peter de Jonge (1996) entitles his *The New York Times Magazine* article on Hartley 'The Jean-Luc Godard of Long Island'.
4. See Elsaesser (1985: 178), Kael (1993: 335) and Bordwell and Thompson (1997: 384).
5. See Russell (1995: 28), Carringer (1996: 19) and Carroll (1998: 153–5).
6. See Wood (1986: 36), Silverman (1988: 90), Sonnenschein (2001: 135) and Keogh (2008: 65).
7. Kozloff (2000: 33–63) divides the functions into either those that communicate the narrative (including those cited above), and dialogue that is used for 'aesthetic effect, ideological persuasion and commercial appeal'.
8. Geoff King (2005), whose writing on American independent cinema will be considered further at later points in the book, also notes that 'dialogue and character-centred films' tend to be cheaper to produce (103).
9. Berliner (1999: 4–5) makes the following five claims (verbatim), which will be referenced at various points throughout this book: 1. Dialogue in American movies either advances the plot or supplies pertinent background information; 2. American movie dialogue tends to move in a direct line, often towards one character's triumph and another's defeat; 3. Characters in Hollywood movies communicate effectively through dialogue; 4. Whereas most real people adjust what they are saying as they speak, movie characters tend to speak flawlessly; 5. When a film breaks one of movie dialogue's rules, the transgression normally serves a direct narrative function.
10. By providing 'a brief primer on film dialogue' Jaeckle (2013b) builds on Kozloff's study, but he aims to provide a more methodological approach to dialogue analysis than Kozloff by outlining a four-step method: (1) Quote film dialogue; (2) Verify the accuracy of film dialogue quotations; (3) Analyse the aural and verbal components of the dialogue; (4) Analyse the literal and figurative components of film dialogue (3–11). Although this book indirectly incorporates each of Jaeckle's steps, my focus on dialogue *integration* and the evolution of the cinematic verbalists' dialogue necessarily differs from Jaeckle's model. For example, while he considers dialogue quotations as an alternative to screen shots (3), I incorporate film stills when arguing that the cinematic verbalists' dialogue is embodied and combined with images in significant ways.
11. Jill Nelmes (2011: 225) also identifies dialogue's ability to 'integrate the aural with the visuals, suturing the story so that the audience is drawn into the film world rather than acting as observers'.
12. The full publication details are as follows: O'Meara, J. (2013), 'Poetic Dialogue: Lyrical Speech in the Work of Hal Hartley and Jim Jarmusch', in M. Santos (ed.) *Verse, Voice and Vision: Poetry and the Cinema*, Lanham: Scarecrow Press,

pp. 165–78; O'Meara, J. (2014a), 'A Shared Approach to Familial Dysfunction and Sound Design: Wes Anderson's Influence on the Films of Noah Baumbach', in P. C. Kunze (ed.) *The Films of Wes Anderson: Critical Essays on an Indiewood Icon*, New York: Palgrave Macmillan, pp. 109–24; O'Meara, J. (2015), 'Character as DJ: Melomania and Diegetically Controlled Music', *The New Soundtrack*, Vol. 5, No. 2, pp. 133–51.

1. MEASURING ENGAGING DIALOGUE

During cinema's initial conversion to sound recording, dialogue was criticised by many film theorists, filmmakers and actors – and yet audiences immediately embraced and demanded 'talkies' to such an extent that they soon supplanted 'silent' films. Although focused on contemporary independent cinema rather than early 'talkies', this study aims to highlight how dialogue can subtly guide audiences towards certain meanings, and the potential of dialogue to increase or decrease the redundancy of textual cues. In doing so, it builds on Kozloff's argument that filmmakers and audiences instinctively 'internalise' certain patterns of speech as the most appropriate (2000: 137), as well as her point that dialogue can be used to guide their responses (49–50). While Kozloff argues that generic speech conventions were established early in the sound era, in this book we consider how – and gauge why – American independent filmmakers manipulate such internalised conventions. This chapter provides an overview of the methodological framework for doing so, including the rationale for studying the significance of dialogue to low-budget cinema more generally. Since the research is partly motivated by a long-standing bias against film dialogue, it is worth reflecting on that context.

From 'Talking Films' to Talking Back to Films

The precarious status that dialogue will hold in film studies, and the film industry, is signalled by Rudolph Arnheim's scathing review of 'talking films' from 1932:

> Not only does speech limit the motion picture to an art of dramatic por-
> traiture, it also interferes with the expression of the image. The better the
> silent film, the more strictly it used to avoid showing people in the act of
> talking. (Arnheim 1967 [1932]: 234)

Here, Arnheim reveals a contempt for speech that was shared by many when
silent cinema transitioned into sound. This contempt was due to restrictions
placed on creative editing styles and the replacement of celebrated silent actors
by those with voices considered more appealing.[1] The main argument levelled
against sound was that it could only ever be of marginal importance since
cinema had existed without it (cf. Altman 1992: 35–46). From the narrower
perspective of speech, such judgements failed to take into account how crucial
dialogue (in the form of intertitles) was to many silent films. As Pauline Kael
(1971: 247) notes, silent films were 'trying to talk to us, crying out for sound',
with action 'choked' by the frequency of explanatory and dialogue titles.
Technological issues also contributed to the contempt for speech, since cumbersome sound-recording equipment restricted actors' movement, as well as
limiting freedom with regard to editing and shot framing. However, with the
introduction of smaller, lighter microphones and mobile mikes by the mid-
1930s, mobility problems were solved (Williams 1980: 53–4). Other technological improvements quickly followed and, by 1935 – just eight years after
the first talkie – 'looping' allowed actors to re-record problematic vocals in
post-production (Bordwell 1985: 300–1).

More enduring than the technical limitations of sound recording was the
view that dialogue was an unnecessary addition to the supposedly *visual*
medium of cinema. The fear that speech would redundantly echo things
already made clear by the images was transnational and particularly strong
in Europe and the Soviet Union. In 1928, V. I. Pudovkin, S. M. Eisenstein
and G. V. Alexandrov wrote a collective statement on sound that suggested
that they were not averse to it per se, provided it was used in counterpoint to
the images. Contrapuntal sound would 'not confine it to a national market,
as must happen with the photographing of plays' (cited in Belton and Weis
1985: 85). In Hollywood, on the other hand, despite several sceptical industrial players, dialogue and sound were quickly embraced by US audiences
and drew record numbers to the cinema.[2] So although Russian filmmakers
experimented with sound but not dialogue, by the time the first Soviet talkie
was released in 1931 the assumption that 'photographed plays' would be
limited to national markets was disproved. Hollywood film exports reached
a record high since international audiences and distributors had embraced
subtitles and dubbing (Segrave 1997: 79). And so, despite enduring critical
opposition to dialogue, including from certain filmmakers,[3] 'talkies' gradually
spread to productions in Europe, and later to Russia, Japan and the rest of the

world: national film industries were unwilling to allow Hollywood imports to dominate.

Writing on dialogue diminished, however, as though critics were unwilling to reconsider its creative functions or admit that they had been wrong about the extent of its impact. Some seventy years after Arnheim's critique, Noël Carroll's (2008) defence of 'verbal texture' reveals the persistent nature of such criticism. Carroll explains how 'it is a mistake to think that elaborate verbal textures have no place in cinema. For, at the very least, the juxtaposition of complex verbiage with imagery can be immensely stimulating' (48). In the lengthy period between Arnheim's critique and Carroll's defence, appraisals of dialogue were uncommon. In 1960, the influential German theorist Siegfried Kracauer reassessed dialogue's role in *Theory of the Film* (1997 [1960]). Since it was still rare for film speech to be discussed, Kracauer's accounts proved influential, with many of his prescriptions still listed in criticism and advice manuals. Like contemporary screenwriting manuals that assert that dialogue should never be obscure or intellectual,[4] Kracauer describes dialogue that introduces discursive reasoning or sophisticated thoughts as 'extremely dangerous' (104). Kracauer's reflections are better informed and less one-sided than much of the writing in the 1920s and 1930s,[5] but he still insists that the communication of meaning in sound films 'must originate with their pictures' (103).

The rise of auteur theory in the 1950s is another factor contributing to the continual disregard for dialogue. When auteur theory spread from the French *Cahiers du Cinéma* writers to the United States, the raised profile of the director came not just at the expense of the screenwriter, but at the expense of his or her dialogue. This point obviously does not hold for writer-directors, although in such cases critical discussion tends to be on writer-director's direction rather than their writing. While critics like Jonas Mekas (1959), Pauline Kael (1971), William Goldman (1983) and Richard Corliss (1973, 1974) struggled to remind people of the screenwriter's role and impact on the final film, by the late 1960s Andrew Sarris's *The American Cinema: Directors and Directions* (1968) had placed the director at the centre of the creative process – a position still held today. So although Corliss notes that a director can do one of three things to the screenplay, 'ruin it, shoot it, or improve it' (1973: 142), the director is generally praised on the assumption that the screenplay, which few have read, has been improved upon.

As a result, television has become regarded more as a writer's medium and, in its struggle to gain cultural prestige, television critics and scholars often highlight the role of the writer(s). For example, when Julian Fellowes's scripts for *Downton Abbey* (ITV, 2010–15) were published in 2012 and 2013, the television drama further aligned itself with the prestige of dramatic plays. In fact, more so than with cinema, linguists have become increasingly keen to analyse television dialogue – perhaps because the long-form structure lends itself better to discourse analysis. Two edited collections have been published in this area in recent years – Kay Richardson's *Television Dramatic Dialogue: A Sociolinguistic Study* (2010) and Roberta Piazza *et al.*'s *Telecinematic Discourse: Approaches to the Language of Films and Television Series* (2011) – and this study will engage at times with related findings.

Film screenplays are also being published with increased frequency, including those by the six filmmakers under discussion here. Critical interest in the screenplay provides one channel through which dialogue can be analysed, albeit with an emphasis on the speech as written rather than as executed. Connecting screenplay analyses to this study is Kevin Alexander Boon's (2008) chapter on 'dialogue as action' in *Script Culture and the American Screenplay*.[6] Boon's chapter focuses on *Glengarry Glen Ross* (Foley 1992) and he coins the term 'active dialogue' to describe speech that is designed so that meaning can be inferred by an audience (but is not stated) (99). He contrasts this with 'didactic dialogue', which lectures audiences and determines conclusions for them through speech (90–1). For Boon, didactic dialogue is the norm in cinema with David Mamet's screenplay providing a rare example of 'active dialogue'. Boon's terms are a succinct way of explaining the dramatic potential of dialogue, and its ability to engage audiences, but his theory can be developed further and extended beyond the scope of a single film. Indeed, the inference process will be shown to be crucial to how meaning is built up but not 'spelt out' in independent film dialogue. Furthermore, Boon asserts that it generally takes a playwright to script a screenplay in this way (90–1), something that this book aims to refute by showing the frequency with which the cinematic verbalists limit didactic dialogue, or undermine it in novel ways.

Although the focus here is on dialogue as executed in the selected independent cinema, I draw at times on screenwriting literature and the filmmakers' published screenplays. This allows for a more thorough consideration of the evolution of dialogue from screenplay through to the finished film. The value of cinematic verbalism as a concept becomes more evident in this context: it involves analysis of dialogue as executed and integrated as much as the way that it is written. Considering how dialogue can be cinematic also aims to shift the norm from focusing on a writer-director's *direction* to also analysing their writing, and the relationship between the two components.

Moving from a critical perspective to the experiences of audiences and those working in the contemporary film industry, even screenwriters tend to be trained to focus on plot over dialogue. Pleas such as the following one, from a script editor Staton Rabin (2009), are rare:

> [I]f you want audiences to remember your work – if you want to be immortal – learn to write better dialogue. Audiences don't go out of

movies quoting the plot ... if they repeat anything, it will be a line of dialogue. (Rabin 2009: 37)

Notably, given this book's focus on the reception of the cinematic verbalists' dialogue, Rabin highlights that speech is the element of a film that audience members can most easily take away with them. Indeed, it is now common for lists of film quotations to be listed on popular websites such as IMDb or even compiled in books.[7] This tendency for dialogue to be remembered and repeated is a feature of cult cinema in particular. Discussing *Blade Runner* (Scott 1982), for example, Louis Paul (2007) refers to lines of dialogue that become ingrained in the minds of 'catchphrase-crazy' fans (117–18). In terms of audiences' attachment to dialogue, we can also think of negative responses to moments when dialogue seems to be withheld. As Justin Horton (2013: 4) explains in 'The Unheard Voice in the Sound Film', we tend to feel uncomfortable in those rare situations when a character is shown to speak but their lines go unheard: 'Audiences, it seems, can tolerate fractured chronology, ellipses, or narrative irresolution, but the withholding or occlusion of the voice is experienced as an unusual and unsettling disrupting.'

Taking a different but related perspective, Janet Staiger has identified several kinds of talk that films can elicit from the audience, thus alluding to another way in which audiences can be verbally engaged. In *Perverse Spectators: The Practices of Film Reception* (2000), Staiger considers 'talking in the theatre', as well as other physical and expressive activities carried out by audience members, both during and after the 'event' of film-watching (44–54). She notes how audience members can not only repeat lines of dialogue, but they can also talk *about* the film to companions and talk *to* the characters or 'the author' during the screening. Staiger's discussion is in contrast to Miriam Hansen's (1991) argument in *Babel and Babylon* that, with the arrival of sound, dialogue stopped audience members from talking in the cinema.[8] Rather than speculating on this element of the reception of American independent cinema, Chapter 7 examines speech that moves in the reverse direction – when these indie filmmakers seem to personally address the audience through their characters. This kind of 'double voicing' is suggested to be a complementary form of verbal engagement to those identified by Staiger, and one that continues to be associated with less mainstream, and more niche, audiences.

NICHE AUDIENCES, NICHE DIALOGUE

Within film studies, considerable attention has been dedicated to determining differences between 'independent cinema', 'art cinema' and hybrids like 'smart cinema' and 'Indiewood' – including attention to their respective audiences. Writing on American independent cinema has surged in the twenty-first century, with scholars including Peter Biskind (2004), Geoff King (2005, 2009) and Yannis Tzioumakis (2006, 2012) considering what constitutes 'independence' from a variety of narrative, formal and industrial perspectives. King describes how the kind of production that qualifies as independent is 'constantly under question, on a variety of grounds' (2005: 1), but the label tends to be applied to films that are produced outside of the Hollywood studio system, and/or films that are more political, polemical or experimental in terms of form and content (2). In her study of art films, Barbara Wilinsky (2001) explains that they are often 'not defined by their thematic and formalistic similarities, but rather by their differences from Hollywood films' (15). In addition to art cinema being associated with the work of individual auteurs, elliptical narratives and formal experimentation, the term can be applied to those films screened in art-house cinemas, or to films that aim to deny the audience the experience of passive entertainment. Somewhat connecting the two is Jeffrey Sconce's influential article on the 'smart' film (2002). He describes 'smart' cinema as a point where mainstream, 'art' and independent film meet (351), and he uses the term to capture certain films emerging in the late 1980s and early 1990s with an ironic and a nihilistic tone. Sconce distills the distinctiveness of these films down to five tendencies, including a 'blank' style and incongruous narration, with Claire Perkins later extending on Sconce's label in *American Smart Cinema* (2012).[9] Lastly, the label of 'Indiewood' has been described by King (2009) as the point on the American film spectrum at which Hollywood and independent cinema becomes blurred.[10] It is not typically compared to art cinema and thus differs from smart cinema. Given our focus on dialogue, these general distinctions between categories matter less than the ways that each one intersects with verbal conventions. And although I refer to these six filmmakers using the term 'independent' – the label that best applies to the group as a whole, although all but Hartley could also be described as 'Indiewood' – it is important to acknowledge the broader links that exist between dialogue and the reception of non-mainstream cinema.

The association between alternative dialogue styles and art cinema can be traced back to its emergence as an alternative to classical Hollywood. Long before the experimental dialogue of low-budget indies, the extra 'work' that subtitled European films required of audiences was considered so unappealing that, as Wilinsky explains, these films were either dubbed in the US or contained to smaller repertory cinemas (30–2). Indeed, Annette Insdorf (2005) briefly identifies a connection between the dialogue of 'art' cinema and the 'abundance of dialogue – especially, intelligent dialogue' in contemporary indie cinema (30). J. J. Murphy (2007: 6) explains similar in his study on screenwriting in independent American cinema: 'The film script is the heart of the creative originality to be found in the independent movement'. Murphy's study currently offers the greatest insight into how independent dialogue differs from that of the mainstream. For instance, he notes that it is often less concise, instead mimicking the rhythms of everyday conversation (23). But Murphy's analysis of independent screenplays is not focused purely on dialogue, nor is he concerned with how the dialogue is integrated or embodied in the finished products. With 'smart' cinema, dialogue's significance to it is most obvious in relation to the 'miscommunication and emotional dysfunction' that Sconce identifies. And yet he deems interpersonal alienation 'so obvious and relentless' that it is paid no further attention (364). In her broader study of related cinema, Perkins does briefly identify a 'smart' verbal style, which she describes as having an 'overtly "talkie" tendency' and 'off-kilter lucidity' (30).

'Active' Audiences and Dialogue as a Meaningful Cue

Building on this context, this study of the design and execution of dialogue is concerned with how speech that complicates and challenges mainstream dialogue norms by being more 'difficult' to follow in various senses (audibility, the content and/or style of the language) both connects the work of the six filmmakers and makes their films more engaging. By extending on the work of selected cognitive theorists, it aims to show that while audience members' cognitive processes are regulated, moulded and directed by textual choices of all kinds, dialogue can be a particularly rich source of cues. For although dialogue is rarely foregrounded in reception studies or cognitive film theory, literature on how we construct and infer meaning, recognise verbal patterns and 'signposts', reconcile inconsistencies and identify with characters can be extended, or reapplied, to include film dialogue.

Psychological and physiological approaches to film audiences have been growing in influence since the late 1980s when – initially separately and then collectively in their edited collection *Post-Theory* – Bordwell and Carroll launched a critical intervention into the propagation of 'fashionable slogans and unexamined assumptions' in film theory based on psychoanalysis, semiotics and Marxism (Carroll 1988: 234). As Bordwell explains in his influential article 'A Case for Cognitivism' (1989b), such theories aim to understand such mental activities as 'recognition, comprehension, inference-making, interpretation, judgment, memory, and imagination' (13).[11] Although a variety of theories have been proposed in relation to how audience members experience these processes, analyses of audiences' responses to dialogue are rare, since the focus tends to be on *visual* processing. Yet definitions of cognitive film studies tend to be drawn broadly, incorporating research from the social sciences as well as psychology and neuroscience. Some of this can prove useful to studies of dialogue's relationship to character, performance and gender. My chapters on these topics thus draw on specific findings from socio-linguistics and social psychology, which are used to illuminate the verbal dynamics between characters.

More generally, of particular use to this study is Richard J. Gerrig and Deborah A. Prentice's (1996) 'participant theory of audience response', which uses selected terms from socio-linguistics and provides a useful model for considering the cinematic verbalists' dialogue design and reception. For Gerrig and Prentice, the skills that individuals require to understand films are the same as those acquired through conversation. Borrowing from speech-act theory, they use the terms 'side-participant', 'addressee' and 'overhearer' to capture various forms of engagement between audience members and the film (although they use the terms to capture the communicativeness of the film in general, rather than just the dialogue). According to Gerrig and Prentice, audience members are generally side-participants since, although the characters on screen do not directly address them, the speaker (or, I would specify, the writer of the speech) formulates utterances so that the audience member is informed (390). 'Overhearing' instead involves a character withholding specialist knowledge that, purposefully or by accident, mystifies those who are 'uninitiated', such as other characters or those in the audience. Throughout this book, we will consider the ways that independent writer-directors design and execute dialogue so that the audience members are treated as 'overhearers', 'side-participants' or 'addressees' (those directly addressed by an utterance, for example, when a character breaks the fourth wall by speaking to the camera).[12]

In *Overhearing Film Dialogue*, Kozloff (2000: 15) cites the same influential article by Clark and Carlson (1982) as Gerrig and Prentice, but she adopts the term 'overhearing' without referring to the other kinds of listeners. Instead, I share Gerrig and Prentice's view that most films position audience members as side-participants rather than overhearers. The rationale for this lies in Clark and Carlson's summation that '[w]hat distinguishes overhearers from [side] participants ... is that overhearers aren't intended to understand' (1982: 350). By contrast, film dialogue is typically designed to aid the audience's understanding of both individual exchanges between characters and the narrative as a whole. And although the performers of film dialogue rarely have the freedom to change their scripted speech, it can equally be designed with a view to the needs of the wider audience. In something of a departure from this, the cinematic verbalists instead incorporate an uncommon amount of overhearing in the sense that their characters' dialogue (or the way the dialogue is performed or integrated) often withholds knowledge from us.

Based on the existing literature on the filmmakers under focus, there are already signs that this is the case, both in terms of their overt intentions and audiences' responses to them. For Mark L. Berrettini (2011: 2), Hartley 'attempts to break away from an unsophisticated model of spectatorship as consumption', with films that instead 'address us as "cocreators" of meaning'. More specifically, Rawle (2011) briefly connects Hartley's dialogue to his expectations for audience engagement when he asserts that 'the tone of

[Hartley's] dialogue and the performance style of his films have long been a blockage for contemporary audiences accessing his work' (272). Indeed, when asked by Peter De Jonge if he wants the audience to enjoy his movies, Hartley (1996: 20) replied as follows: 'Enjoy? No, they have to work. Anything worthwhile necessitates work.' The issue of audience accessibility is implied by Carole Lyn Piechota's (2006) description of Anderson's dialogue in *The Royal Tenenbaums* (2001) as 'often obtuse', and it is explored more fully in Kim Wilkins' (2013) study of what she refers to as 'hyper-dialogue' in selected contemporary cinema, including that of Anderson. In her article, Wilkins connects dialogue to the role of the audience when she argues that it 'encourage(s) the audience to recognise the conventions of mainstream dialogue while simultaneously subverting these expectations through their uneven ironic employment' (411). Although Wilkins is focused on existential anxiety and a different range of films (including the work of David O. Russell), we will consider her findings further at several other points.

Returning to the more theoretical underpinning, our analysis here is also informed by Bordwell's early work in *Making Meaning: Inference and Rhetoric in the Interpretation of Cinema* (1989a) and by Joseph D. Anderson's *The Reality of Illusion: An Ecological Approach to Cognitive Film Theory* (1998).[13] While Bordwell's (1989a) discussion of meaning-making in cinema as a constructive process does not consider speech, it can help our understanding of how the cinematic verbalists design dialogue to engage the audience. According to Bordwell:

> The perceiver is not a passive receiver of data but an active mobilizer of structures and processes (either 'hard-wired' or learned) which enable her to search for information relevant to the task and data at hand. In watching a film, the perceiver identifies certain cues which prompt her to execute many inferential activities.[14] (Bordwell 1989a: 3)

More generally, Bordwell focuses on how 'active' audience members fill 'textual gaps' (251), and the cinematic verbalists will be shown to leave gaps in the dialogue, both perceptually (when the words are unclear, for instance) or cognitively (when they require inferences to be made). The mainstream dialogue norms from which they playfully depart can also be framed in terms of Bordwell's argument that the perceiver actively mobilises learned data structures – in this case, the kind of internalised generic dialogue norms that Kozloff (2000) and Berliner (1999) have identified. To this end, analysis of American independent cinema's experimental dialogue necessitates a degree of reference to the mainstream norms from which they depart.

Kristin Thompson's (1977: 56) discussion of 'cinematic excess' is also useful here. With a focus on visual aesthetics, she notes that excessive stylistic elements are those that can encourage an audience 'to linger over devices longer than their structured function would seem to warrant', and that this provides a kind of 'perceptual play'. By identifying a range of verbal excesses, this kind of play – only one based on dialogue rather than visual excess – will be explored.

Verbal Signposts and Detective Work

Joseph Anderson (1998: 10) follows on from the cognitive theory of Carroll and Bordwell to demonstrate how the perception and comprehension of motion pictures should be regarded 'as a subset of perception and comprehension in general'. He details how, psychologically, a film functions like a computer programme with which 'the mind interacts ... utilizing the same perceptual system' (90). But Anderson's study generally highlights how the mind interacts with the succession of *images*, not dialogue:[15]

> If indeed the problem of integrating a succession of disconnected shots provides the opportunity for the filmmaker to organize these shots in a way that will be precisely meaningful to the viewer, then it is reasonable to ask, [h]ow does the viewer perform this integration? (Anderson 1998: 90–1)

Similarly, screenwriting theorist Adam Ganz (2011) compares the screenplay to computer software interaction design. He too considers how individuals process information and argues that audiences enjoy being made to 'add two and two together' (127).[16] Although Ganz does briefly mention the role of sound, like Joseph Anderson he generally focuses on visual components of the 'programme'. He describes the process as 'a piece of visual detective work' whereby the screenwriter designs 'a set of images to be scrutinized and deduced from' (134), with audience speculation followed by 'visual proof' (ibid.).

It is disconcerting that even Ganz, a proponent of screenwriting theory, disregards the role of verbal detective work and proof. Similarly, although historical conceptions of the art film are bound up with the role of the audience,[17] such discussion tends to focus on their active *viewing*. Wilinsky (2001: 18), for instance, describes how the use of long shots and deep focus in neo-realism gives the audience some freedom when deciding 'where to look within a frame', with a lack of visual 'signposting' also making the experience more active (ibid.). Instead, by focusing on the way that independent cinema uses verbal 'signposting', this study aims to demonstrate how the precise organisation and treatment of the speech plays a key role in our interpretation of the succession of disconnected *words*, or words and images.

The Appeal of Alternative Dialogue Styles

Joseph Anderson (1998: 119–20) does not discuss different kinds of audiences in detail, but notes that there exist more experienced viewers who are 'better able to assimilate novel or unexpected filmic techniques', and may even become 'more demanding' in this regard. Like King discusses in relation to independent cinema, Anderson cites art cinema's 'less conventional techniques' as an appealing challenge to such audiences. He discusses the things that people can do to avoid being under-stimulated, and equates this with how viewers seek 'pacers'[18] (optimally arousing stimuli) appropriate for their individual 'level of film experience' (ibid.). For although we need stimulation in order not to get bored, we are generally most satisfied by things that are:

> new but not too new. The stimulation must be something that can connect to existing schemata but will modify them only slightly, stretching them a little bit – not something so totally novel as to have no associations, no sense of familiarity in any way whatsoever, with nothing to relate to or connect to in our attempts to assimilate the new information. (Anderson 1998: 117–18)

This reasoning can also be applied to explain the rewarding nature of independent film dialogue. If its design in mainstream cinema is not optimally stimulating due to its simplified design (for example, didactic dialogue that spells out character motivations or is full of expositional information) then audience members for whom these traits are overly familiar may find alternative forms of dialogue more pleasurable. By demonstrating that the cinematic verbalists use more 'active' forms of dialogue and dialogue integration, it can be argued that this constitutes an 'unexpected filmic technique' (albeit one somewhat expected in the context of non-mainstream cinema) that is pleasurable for audience members who, as Kozloff suggests, have internalised generic film dialogue conventions.

The notion that audience members can find verbal novelty inherently rewarding also seems to complement certain sociological explanations related to audience preferences. King (2002), Wilinsky and Shyon Baumann (2007) cite Pierre Bourdieu's (1984) argument that taste is socially defined. For King (2002: 198), '[w]hat we "like" is a matter less of individual choice than of social background. A "taste" for subtlety does not spring from nowhere. It is the product of a particular kind of education.'[19] The mental stimulation that comes with the stretching of familiar schemata or 'pacers' can be considered as a more concrete way of discussing what King refers to as 'subtlety'. Additionally, in *Indiewood, USA: Where Hollywood Meets Independent Cinema*, King (2009) locates the audience for 'Indiewood' in terms of taste cultures and niche marketing techniques. He argues that the implied audience (as targeted, if not the actual audience) is one that is 'receptive to the presence of some markers of difference or distinction within the context of frameworks broadly familiar from the Hollywood mainstream' (35). Crucially, King argues that such an audience is assumed to 'find pleasure' in these distinctions (ibid.).[20] In theory, then, distinctive dialogue can be used to provide, or at least it can be *designed* to provide, similar audience pleasures. And although individuals from certain social backgrounds may be more likely to seek out novel dialogue (as well as other distinctive cultural markers), they may also seek novelty because the 'stretching' of verbal norms is inherently pleasurable as a result of being cognitively rewarding.

As will become apparent in the chapters to follow, attending to dialogue's role in the construction of meaning is complex and the level of detail that such analysis requires indicates why the way that dialogue is integrated and received is rarely studied. But, ignoring or downplaying dialogue leads to blind-spots in our conception of how films work, something that Kozloff (2000: 14) stresses when she explains that often it is the *interaction* of visuals and words that permits themes to be conveyed, empathy to be elicited and narrative causality to be communicated. It is with these aims and blind-spots in mind that I begin my analysis of the cinematic verbalists' dialogue.

But first, a few points about terminology: first, despite 'dialogue' generally referring to a verbal exchange between two or more people, I also use the term to discuss speech more broadly, for example, when referring to a character's personalised style of dialogue. Second, in keeping with the use of the term 'audioviewer' (as opposed to 'viewer' or 'spectator') by various scholars studying film sound,[21] the word is used throughout to refer to cinema as a bi-modal (aural and visual) experience. Third, audioviewers and the implied 'audience' or 'audiences' are referred to interchangeably. I do so not because individual audioviewers have been surveyed, or because the implied audience constitute a unified, knowable body, but because the use of reception studies and cognitive theory aims to grounds the discussion in shared human psychological processes as much as cultural forms of knowledge and experience.[22]

NOTES

1. For a more detailed discussion of the impact of 'talkies' on actors of this period, see Chapters 1 and 18 of Donald Crafton's *The Talkies: American Cinema's Transition to Sound, 1926–1931* (1999).
2. For example, although Warner Bros was one of the main proponents of film sound, even studio head Jack Warner (1926) was unconvinced; he claimed that the viewer enjoyed creating 'the imagined dialogue for himself'.
3. Despite praise for Alfred Hitchcock's experimental use of sound, including dialogue, in *Blackmail* (1929), he maintained that silent pictures were a pure form of

cinema as opposed to most talkies that were merely 'photographs of people talking' (Hitchcock quoted in Truffaut and Scott 1984: 61).

4. See Kozloff (2000: 28) for a list of the most commonly listed prescriptions in screenwriting manuals, including that dialogue should be kept to a minimum and be subtle, but 'should never be' repetitious, flowery or ostentatious, obscure or intellectual.

5. Kracauer admits that dialogue had been a necessary step in cinema's evolution: 'For with plots becoming ever more ambitious and intricate, only the spoken word would be able to relieve the silent film from the increasing number of cumbersome captions and explanatory visual inserts' (1997 [1960]: 102).

6. Two other relevant studies are Jill Nelmes' (2011) chapter 'Realism and Screenplay Dialogue' in *Analysing the Screenplay*, and Mark Axelrod's (2014) *Constructing Dialogue: From Citizen Kane to Midnight in Paris*, which does attend to the ways in which dialogue influences the construction of the scene in the finished film.

7. For a book-length list of quotations, see Robert Cettl's *Film Talk* (2010). Cettl does not attempt to theorise the phenomenon of quoting films; instead he isolates memorable lines from a diverse range of genres with the premise that dialogue can capture 'the entire breadth of the movie going experience' (5).

8. Jeffrey Weinstock's (2007) study of *The Rocky Horror Picture Show* (Sharman 1975) incorporates significant analysis of fans' verbal engagement with the cult film. Weinstock considers why 'the convention of talking back to the screen' developed around that particular film (34), and why fans construct and overlay 'a secondary script' on top of that original script (39).

9. While Sconce cites Anderson, Hartley and Linklater as expressing a 'smart' sensibility, Perkins more fully incorporates Anderson and Baumbach into the 'smart cinema' category. I agree with Perkins's use of the 'smart' label as something that is 'open and partial' (2012: 29), an approach that leads her to make a distinction between Anderson and Baumbach and Stillman and Hartley; she cites the latter pair as 'adjunct' smart directors (16). Perkins makes a further distinction between them and Jarmusch who is only 'potentially' another 'adjunct' (40).

10. There is some disagreement as to who coined the term 'Indiewood', with Biskind (2004: 194) suggesting that it started being used in 1994. According to King, use of the term gained momentum on the *indieWIRE* website, which attributes the term to a 1997 article on the website by filmmaker Sarah Jacobson (2009: 3; 39).

11. It should also be noted that although the phrase 'cognitive film theory' is frequently used, its proponents are careful to distinguish that they use cognitivism less as a grand theory and more as a perspective or approach to material. Carroll (1992: 200) explains various reasons why cognitive theory is not 'unified' with its proponents but rather shares certain convictions. Furthermore, given that many fields other than cognitive science are drawn on in such discussions, several scholars suggest that 'rationalist theory' would be a more suitable term (cf. Nannicelli and Taberham 2014: 6–7; Currie 2004: 154).

12. For an alternative, psychoanalytic analysis of the cinema as overhearing see Elizabeth Weis's (1999) 'Eavesdropping: An Aural Analogue of Voyeurism?' Weis proposes the use of the term '*écouteur*' as an aural equivalent to the 'voyeur' and equates eavesdropping by the cinema audience with a child overhearing the primal scene.

13. In the chapters to follow, references to Anderson refer to Wes Anderson, unless the forename of Joseph Anderson – or other scholars named Anderson – is also cited.

14. For a more detailed analysis of the construction of meaning by audience members, see Bordwell's (1985) *Narration in the Fiction Film* (30–40).

15. Although Joseph Anderson (1998: 80–9) dedicates a chapter to 'sound and image' he focuses on issues of synchrony, sound effects and music, but not dialogue.

16. Ganz (2011: 131) argues that the screenplay can be thought of as 'one side of a dialogue with an audience … The pleasure of the film lies in the interactions the audience will have with it'.

17. While acknowledging that viewers of Hollywood films are also required to 'make meaning', Wilinsky (2001: 88–9) stresses how art cinema of the 1950s and 1960s placed emphasis on their 'intellectually participatory' nature, regardless of whether they 'actually required more "activity" on the part of the spectator' than did classical Hollywood films.

18. Joseph Anderson takes the term 'pacers' from Michael J. Ellis's *Why People Play* (1973: 47).

19. For an informative application of Bourdieu's theories to cinema audiences see Baumann's *Hollywood Highbrow: From Entertainment to Art* (2007).

20. King gives as example Charlie Kaufman's self-referential narratives and Steven Soderbergh's 'stylized touches' (2009: 35). Furthermore, King argues that while Indiewood films are 'not generally designed to be difficult to access', their distinctive features nonetheless imply 'an audience role that can differ in some respects from that associated with mainstream cinema' (33).

21. Scholars of film sound to use the term 'audioviewer' or 'audio-viewer' include Michel Chion in *Audio-vision: Sound on Screen* (1994) and John Richardson in *An Eye for Music – Popular Music and the Audiovisual Surreal* (2011). By contrast, in linguist Michael Toolan's (2011: 161–2) analysis of dialogue in *The Wire* (2002–8), he uses the more cumbersome term 'viewer-listener'.

22. David Bordwell (1985: 29–47) discusses the 'real' spectator in more detail in a chapter dedicated to 'The Viewer's Activity' in *Narration in the Fiction Film*.

2. VERBAL-VISUAL STYLE AND WORDS VISUALISED

Unless distracted or multi-tasking, audiences rarely listen to film dialogue without also watching what is happening on-screen. Likewise, unless experiencing a film in a noisy environment, they rarely witness on-screen events without them being framed by characters' spoken words, and the soundtrack more generally. But what can make certain combinations of words and images jarring, or pleasurable, for an audience – and why? This chapter examines the relationship between dialogue and what is simultaneously shown on-screen, in order to develop an understanding of verbal-visual style in contemporary indie cinema. Given that the low budgets of independent cinema can place severe restrictions on the visual aesthetics, it is unsurprising that at times the six cinematic verbalists substitute verbal interest for visual interest, or for visual interest that depends on the verbal for its impact. We can see this in the decision to shoot more cheaply using black-and-white film, as with Jarmusch's *Stranger Than Paradise*. But, given that Baumbach also opted for black and white with *Frances Ha*, albeit a high-quality and digitally captured version, we may also consider a monotone colour scheme as particularly well-suited to films with 'colourful' dialogue.

In the films under focus, verbal-visual style generally depends on meaningful relationships between what is spoken and what is shown; although this interdependence does not necessarily involve a redundancy in relation to words and the images shown simultaneously. Instead, the cinematic verbalists can take advantage not only of the way that we perceive things both visually and aurally, but also of the way that we can recognise and remember patterns built up in this way. Although independent writer-directors can use visual techniques that are stylised to a similar degree to their speech, their work also reveals a less prominent trend for an observational visual style that aligns with the way that, at times, audiences have to work at 'overhearing' their dialogue. In fact, analysis of the interaction between their respective visual and verbal styles can reveal how the mise en scène is often subordinate to a fascination with language, and that spoken words can be used to alter, rather than repeat, meaning signified visually.

In *Audio-Vision: Sound on Screen* (1994), Michel Chion maps out various ways that the filmgoer can perceive combinations of image and sound. His principle of 'audiovisual analysis' provides a useful technique for determining how speech is presented and undermined or reinforced by visual cues. Chion recommends alternately masking the image or muting the sound in order to 'hear the sound as it is, and not as the image transforms and disguises it; [and to] see the image as it is, and not as sound recreates it' (185). Alluding to cognition and the audience experience, Chion describes an audiovisual contract through which 'the two perceptions mutually influence each other' (9). In *Film, A Sound Art* (2009), he helpfully outlines various terms for the range of relationships between sound and image, including dialogue and image, with 'verbocentrism' and 'verbo-decentrism' two particularly useful concepts for our examination of verbal-visual style in the contemporary films under discussion. Verbocentrism captures situations in which 'speech is the center [*sic*] of attention without seeming to be, because it dovetails with parallel visual actions' (73). Chion argues that verbocentric cinema was established by the end of the 1930s and continues to dominate today. Conversely, verbo-decentric cinema aims for no such pretence; dialogue both seems to be and *is* the main source of action (497–8). For Chion (2009: 73–4), the crucial condition of verbocentrism is the absence of a relationship between a discussion's general content and accompanying visual actions. By this he means that a verbocentric director tries to disguise the significance of the dialogue by having the actors engage in small, unrelated actions like cleaning, driving, eating or smoking. Indeed, characters in Jarmusch's, Hartley's and Stillman's films do tend to talk and smoke, drink or walk. Yet because there is limited narrative action, and because the dialogue can be meandering and verbose, speech is still foregrounded rather than disguised, somewhat confusing Chion's formulation. In fact, in many ways, the verbal-visual style of the writer-directors under discussion complicates and avoids both of these principles to instead harmonise speech and images in exceptionally detailed ways. Indeed, although the term 'audiovisual' is appropriate for discussion of how visual images relate to the *four* components of sound (music, sound effects, dialogue and voice), this chapter instead uses the term 'verbal-visual' to reflect our narrower focus on the dynamics between the words and images. As case studies of voice-over narration, embedded text and 'textual speech' in the work of Anderson, Baumbach, Linklater and Stillman will now reveal, the cinematic verbalists craft a complex and complementary verbal-visual style.

Voice-over as Double-layered Structure in the Films of Anderson and Baumbach

In Sconce's discussion of the 'smart' film, the single argument he makes in relation to dialogue concerns the ironic voice-over that opens *Election* (Payne 1999).[1] Sconce explains that while initially the voices of the student (Reese Witherspoon) and teacher (Matthew Broderick) suggest 'the film will play as a pedestrian teen comedy', it ends with a shocking revelation that quashes the boundaries it seems to be operating within:[2]

> As a result of this sudden juxtaposition, the calculatedly banal voice-overs and opening generic cues become increasingly ironic for the rest of the film, so much so that by the film's end voice-over and image are often in direct conflict. (Sconce 2002: 361)

By arguing that a single sentence in the opening scene impacts the entire narrative, Sconce indirectly highlights the power of dialogue in selected 'smart' cinema. Furthermore, like Sconce notes of *Election,* Anderson and Baumbach use voice-overs to create an ironic disjuncture between words and image. In *Greenberg* (2010), Baumbach mocks voice-over connotations through title character Roger's (Ben Stiller) pseudo-literary narration of a stream of pedantic letters. Baumbach was inspired by the title character of writer Saul Bellow's *Herzog* (1964), who writes to various people in his life and throughout world history. But while Bellow uses the letters to reveal that there is still some good in Herzog, Roger's letters satirise his ability to find fault in *anything*. He writes to companies like American Airlines, the Yellow Pages and Starbucks, and through editing and mise en scène, these letters are indicated to be Roger's main purpose in life. For instance, when an old friend visits, the scene jumps to a shot of Roger reading an entire letter to the friend while he waits, bored, to be let inside. Ironic contrasts are created between the impression Roger tries to project through the letters (of a mature, well-educated adult) and the images accompanying the words that convey him as childlike (such as looking at his eye in the mirror through a magnifying glass, or struggling to swim).

Kozloff devotes a chapter of *Invisible Storytellers: Voice-Over Narration in American Fiction Film* (1989) to voice-overs used ironically, and, like Sconce, she explains how the double-layered structure of the voice-over is perfect for creating irony through narration that either overinflates or understates what the images show (110). More narrowly, a comparison can be made between

Kozloff's discussion of Godard's 'romantic irony' – described as deliberately questioning or demolishing a work's dramatic illusion (112) – and Baumbach's voice-over in his second film, *Mr. Jealousy* (1997). As Kozloff notes of *Bande à parte* (1964), ten minutes into the film Godard narrates 'a few clues for later-comers' (ibid.). Similarly, *Mr. Jealousy* has an omniscient narrator who also draws attention to his own role in the fiction with asides like 'but I'm getting ahead of myself'. In contrast to the authoritative narrator who clarifies the image, *Mr. Jealousy*'s narrator admits his own ignorance and complicates matters rather than simplifying them: 'And so, as agreed upon, Vince became Leo, while Lester remained Vince. Although why Leo spoke with an English accent, Lester couldn't even begin to imagine.' While Godard uses voice-over as a distancing technique, Baumbach copies elements of Godard's self-conscious voice-over so that it serves as an intertextual homage to engage audioviewers familiar with Godard's work.

Like Baumbach's voice-overs, Anderson's often take the form of characters narrating letters containing their own bizarre thoughts in a matter-of-fact tone, to create an overall effect of ironic disjunction. Anderson also makes use of what Kozloff identifies as one of the most complicated ways to create an ironic effect through narration. When voice-over dialogue is synchronised with images of the same words it tends to be redundant, as when the voice speaks the words also printed on-screen (103). In *Rushmore* (1998), Anderson instead takes advantage of Kozloff's exceptional case, which exists when there is a significant discrepancy between the tone of the voice and the look of the text shown in the image. Dirk (Mason Gamble) writes Max (Jason Schwartzman) a letter and we see an insert of it as Dirk's disembodied voice narrates. He refers to Max as such a 'good friend', with the two words shown in the letter as underlined. Based on the insert alone, we (like Max) could take the letter as sincere. But while Max assumes that Dirk has underlined the text to stress the strength of his feelings, the audioviewer can detect Dirk's resentment through his sarcastic tone.[3] Audiences are thus required to recognise and resolve the ironic tension. By undermining the words of the letters visually (as in *Greenberg*) or aurally (as in *Rushmore*), Anderson and Baumbach take advantage of film's mixed media, which makes the voice-over more 'cinematic' than those in which words and images redundantly overlap.

Arguably, Anderson's most cognitively complex voice-over is the antiphonal narration between Suzy (Kara Hayward) and Sam (Jared Gilman) in *Moonrise Kingdom* (2012), in which each is heard reading letters to the other over a montage of related images. The voice-over is clearly indebted to Marianne (Anna Karina) and Ferdinand's (Jean-Paul Belmondo) alternating lines of narration in Godard's *Pierrot le Fou* (1965). But, rather than closely following Godard's antiphonal voice-over, Anderson incorporates elements of his own efficient verbal style by cutting characters off mid-sentence. In just under a minute and a half the viewer hears excerpts from fifteen letters written by Suzy and Sam, with much of the written exchange kept private since the excerpts end openly: for example, 'Please find enclosed –' and 'Unfortunately, it is –'. Like Richard Roud notes of Marianne and Ferdinand's alternating commentary in *Pierrot le Fou*, 'one [can] just about put it all together' (2010 [1970]: 97). Roud points here to the audioviewer's role in constructing meaning from the voice-over, something that equally applies to *Moonrise Kingdom*. When Suzy is cut off while saying 'My favourite colour is –', we learn that Sam questions her about even mundane details, but we never hear him ask the question, nor do we hear her answer. Even in these brief exchanges, dialogue is efficiently loaded with meaning.

Sam and Suzy's exchange is also in contrast with Chion's (2009: 80) summation that films with voice-overs have a habit of opening quotation marks for a story but often '"forget" to close them'. He refers here to voice-overs that introduce a film, then fade in and out, allowing an audience to temporarily forget that they are watching an 'embedded story' (ibid.). Sam and Suzy's quotations are cut off so abruptly, and so frequently, that it is impossible to ignore the narration's heavy manipulation. By drawing attention to its own artifice, Anderson's voice-over can thus increase our awareness of how voice-overs typically function.

These experimental voice-overs can again be considered from the perspective of Joseph Anderson's (1998: 119–20) discussion of how audiences seek 'pacers' appropriate for their individual level of film experience, since voice-overs that are ironic or antiphonal can stretch our expectations of what to expect from such a narration device. In these ways, the cinematic verbalists' experimentation can be seen to reflect a certain tendency in art cinema for the narrative authority of voice-overs to be questioned. This questioning is evident, for instance, in Stanley Kubrick's *Dr. Strangelove or: How I Learned to Stop Worrying and Love the Bomb* (1964). As Jason Sperb (2006: 68) argues, the film's opening voice-over appears to mock the self-importance and seriousness of Kubrick's earlier voice-overs. Sperb also identifies how the film creates an analogy between some of the characters' words and standard voice-over conventions. When characters in *Dr. Strangelove* speak to others through intercoms, they evoke for Sperg the voice-over's 'aural feeling and narrative power' (64).

Anderson creates a similar effect when loud-speakers and pipes are used to amplify voices in *Rushmore* and *Moonrise Kingdom* (64), with Hartley employing a related technique to ironic effect in *The Girl from Monday* (2005), a science-fiction film that includes a series of disembodied voices. On the streets of the dystopian city, we hear a robot speaking on behalf of the 'Big Brother' style government. There is also a female voice that speaks to Jack (Bill Sage) over an intercom in work – but who is never anchored visually – along with another robotic voice who speaks to Cecile (Sabrina Lloyd) from her computer. In contrast to the voice from the police cars, which issues concrete instructions ('Go back to your homes. All is well. Details at 11'), Cecile's computer makes idealistic declarations ('Be empowered. Live your own way. Take control. You're in charge'). Again, the voice-overs create ironic dissonance, although not as a result of the images; the computer's messages have been programmed by government officials who have imprisoned Cecile in the school, and who refuse to let her live her own way or 'take control'.

If, as Sconce argues, an ironic tone instantly bifurcates an audience into 'those who "get it" and those who do not' (352), then it is unsurprising that the cinematic verbalists employ ironic voice-overs and disembodied voices among their arsenal of verbal techniques designed to actively engage us. More generally, their combinations of words and images can also advance an ironic commentary. In Hartley's *Trust* (1990), Maria (Adrienne Shelly) expects to identify a man based on his wife's description of him (as carrying a briefcase and smoking a pipe). Instead, she watches disappointed as a large group of men, all matching the description, emerge from a train. Here Hartley uses an image to 'respond' ironically to a line of dialogue in order to undermine the power normally attributed to convenient character descriptions, which serve to advance exposition.[4]

Verbal irony has been touched on previously by Bordwell in relation to 'dialogue hooks' (1985: 158), a term he later developed to describe four possibilities through which 'the audiovisual texture links a specific causal element at the end of one scene to that at the very start of the next' (2008).[5] Bordwell explains that while dialogue hooks generally increase cohesion between scenes, they too can be used ironically. This is often the case with Anderson and Baumbach, who regularly start one scene with an image that is unexpected or in conflict with the closing line of the last. Dignan (Owen Wilson) in *Bottle Rocket* (Anderson 1996) is determined to prove that 'crime does pay' and he announces that when they get to the motel he will rent them 'the best room in the house'. Yet the scene cuts to a shot of Dignan, Anthony (Luke Wilson) and Bob (Robert Musgrave) in a room so small that their three beds touch. Similarly, in Baumbach's *Greenberg* there is an incongruous visual of Roger handing Florence (Greta Gerwig) a burger after she comes out of surgery, in response to Ivan's (Rhys Ifans) suggestion – at the end of the last scene – that he could get her flowers. Like Roger's choice of words, his actions are well-intentioned but somewhat misplaced, and the ironic hook captures this in a way that depends on both words and images for effectiveness. Although the use of such hooks is a familiar technique in film comedies, it is important to recognise their role in these films' broader, ironic verbal-visual style.

LINKLATER'S AND ANDERSON'S TEXTUAL SPEECH

Although Chion (2009: 68) considers voice-over to be the dominant form of 'textual speech', he uses the term to capture any dialogue that summons the image it describes through the speaking of the words. He asserts that, with few exceptions, textual speech is used sparingly and voice-over tends to disappear discreetly after setting the scene, so that a film does not simply become a visual stream 'that one flips through like a magazine according to the directives of words' (68). The cinematic verbalists stand apart here, in that they also employ other forms of textual speech. Linklater's dynamic use of this in *Waking Life* (2001), an animated film that explores human consciousness, is particularly revealing and worth considering in some detail.

Filmed in digital and then animated with rotoscope, *Waking Life* includes countless examples of characters and their surroundings altering to reflect that which is discussed. One nameless man considers humans in terms of the laws of physics and, as he describes how people are 'complex arrangements of carbon, mostly water', his body fills up with liquid and bubbles emerge from his mouth. When he talks about being 'a gear in a deterministic, physical machine', his head turns into a grey cog, surrounded by smaller yellow cogs (Figure 2.1). In another sequence, Kim Krizan (co-writer of Linklater's *Before Sunrise*) shares her view that language is more interesting when used to discuss 'abstract and intangible things'. Somewhat undermining this, Linklater cleverly uses animation to make language more *tangible*: when Krizan points at her mouth as she says, 'When I say love', continuing, 'Sound comes out of my mouth and hits the other person's ear.' As she says 'my mouth', a faint smoky shape emerges from it. Krizan subsequently describes how the word then 'travels through this byzantine conduit in their brain, through their memories of love, or lack of love'. As she does, a tunnel of curved lines appears to her right to represent the 'conduit' (Figure 2.2).

In these ways, Linklater maximises cinema's potential to give words a *physical* presence. Animation allows for the ultimate form of textual speech; Linklater's words not only set a series of images in motion, but the characters come to embody their own words while speaking them. Additionally, since he uses a different animator to create each character, then they are as individualised visually as their semi-improvised styles of speech. As a result, the close connections between Linklater's verbal and visual style is further established.

Characters' embodiment of words in *Waking Life* aligns them with Noël Carroll's (1996) discussion of 'verbal images', a concept that tangentially addresses dialogue. Carroll defines verbal images as those that evoke, individually or in succession, words or groups of words in the form of phrases, sentences and clichés (188). In keeping with this, at selected points in *Waking Life*, Linklater and his team of animators visually suggest that a character is

Figures 2.1 and 2.2.   Rotoscoped characters embody their words in *Waking Life*
(Linklater 2001). (Source: screenshots by author)

embodying a common expression – as when a man shouting about freedom literally goes blue in the face, and then red with anger. As Carroll's term suggests, 'verbal images' are a complex way for a visual medium like film to draw on audiences' broader understanding of language, in *Waking Life*'s case, a figure of speech. The relationship between Linklater's verbal images and the cinematic verbalists' broader use of dialogue can be considered a complement to their other forms of poetic dialogue, as examined in the next chapter. For Carroll, verbal images are based on a shift between a word's literal and descriptive use and its extended meaning. Since the images take on additional meaning by pointing to another, verbal layer, such devices are metaphorical in a particularly cinematic way.

Anderson also complicates traditional applications of textual speech by incorporating certain properties of external voice-over narration into the standard dialogue. His characters often discuss themselves in the third person, as though narrating their lives as they happen. In *Bottle Rocket*, for instance, Dignan tells his friend, 'Dignan got fired. Laid out on his ass.'[6] Anderson's use of textual speech is also unconventional when he includes moments in which a question is answered not by another character, but by an insert of text (sometimes accompanied by voice-over narration). In *Moonrise Kingdom*, when the scout master asks Sam's foster parent why there is no mention of him being an orphan in the register, Mr Billingsley (Larry Pine) responds: 'I don't know. What register?' We cut to an insert of Sam's detailed registration card, complete with a Polaroid photo and Mr Billingsley's signature in the designated space for 'parent or legal guardian'. Furthermore, like in Jarmusch's *Ghost Dog: The Way of the Samurai* (1999), when Sonny (Cliff Gorman) paraphrases from a note he has received with words that *later* appear in an intertitle, Lionel (Jake Ryan) in *Moonrise Kingdom* quotes from the letter left for him by his sister Suzy. Lionel's focus on the 'ten days' ('she borrowed my record player for ten days without asking') echoes Suzy's description in the letter of giving it back 'in ten days or less'. In this way, there is a spill-over from precision in the voice-over (and embedded text) to precision in the dialogue.

Although voice-overs are typically associated with mobilising images, Anderson reverses the technique when diegetic speech instead mobilises images of text to appear in the mise en scène. Indeed, Jaeckle (2013a: 163–6) has already outlined Anderson's use of printed texts, which he identifies as one of the 'verbal embroideries' that Anderson shares with Preston Sturges.[7] As Jaeckle notes, such printed text reminds audiences 'that film language is necessarily composed and shaped' (163). Yet Anderson is not the only independent filmmaker to do this, with shots of written text also common in the work of the other cinematic verbalists, thus allowing them to overtly (and cheaply) visualise their fascination with words.

Words, Visualised: Intertitles and Embedded Text

Our understanding of the cinematic verbalists' use of images of words – in the form of embedded texts, intertitles and subtitles – are in keeping with those in independent and art cinema more generally. Geoff King notes that indie films use intertitles self-consciously and he provides examples from *Clerks* (Smith 1994) and *Magnolia* (P. T. Anderson 1999).[8] The same can be said of the cinematic verbalists' use of visualised words. In *Waking Life*, a character passes through a shot wearing a T-shirt with the word 'Slacker' printed above the outline of a box where an image would normally be. The text references the cult following and subsequent merchandising of Linklater's film of the same name, becoming a reflexive comment in the process. Similarly, while the narrative of Hartley's *The Girl from Monday* satirises aspects of capitalism and consumerist society, he also incorporates this into a central character's clothing, with the word 'Anything' plastered across them as though a designer label. Like Linklater, Hartley uses text as a self-conscious comment on his earlier films, as when he reuses titles from *The Unbelievable Truth* (1989) eighteen years later in *Fay Grim* (2007). Rawle (2011: 288) considers Hartley's experimental use of captions in both films, and explains how *Fay Grim* uses captions rather than dialogue to externalise the protagonist's thought processes. At one point Fay (Parker Posey) looks at the camera, the frame freezes, and we read 'ottoman + thanksgiving = turkey/wild party = ?' As is often the case with Hartley's dialogue, expositional information is eschewed here for nonsensical combinations of words that serve to amuse.

Similar to Hartley's 'recycling' of intertitles from his previous films, Baumbach uses written words to quote intertextually from other films. In *The Squid and the Whale* (2005) we see the movie poster for *The Mother and the Whore* (*La Maman et la Putain*) (Eustache 1973). The audioviewer is invited to draw parallels between the compositions of the two titles, not to mention the films' verbal and narrative similarities. Jarmusch also uses written words to quote intertextually, as well as to further highlight the breakdown in communication due to language barriers. *The Limits of Control* (Jarmusch 2009) opens with a quote by poet Arthur Rimbaud ('As I descended into impassable rivers I no longer felt guided by the ferrymen ...'). The words appear first in French, then English, a trope continued throughout when characters repeat the exact same words but in different languages. Anderson's and Jarmusch's use of non-English dialogue also extends to signs. In *Bottle Rocket* a neon sign reading 'BARRA' (Spanish for bar) hovers above Anthony's head as he listens, clueless, to two characters speaking Spanish. The sign serves as a visual reminder that he cannot understand the words spoken around him. Indeed, in another example of a 'verbal image', Spanish words literally and figuratively go 'over his head' (Figure 2.3).[9] As embedded texts go, neon writing (which Jarmusch also likes to include) inherently draws our eye to the text.

Again, modernist French cinema is an important antecedent. Valerie Orpen (2003) discusses the significance of particular titles and words embedded visually in *À bout de souffle*. Referring to words on a poster, she notes that 'we notice it not because it carries the narrative forward, but for its symbolic resonance' (72). Similarly, she describes as 'poetic' the meaning conveyed throughout by the filmed words. This recalls the lyrical components of the cinematic verbalists' dialogue, as well as Carroll's description of verbal images as poetic.

Figure 2.3   Embedded text goes 'over his head' in *Bottle Rocket* (Anderson 1996).
(Source: screenshot by author)

In each case, not only is the dialogue poetic (in and of itself), but the words are integrated with the visuals, including images of other words, in ways that are figuratively rich.[10]

The significance of embedded texts to cinema has been most fully considered by Tom Conley in *Film Hieroglyphs: Ruptures in Classical Cinema* (2006). Conley discusses the creative and narrative potential of writing that appears in the mise en scène and 'unites and divides word and image' (xxv). Although Conley's discussion of the functions of embedded texts generally apply to the cinematic verbalists, their use of them departs from Conley's model in certain ways. He describes how such writing can appear to fall into a film as though 'by chance' and 'unbeknownst either to the storyteller or the spectator' (xxiv). By contrast, in keeping with other highly unified elements of the cinematic verbalists' diegetic worlds, they encourage audiences to notice overlaps between dialogue and embedded text.

Given the constructed nature of animation, it is particularly unlikely that words are casually inserted into Linklater's animated features, *Waking Life* and *A Scanner Darkly* (2006). Linklater instead takes advantage of the potential of animation to control the timing and movement of words. In a scene in *Waking Life*, words are projected onto a white screen with film strip visible at the edge. Over four seconds, new words appear and rearrange to change the meaning: we initially see the word 'BEGINNING', then 'BEGIN AGAIN ... FROM BEGINNING'. This turns into 'BEGIN AGAIN ... FROM THE BEGINNING', before finishing with 'TO BEGIN AGAIN ... FROM THE BEGINNING'. Thus, like the oblique nature of much of Linklater's dialogue, his visual text requires the audioviewer to fill in the gaps – in this case literally.

Certain embedded texts in *Waking Life* also include wordplay of a verbal-visual nature, and so constitute what Carroll refers to as 'primed verbal images'. By 'primed' Carroll distinguishes that the words accompanying the images direct us to focus on specific features of the images. 'Proper' verbal images instead require us to find the words *through* what is seen; instead of text accompanying the images, the audioviewer supplies it (187). Although primed verbal images typically require us to engage in less inferential activity than their 'proper' versions do, a metaphorical deduction is nonetheless required. A deduction of this nature is evident in a scene in *Waking Life* in which André Bazin's concept of 'The Holy Moment' is discussed. The three words gradually expand and turn, appearing to fly towards the audience. We finally see a close-up of the 'O', which becomes like a tunnel that we are taken through. This verbal image is 'primed' in the sense that the audioviewer should recognise that their attention is being drawn to the hole in the 'o' of the word 'holy' and notice the wordplay between the word 'hole' and how the word is represented visually.

More generally, it is worth considering the broader impact on the audioviewer of texts embedded in the mise en scène. Amresh Sinha (2004) argues that the act of reading text tears the mind away from what Peter Thompson (2000) calls 'the bodily presence of the film' (Sinha 2004: 173–4). Discussing subtitles in particular, Sinha argues that the work required to synthesise visual, audio and textual signifiers simultaneously can be considered a barrier between the audience's access to pleasure (ibid.). Yet, as this analysis of various uses of text demonstrates, there are various forms (other than subtitles) that equally require us to read and synthesise what is read with the rest of the data on the sound and image tracks. Significantly, given that the cinematic verbalists carefully select words (and their colour, size, language, and relevance to the character), their use of text tends to engage the audience rather than push them away. In other words, rather than being a barrier to pleasure, as Sinha suggests, their texts become an alternate kind of pleasure.

STILLMAN'S TEXTUAL SIGNPOSTS

Just as audiences can be conditioned to hear certain words when they form a broader pattern (as considered in Chapter 3), speech can prime us to look for certain things in the images, and vice versa.[11] Indeed, in Wilinsky's discussion of art cinema, she describes how a visual style that lacks 'signposting' can give audiences more freedom when deciding which elements of the image to focus on (2001: 18). By contrast, the cinematic verbalists can include actual text as signposts, and these can direct our attention and encourage us to focus on certain elements of the dialogue. A relationship of this nature is central to the working of text in Stillman's *Damsels in Distress* (2011), particularly to the way that embedded texts refer back to the characters' spoken words. In numerous scenes, dialogue revolves explicitly around language (Greek or Roman letter systems, and the correct spelling, pronunciation or plural of a word), and Stillman's intertitles extend on this. In one sequence, two girls debate the spelling of the name Xavier:

HEATHER: Zavier. with a Z?
LILY: No, I think it's with an X.
HEATHER: No, I'm certain it's a Z. Zavier, like Zorro. It's the same sound. Zorro marked his name with a Z.

Twelve minutes later an intertitle reading 'Xavier' appears, introducing the character, and a second later 'Zavier' appears underneath in quotation marks. The intertitle therefore reflects Lily's (Analeigh Tipton) words, but also Heather's (Carrie MacLemore) insistence on an alternate spelling. Like in Linklater's 'Holy Moment' sequence, Stillman also alters the structure of signs in the mise en scène, as when we have considerable time to observe the words 'SUICIDE CENTER' on the side of the building, before Violet (Greta Gerwig) slots a panel reading 'PREVENTION' in between them (Figure 2.4). On the walls inside the building, there are hand-made signs with messages like 'Look B4U Leap' with 'B4U' partially obscured by another sign that has been stuck over it, changing the message to 'Look Just Don't Leap'. In each case,

Figure 2.4   Characters speaking through text in *Damsels in Distress* (Stillman 2011). (Source: screenshot by author)

the signs require us to consider both versions and draw a conclusion from the difference.

Chion (2009: 176) notes that words embedded in the image remain unpronounced yet 'shout out their silent message to be read'. Specifically, he notes that audience members are engaged in a linguistic process called 'endophony', which involves the soundless mental enunciation of words (175). In the case of *Damsels in Distress*, audience members likely read the messages on the signs in Violet's voice, in large part due to the way that Stillman integrates them with her dialogue. Violet explains, on entering the room with the signs, how she loves 'clichés and hackneyed expressions'. The close, contrived relationship between the words and images is thus cemented by the way in which Violet speaks to the audience through the signs she is implied to have made. Elements of Violet's dialogue also gain greater significance in the form of Carroll's 'verbal images'. When her boyfriend is unfaithful, Violet flees to a nearby town and describes herself as 'in a tailspin'. The scene cuts to the editor of the college newspaper who explains that they're going to circulate her photo, after which the shot dissolves into a revolving newspaper with Violet's picture on it. When the paper spirals towards the camera it literalises Violet's 'tailspin'.

Although intertitles are used throughout *Damsels in Distress*, the film closes with the incorporation of more experimental superimposed text. Violet's mission in the film is to launch a worldwide dance craze, and Stillman ends with a cast dance sequence, with the following lines of text run up the screen from bottom to top, while the characters execute the moves:

> The Sambola! is an easy dance to do.
> If you can count to 8 you can do the Sambola!
> First, spin clockwise for a count of eight.
> Walk 'a la tango' for six – come face to face for two.
> For the next two 8s it's a cha-cha move.
> And so on.

The text addresses the audience directly by taking on the role of a dance instructor, most likely Violet since the dance is her invention. Stillman also reveals the inherent artifice of it with the line 'And so on'; this is not a real dance and so there are no more steps. After several other lines, another title appears – 'Footnotes to come' – in a further reference to the film's self-consciously literary style. Significantly, the omniscient narrator who is responsible for the on-screen text directly quotes Violet in the final 'footnote': 'The spelling of "doufi" is non-standard, but preferred.' Earlier in the film, Violet suggests two plurals for the word 'doofus', as well as referring to certain spellings as 'non-standard'. Stillman's texts again refer back to one character's dialogue, with Violet getting the last word in the text, as she does in most of the scenes. Therefore, like the cinematic verbalists' use of embedded texts as a whole, Stillman demonstrates how even mise en scène can be somewhat subordinated to the verbal style.

As will be considered further in the next chapter, Perkins (2012: 17) describes the excessive use of music in American smart cinema as 'emphasising the plasticity of the image' by unbalancing the narrative flow. The same could be said of the excessive use of texts that, like their excessive dialogue, highlight the contrived aesthetics in their films. Perkins argues that by refusing to subordinate music to image 'songs *become visible* in the films in the construction of a type of music-image' (129; emphasis in the original). Although the cinematic verbalists generally refuse to subordinate dialogue to images, embedded texts make this refusal more explicit, particularly when the spoken words are echoed visually on-screen.

A Complementary Verbal-visual Style

Like the cinematic verbalists' dialogue, their image tracks can be somewhat fragmented and thus require audioviewers to bridge gaps in visual as well as verbal meaning. For example, shots of characters watching television recur in Jarmusch's work, but only rarely does the audioviewer see what they see. Instead, the type of show is determined by the sound properties alone, either through dialogue or sound effects.[12] Similarly, although *Ghost Dog: The Way of the Samurai* (Jarmusch 1999) includes many point-of-view shots from the perspective of the title character (Forest Whitaker), at other moments the camera is notably restrained. In one scene, Ghost Dog stops his car and goes down a dark alley after a couple. The camera stays in the original wide shot, focusing on the whole street, with no cut to the action taking place in the blackened space. Eventually he emerges wearing different clothes. This is followed by a shot of the couple walking hesitantly back on to the street in their underwear. Jarmusch deprives the audioviewer of shots of them being coerced and forced to strip, ones that could easily be made gratuitous for dramatic effect.[13]

Stillman similarly chooses subtle visual clues over more concrete visual evidence. Based on words and actions, it can be obvious what the characters are about to do or have done, but the camera does not necessarily capture it. In *The Last Days of Disco* (Stillman 1998), Alice (Chloë Sevigny) and Tom (Robert Sean Leonard) disappear into the shadows of his bedroom and Tom closes the door. The scene cuts not to inside the room, but to Alice leaving the following morning. As Perkins (2012: 34) rightly notes, Stillman's limited depiction of sex and violence is compensated for with characters' dissection of the events in dialogue.[14] Like instances in which the cinematic verbalists' dialogue provides minimal background information for characters, the camera grants them a sense of privacy at the risk of frustrating the audience.

In their editing of dialogue sequences, the cinematic verbalists at times subvert Rick Altman's (1980) assertion that the right to speech 'carries with it a secondary right, the right to appear in the image' (68). Indeed, Altman is generally right since there has been relatively little experimentation with editing dialogue scenes since the norms for classical continuity were established in the mid-1930s. Again, dialogue reception played an important role with editing practices attributed to audience demand. Writing on early 'talkies', Mary Ann Doane (1980) explains that viewers 'would have felt that a trick was being played on them if they were not shown the words coming from the lips of the actor' (34). American independent cinema does not always abide by this convention and considering things from an audience perspective can help to explain why not.

In *The Reality of Illusion: An Ecological Approach to Cognitive Film Theory* (1998), Joseph Anderson highlights the perceptual impact of synchrony when sound and images are combined. He recaps findings from studies on infants that reveal how, when perception occurs simultaneously in two or more sensory modes, we actively seek connections between them (82). As Anderson explains, 'We seek speech synchrony, and when we find it, we lock our eyes onto the lips of the speaker and our ears onto the stream of utterances' (84). When we can easily connect the words heard on the soundtrack to the mouth of a character on screen then the figure will hold our attention. Although dialogue scenes are generally still treated in this way,[15] there are various moments in which these filmmakers avoid synchrony between who we hear speaking and what we see. If a character is not central to the narrative, then, contrary to Altman's assertion, they may appear on the sound but not image track. For example, *Ghost Dog*'s title character befriends a girl called Pearline (Camille Winbush) whose mother shouts things at her from off-screen, but is never actually shown. Likewise, despite their prominent speech, Audry's (Adrienne Shelly) parents are often kept outside the frame in Hartley's *The Unbelievable Truth*.

Indeed, at various moments in this independent cinema, the pleasurable 'cross-modal confirmation' that Joseph Anderson refers to is frustrated (87). At times, verbal-visuals are designed so that we hear one of the cinematic verbalists' characters in voice-off, or using an angle that means their mouth cannot be seen. At other points, the cinematic verbalists' dialogue precedes the image track and thus avoids the norm for speech to be synchronised with shots of the speaker. In Baumbach's *The Squid and the Whale*, the pace is increased when the closing images of one scene are overlapped with the opening dialogue of the next. Perhaps the best example of this is how Lili (Anna Pacquin), Bernard's (Jeff Daniels) student, is introduced. At home, Bernard has asked Walt (Jesse

Eisenberg) if he would like to come to one of his classes. He agrees and, after convincing his father to sign a book for him, Walt stares at the signature and smiles. As he does this, a female voice-over enters the soundtrack. The camera then cuts to the source of the voice (the next day), and circles the room of students while Lili continues to read. The shot rests on Walt and Bernard before cutting to the drive home. The short scene lasts for twenty-seven seconds, but Lili is only *seen* for three of these. Instead, her provocative prose precedes and follows her appearance in the shot. Like Baumbach, Anderson also uses sound bridges to increase the pace, as in *Moonrise Kingdom* when we hear the start of the scout master's (Edward Norton) log over the unrelated closing images of Suzy spying on her mother.

Similar to Lili's introduction, Roger is introduced by his voice in *Greenberg*, as is Xavier (Hugo Becker) in *Damsels in Distress*. In the latter, Stillman often has a character start to speak either over an intertitle or a point-of-view shot. Since the image is not easily attributable to one character, for several seconds we must try to identify who is speaking based on voice alone; cross-modal confirmation is delayed if not withheld altogether. Such techniques can also have the effect of focusing our attention more on the verbal than the visual. The nuances of characters'/actors' voices also take on greater significance when we hear them over a black screen and with less visual clues.

Overall, the cinematic verbalists' decision to at times avoid synchronicity constitutes another method for increasing audience engagement. In a variety of ways, they ignore the convention – established by dialogue editing norms in classical cinema – for speech to determine who is shown in a given shot. With the visuals of one scene merged with dialogue from the next, largely unrelated, sequence, the audioviewer must process the two streams of sensory data simultaneously and without (or with delayed) cross-modal confirmation. Yet, at the other extreme, they occasionally make images and dialogue reinforce one another in creative but more redundant ways.

Visual and Verbal Synchronicity

A line can be drawn between the highly structured aspects of Hartley's dialogue (extreme repetition of particular words), or Anderson's dialogue (heavy use of wordplay and precise numbers) and the filmmakers' claustrophobic mise en scène.[16] Consider the way that Anderson's dialogue makes a feature of numbers: in *The Life Aquatic with Steve Zissou* (2004), Steve discusses their route on the map in terms of inches ('four' versus 'an inch and a half'), and, in *Fantastic Mr. Fox* (2009), Bean asks for 'three shovels, two pick-axes, [and] 500 rounds of ammunition'. Such unnaturally specific dialogue can be considered the textual equivalent of Anderson's detailed visual style, which Joseph Aisenberg (2008) describes as showing the calculation of a museum curator. Comparisons can equally be made between Anderson's formalist reliance on symmetrical shots and his alliterative verbal patterns, which, as in the following example from *Rushmore*, come close to symmetry: 'Anthony, I'd like to introduce you to Applejack. Applejack, this is Anthony.' So, while James Mottram (2006: 217) describes *Rushmore* as 'a visually unified world that hermetically seals its characters',[17] *verbal* repetition and detail is equally used to 'seal' in Anderson's characters. The same could be said for Hartley's, Jarmusch's and Baumbach's characters and, to a lesser degree, Stillman's.

Writing on narrative techniques in the 'New Hollywood', Thompson (1999: 17) explains that, because filmmakers assume that audioviewers will miss visual or verbal cues, they often follow 'the rule of three', whereby '[t]he same event may be mentioned by a character as about to occur, we may then see it occur, and other characters may then discuss it'. This is the kind of redundancy that early theorists feared would result from dialogue – as when Arnheim (1967 [1932]: 216) notes that sound and image should complete each other by dealing differently with the same subject, thereby expressing something not possible by one of the media alone – and the cinematic verbalists tend to avoid such immediate overlaps. Instead, their verbal-visual repetition can involve the creation of motifs across words and images. Returning to Linklater's *Waking Life*, the verbal-visuals of one character are so in sync that he becomes a caricature as well as a cartoon. The man, who is wearing a sailor hat and driving a boat converted into a car, speaks almost entirely in sea-related puns like 'don't miss the boat' and 'keep things on an even keel'. There is no narrative motivation for these inclusions, but the audience can nonetheless be engaged through the recognition of patterns across the sound and image tracks.

Consider also how *Rushmore* separates images and speech related to water and the sea; there are visual references that are not commented on through dialogue – such as shots of a Jacques Cousteau book, and Herman (Bill Murray) swimming under water – but also verbal references that take place *away from* the film's watery locations (a pool and two aquariums), as when Max lists types of fish when in a factory. Redundant overlaps are avoided to instead create a kind of thematic motif that flows between visual and verbal channels throughout.

Therefore, similar to the carefully integrated relationship between dialogue, music and sound effects that will be explored in Chapter 3, there are a variety of instances in which verbal-visual style in this independent cinema is more excessive than that of mainstream Hollywood cinema. This is often achieved by creating clever synergies between dialogue and mise en scène. This relates back to, but amends, Sconce's discussion of coincidence and synchronicity as an organising *narrative* principle in smart cinema. Sconce (2002: 363) argues that excessive coincidence is seen as an unrealistic plot device that is largely avoided within classical Hollywood narration, but in smart cinema it is a common way to represent 'the fundamentally random and yet strangely meaningful structure of reality'. Although Sconce identifies Linklater's *Slacker* (1991) and Jarmusch's *Night on Earth* (1991) and *Mystery Train* (1989) as three smart films that highlight synchronicity, their formal verbal-visual style is as marked by synchronicity as is the narrative structuring on which Sconce focuses.

In addition to dialogue being overshadowed in Sconce's discussion, it is overshadowed by critics who describe how Anderson and Jarmusch create diegetic worlds that are 'closed' (Suárez 2007: 63), 'unified' (Mottram 2006: 217) or 'self-contained' (Felando 2012: 73). Dialogue that is heavy on coincidence (both in terms of what words keep reappearing, and how they are reflected in the images) creates the impression that we are entering a highly contrived, fictional world. It thus reminds us of cinema's verbal artifices, in contrast with Nelmes's (2011: 217) description of dialogue that gives us the impression that we 'are entering a living, transparent world'. By highlighting cinema's contrivance through diegetic worlds that are 'closed', 'unified' and 'self-contained' in terms of their verbal-visuals, these films acknowledge the tendency for mainstream dialogue to also be contrived, but in more subtle ways. This is not yet the full picture, however. Elements of a less contrived verbal-visual style can also be identified in this cinema, and these link reasonably well with Chion's classification of verbodecentrism.

VISUAL OBSERVATION AND VERBAL OVERHEARING

While Jarmusch and Linklater incorporate elements of a 'realist' visual style, Baumbach and Hartley also include more naturalistic visual elements in later films. Given Linklater's sustained interested in a less polished look, it is fitting that King uses *Tape* (2001) as an example of an indie film that, although shot on a sound-stage, gives the impression of reality due to a variety of shooting choices. King (2005: 111; 120) notes how fast pans are made from character to character, with digital cameras providing glared light and allowing for uncomfortably intimate shots. Visual elements, such as these, which contribute to a sense of pseudo-documentary are in keeping with my claim that the cinematic verbalists often position the audioviewer as an 'overhearer' who is excluded by design from characters' conversations. In cinema, the conception of both 'overhearing' and pseudo-documentary tend to align with certain notions of 'realism' since both aim to more closely approximate reality; we often overhear or observe things that are not meant for us.

Perkins (2012: 60) applies the term 'observational' to Baumbach's *The Squid and the Whale*, *Margot at the Wedding* and *Greenberg*, and notes this style as a departure from the overt stylistic allusions of Baumbach's earlier films.[18] A preference for intimacy and immediacy (combined with a small budget) led to much of *The Squid and the Whale* being shot on location, with hand-held cameras and natural light.[19] Indeed, in a fitting analogy between the film's visual style as observational, and the verbal style as creating a sense of overhearing, one reviewer suggests that the roaming camera evokes 'the primal anxiety of a child listening to his parents whispering angrily in an adjacent room' (Malcolm 2005 cited in Perkins 2012: 60). Indeed, in several scenes one or both sons literally try to listen in on conversations. This situation is replicated in Linklater's *Boyhood* (2014). In both films, the children (and audience members who share their point-of-audition) are unable to hear the argument between the parents. Such scenes are in contrast with the tendency in mainstream cinema for the camera to cut to the scene where the conversation is taking place, or for the volume of actors' dialogue to eschew realist conventions so that conversations can be heard through walls and windows.

When discussing visual style that is more naturalistic than that of mainstream Hollywood, it is important to keep in mind economic and industrial factors that impact on form. King (2005: 158) explains how low-budget productions can be limited in their ability to create smooth movement, with insufficient film stock or shooting time preventing seamless continuity editing. Crucially, although King notes the difficulty of determining when the budget has determined the film's visual aesthetic, it is difficult to identify a situation in which a low budget would determine the verbal style. The cinematic verbalists appear to be aware of this important distinction. Hartley (cited in Wyatt [1997] 2011: 75) explains that when the final budget is lower than anticipated, the script stays the same while *other* elements (such as the number of crowd scenes) have to change.

But it would be incorrect to assume that naturalistic sound design cannot be a stylistic choice. Although the budget for *Margot at the Wedding* was considerably higher (approximately ten million dollars), Baumbach's visual choices are in a more pseudo-documentary style than those in *The Squid and the Whale*: with hand-held cinematography, haphazard framing, dark naturally lit interiors and tracking shots, it is no wonder that critic Scott Tobias (2007) compares the film's 'kitchen-sink realism' to the work of Cassavetes. This complements the film's partly inaudible dialogue that, as is discussed in Chapter 3, is intentionally designed to be difficult to hear – thus distinguishing it from Hollywood sound mixing that ensures that every word is heard.

We can relate Chion's concept of verbodecentrism to these attempts at verbal-visual realism. Chion describes verbodecentrism as:

> the seemingly paradoxical case where dialogue is abundant, but its abundance is not obscured or absorbed by the *mise-en-scène* and instead is foregrounded, as such, for lack of other filmic elements such as acting to make it easier to listen to. (Chion 2009: 497)

His description of verbal-visual style that does *not* make the dialogue 'easier to listen to', is paralleled in performance or recording practices that literally make listening a challenge, such as those in *Margot at the Wedding*. The cinematic verbalists also include other elements that may be considered to be visual equivalents to unintelligible speech, such as the blurring of moving figures in some of Hartley's digital productions. Jim Deneault, cinematographer for *The Book of Life* (Hartley 1998), notes that the shutter speed was reduced to just fifteen frames per second (Rawle 2011: 261). The film was one of the first features to be shot entirely on digital video and, in addition to Hartley showing awareness of complementary sound and visual techniques, he explains that he wanted to make the most of qualities endemic to the medium:

> I've always thought of [digital video] as the visual equivalent of what electronic popular music or amplified electric music has been making for fifteen years now. Distortion has a visual texture. All that blurriness comes out of that aesthetic. (Hartley cited in Eaves 2005)

Hartley's reference to visual texture gains in significance when compared to dialogue. If the cinematic verbalists' deliberate inclusion of a range of non-verbal vocalisations (such as sighs and expressive breathing) are considered as textured sound, then visual texture is another point of comparison. Indeed, in his discussion of Jarmusch's *The Limits of Control*, Adam Nayman (2009) describes Christopher Doyle's cinematography as 'tactile', with the film accumulating 'disparate textures', including strong creases on a suit, or the swirl on an espresso (48–50). Such small details can benefit from being captured by an expert cinematographer and projected onto a large screen. Similarly, vocal texture that depends on cinema's recording and screening equipment is also endemic to the medium, as reflected in discussions of 'the grain' of the voice.[20]

Considering these filmmakers use of (1) visual and verbal synchronicity and (2) an observational visual style as an equivalent to verbal overhearing, one could conclude that the interplay between their verbal and visual tracks is highly complementary. It is therefore fair to say that, as Chion (1994: 9) suggests with his description of the 'audiovisual contract', the two perceptions mutually influence each other in their work. Even when one sets aside the two other components of the audio track (music and sound effects), such analysis reveals the potential for a powerfully harmonised relationship between the verbal and visual.

'BEYOND' VERBOCENTRISM

Discussing independent cinema from the perspective of formal characteristics, King (2005: 106–7) defines form as: 'positioning, movement and framing established by the camera; image quality and textures created through the use of different types of camera, film stock, processing or lighting conditions; sound; and editing regimes'. His discussion of sound is somewhat limited, however, with just one reference to expressive dialogue.[21] More useful to this chapter's analysis of verbal-visual style is King's classification of conventional Hollywood style as 'neutral' (albeit highly constructed), with two opposing effects that indie films generally opt for instead; 'beneath' and 'beyond'. Style that falls 'beneath' aims for an increased sense of 'reality' with devices more associated with documentary, such as handheld cameras and untidy frames. On the other hand, when more self-consciously stylised options are chosen, King describes their form as going 'beyond' that of the classical style. These three points fall along what is obviously a broad spectrum, and one film-maker's work may rest at varying points. While King focuses on the formal properties of *visual* style, these classifications can also be extended to the cinematic verbalists' verbal-visual style, especially when combined with Chion's conception of verbocentrism and verbodecentrism.[22]

The analysis here suggests the operation of a third mode in these film-makers' work – 'beyond verbocentrism' – when dialogue does not necessarily parallel visual actions (as in verbocentrism) or avoid visual interest altogether (as in verbo-decentrism), but is harmonised with other filmic elements in an exceptionally detailed way. Verbo-decentrism generally aligns with King's description of indie films with a formal style 'below' that of classical Hollywood, while verbocentrism conforms with King's conception of a 'neutral' mainstream Hollywood visual style. 'Beyond verbocentrism' instead consists of overtly staged relationships between the cinematic verbalists' image and soundtracks, such as (1) clear overlaps in words and images or (2) ironic disconnects between the two. Such a style accommodates the cinematic verbalists' use of 'verbal images'; intertitles that quote the characters themselves; embedded texts that extend on what has been explicitly verbalised, and spoken sound bridges that increase pace by allowing the words to precede rather than accompany the images.

This verbal-visual style tends to complicate the process through which an audience seeks connections between perception occurring simultaneously in two or more sensory modes – thus taking advantage of cinema as a bimodal experience. Writing on reception and cognition, Joseph Anderson (1998: 86) stresses the propensity of the human mind to 'bridge modalities', and this is a central feature of the way that these indie filmmakers integrate dialogue with moving images. Unlike sound and visuals that redundantly overlap, and so require little bridging, a gap in one element (for example, not seeing the mouth of a speaker) forces another element of perception or cognition to step in – by recalling voices from an earlier scene, or deducing from the content of the speech who is most likely to have said it.

The cinematic verbalists often take a well-established verbal-visual norm, such as the 'rule of three', and subvert it by keeping repetitive elements, but separating out the repetition between images and words so it is less redundant and more of a thematic motif. Such a verbal-visual style departs from Chion's concept of verbocentrism that, while highly constructed, simply tries to mask dialogue's role. Instead, the visuals can be used to remind us what has been said, or to question the authority of its meaning. Dialogue and images are connected in overtly staged ways, thus creating diegetic worlds that are formally 'closed'. Often the filmmakers' verbal-visual style draws attention to contrived overlaps in words and images, or to disconnects between the two. When the cinematic verbalists' dialogue and images overlap then cognitively rewarding patterns are established. Since Sconce identifies the importance of coincidence to 'smart' narratives, then discussion of verbal-visual style in related cinema again demonstrates the role that dialogue can play in establishing the 'smart' aesthetic.

These filmmakers pay close attention not only to *spoken* words, but those incorporated visually. They complicate certain traditional applications of textual speech and the voice-over. Their incorporation of embedded texts demonstrates how mise en scène can be somewhat subordinated to verbal style, while creative intertitles can give the impression that a character is speaking to the viewer through written as well as spoken text.

Notes

1. Sconce's (2002: 359) only other reference to dialogue is when he notes that editing in *Safe* is 'wholly subordinate to character and dialogue'.
2. The line in question implies statutory rape of the student by her teacher when he says: '[T]here's one more thing you should know about Tracey Flick – her pussy gets so wet you wouldn't believe it' (Sconce 2002: 361).
3. Jaeckle (2013a: 166) also discusses this letter when discussing Anderson's use of explicitly scripted speech. Jaeckle notes a complementary ironic contrast between Dirk's mature language and 'the prepubescent voice of Gamble, whose voice-over narration strikes a clear note of sarcasm when reading the boldly underlined phrase "good friend"'.
4. Moments of verbal-visual irony also feature in some of classical Hollywood's more experimental treatments of dialogue, including that of *Citizen Kane*. For example, as Sellors (2010: 74) identifies, Kane's sled is thrown into the fire with Raymond oblivious that 'Rosebud' is painted on it.
5. Bordwell (2008) explains that while an image can link directly to a sound or image in the following scene, it is more common for a sound – usually a line of dialogue – to serve as the connecting device.
6. Similarly, when Anthony in *Bottle Rocket* speaks to his romantic interest through a translator, he discusses his vision for their future impersonally: 'And they meet. And they fall in love. And it's perfect.'
7. Focusing on *Rushmore*, Jaeckle (2013a: 165) identifies how Anderson 'weave[s] three instances of explicitly scripted language into a film that, given its playwright protagonist, is already highly concerned with the power of words'.

8. For example, King (2005: 90) explains how *Magnolia*'s intertitles – in the form of detailed weather conditions – somewhat reflect the film's 'rising and falling dramatic arc'.
9. Similarly, in *Ghost Dog* we not only hear Raymond speak French, but his van has been hand-painted with French words.
10. Chion (2009: 177) also captures the various uses of written text in *Film, A Sound Art*. He explains how such texts can include 'a sense of personal fate for a character, or advice or foreshadowing, or ironic commentary'.
11. This is a variation on John Berger's (1972: 27–8) argument in *Ways of Seeing* that an individual's experience of a painting can be strongly influenced by the description that accompanies it.
12. In *Stranger Than Paradise*, for instance, based on the distinctive sound effects coming from the television, Eva seems to watch science-fiction and cartoons. In *Ghost Dog*, the camera also focuses on Louise (Tricia Vessey) rather than showing the audience what she is watching.
13. King (2005: 72–3) identifies another 'prominent elision' in relation to *Down by Law*, when the audience is not shown how the three main characters manage to escape from prison.
14. Berrettini (2011: 35) notes similar of Hartley when he explains that despite *Amateur* (1994) being centred on sexuality, it 'includes no "explicit" sexual images'.
15. There are exceptions, such as 'New Hollywood' filmmakers in the 1970s who used a more subjective style of editing. For a more detailed example, see Ken Dancyger's (2007: 289–90) discussion of the editing of dialogue sequences for emotional effect in *Chinatown* (Polanski 1974).
16. In terms of Hartley's highly structured mise en scène, Bordwell (2005) has detailed Hartley's 'proclivity for certain tactics of depth staging' and the way in which his economic two-shots often 'squeeze characters into almost cramping proximity'.
17. Similarly, Felando (2012: 73) describes Anderson's diegetic worlds as 'self-contained'.
18. Baumbach's stylistic flourishes in earlier films include intertitles and iris shots. Furthermore, both *Kicking and Screaming* (1995) and *Highball* (1997) are staged theatrically, with limited spatial mobility. When actors move temporarily out of the frame, the camera films their absence and leaves it up to them to return to their mark. However, it could be argued that stagnant camera-work is fitting for plots revolving around people reluctant to move on.
19. However, the film occasionally includes montage sequences set to music, and highly stylised shots, including a circular pan around a table of people.
20. Discussion of 'the grain of the voice' originates with Roland Barthes (1977: 181), but the term has subsequently been applied by scholars discussing the voice in cinema, including James Naremore (1988: 46), Kaja Silverman (1988), Susan Smith (2007) and Donna Peberdy (2007). Vocal qualities are discussed in more detail in Chapter 5.
21. King does make some references to dialogue in his chapter on narrative in independent American cinema, however, revealing the workings of dialogue in such cinema is not the focus.
22. Nessa Johnston (2012) has already extended King's terms to discuss the use of naturalistic 'below' Hollywood dialogue, as part of her broader analysis of the low-budget science-fiction sound design in *Primer* (Carruth 2004).

3. THE INTEGRATED SOUNDTRACK AND LYRICAL SPEECH

Writing in what can be seen as one of the earliest attempts to rid film dialogue of the charge of redundancy, John Fawell (1989) focuses on the 'musicality' of the film script. He explains how Howard Hawks repeats lines so that each 'comes to assume, like a musical refrain, a greater savor and significance' (45). A similar kind of musicality can be identified in independent film dialogue, one that extends to include speech that draws attention to language's rhythmic and aesthetic qualities. This chapter considers the cinematic verbalists' soundtracks as a whole, arguing that their careful approach to dialogue extends to include a creative strategy when combining dialogue, music and sound effects.

Despite the prominence of dialogue and the voice on the soundtrack or – to use Chion's terms – its 'verbocentrism' and 'vococentrism' (1994: 5–6), dialogue does not receive commensurate attention in sound theory literature – although it can in practical handbooks. Integrated approaches to the soundtrack are also rare but, as Paul Thebérge (2008: 66) notes in his study on the interplay of sound and silence, research that analyses each aspect separately is removed from how the sound designer conceives it, the mix engineer creates it and the audience hears it.[1] Instead, the aesthetic and emotive significance of music is often highlighted over the other components.[2] In dedicating a chapter of *American Smart Cinema* (2012: 107) to the 'peculiar "musicality"' of films grouped under this heading, Perkins considers music that serves as 'an excessive element that unbalances narrative flow by emphasising the plasticity of the image' (17). Her discussion of 'smart' soundtracks helpfully examines the importance of music to such films, but it somewhat downplays the significance of dialogue to the sound mix, including its ability to similarly emphasise artificiality through excess. Thus, instead of focusing purely on the music, the discussion of soundtracks here is focused on the interaction of music and sound effects with the dialogue (and other vocal noises): this will include how musical choices made by characters are verbally contextualised, and how these indie filmmakers blur the boundaries between sound effects and dialogue. In particular, by incorporating portions of inaudible dialogue, they seem to position audience members as eavesdroppers rather than sanctioned listeners – calling on us to listen selectively, and engaging us in the process. The films of Baumbach and Jarmusch are particularly distinctive in this regard, as is their general foregrounding of music and approach to sound design, and so the analysis pays special attention to their work.

MELOMANIA AND THE VERBAL CONTEXTUALISATION OF MUSIC

By casting musicians as actors, Hartley, Jarmusch and Linklater immediately signal the significance of music to their work, and often to their characters' identities. Take, for example, Hartley's casting of P. J. Harvey as an unlikely Mary Magdalene character in *The Book of Life*, and Jarmusch's inclusion of musicians such as Tom Waits, Iggy Pop and members of The Wutang Clan and The White Stripes in various films such as *Down by Law* (1986) and *Coffee and Cigarettes* (2003). Their choices of artists are in keeping with the trend in the 1990s, noted by Pauline Reay (2004: 77), for independent films to feature music by independent musicians.[3] In Claudia Gorman's examination of 'auteur music', she uses the term 'melomania' to describe 'music-loving directors who treat music ... as a key thematic element and a marker of authorial style' (149–51). Although acknowledging that directors like René Clair and Alfred Hitchcock used music creatively, Gorbman reserves the term for a more recent group including Jarmusch (151). Melomania has also been extended to Anderson (Hrycaj 2013), and the term could equally be applied to the other four filmmakers under focus. Of course, they are not necessarily responsible for every aspect of music or sound. As in most productions, the music supervisor plays a role in the choices and placement of musical numbers, with Randall Poster working with Anderson, Linklater and Baumbach.[4] Hartley perhaps comes closest to total sonic control since, as well as choosing pre-existing songs, he scores the vast majority of his films under a pseudonym.[5]

Of particular interest to the relationship between dialogue and music, however, is the way that characters in this independent cinema also demonstrate melomania – through the use of significant pre-existing source music, and when the character's musical device is located in the mise en scène. The character's role as DJ has already been noted of Jarmusch's and Anderson's work, as well as by Perkins (2012: 117) in relation to smart cinema more generally. Ben

Winters (2012) has considered how Anderson's characters shape their own sonic environment, and Juan A. Suárez explains that Jarmusch's characters 'traverse the world listening to their own music' (57).[6] The influence of the *Nouvelle Vague* is again clear, with character-chosen music a common feature of Godard's films. As Marie notes of *All the Boys are Called Patrick (Charlotte et Véronique, ou Tous les garçons s'appellent Patrick)* (Godard 1959), we see a young woman listen to pop music on her transistor radio (106), just as we do in several of Hartley's and Jarmusch's films, not to mention the playing of music on other devices (record players, Walkmans, iPods and so forth) in their films more generally.[7]

This trend is of particular relevance to dialogue and audience engagement. In considering the advantages and disadvantages of the lyrics to pre-existing music, Jeff Smith (1998: 166) notes that lyrics 'carry a certain potential for distraction, but their referential dimension can also be exploited to "speak for" characters or comment on a film's action'. But, rather than using non-diegetic songs to verbally comment on characters, when the cinematic verbalists' characters choose the music they often contextualise it for themselves through speech. In Jarmusch's *Stranger Than Paradise*, Eva (Eszter Balint) repeatedly plays the same song: Screamin' Jay Hawkins' 'I Put a Spell on You'. When, several times, Willie (John Lurie) objects to it or asks why she keeps playing it, our attention is drawn to the sound artificiality of character leitmotifs that play non-diegetically whenever they appear. The related dialogue also highlights Eva and Willie's conflicting tastes, which, like the song, is a trope throughout. Comments about Hawkins are also a way for Eva to reveal the American slang that she is learning; she refers to the singer as her 'main man' and counters Willie's negative remarks to her replaying the song with 'He's a wild man, so bug off!'[8] Thus, as well as underlining the contrived nature of the soundtrack, the song becomes a device on which their character dynamics can be explored.

According to Smith, '[b]ecause of its formal autonomy, the compilation score is much less likely [than an original score] to be used as an element of structural and rhythmic continuity' (155).[9] Be that as it may, the cinematic verbalists provide clear exceptions. Jarmusch's *Mystery Train* has been considered as a homage to Elvis, as well as to Memphis as a key location for contemporary pop music (Suárez 2007: 69),[10] while Pink Floyd's 'Hey You' helps to structure the narrative in Baumbach's *The Squid and the Whale*. As we will now explore, dialogue is crucial to the effectiveness of this strategy.

BAUMBACH'S VERBAL INTEGRATION OF MUSIC

Various formats and performances of 'Hey You' are included over the course of *The Squid and the Whale*. On a basic level, it is included because Walt (Jesse Eisenberg) claims to have written it to play in a school talent contest, with parts of it performed live in three locations. The original version of the song is also played on vinyl and heard non-diegetically. The recurrence of the song and its lyrics are used to tie together various strands of the narrative – namely, creative authorship, deception and being torn between different family members and romantic interests. Although most of the lyrics do not resonate, the final line ('together we stand, divided we fall'), recalls the film's opening line, when younger brother Frank (Owen Kline) says over a black screen, 'Mom and me versus you and dad.' The spoken line summarises much of the film's dysfunctional family dynamics, while the final line, as sung, is particularly resonant since Frank accompanies Walt in a performance of the song for their parents. The significance of the song is further highlighted through speech since Joan's (Laura Linney) and Bernard's (Jeff Daniels) reactions to what is supposedly Walt's song are in keeping with the division in the family that runs throughout the narrative. Bernard validates Walt by describing the song as 'very dense, very interesting', while Joan is more realistic than supportive when she stresses how much Walt needs to practice so that he does not embarrass himself at the talent contest. Walt goes on to win the contest and, when he is eventually found out, Bernard's defence of him further connects the father and son. Bernard insists that Walt 'made his own interpretation', echoing Walt's own defence, 'I felt I could have written it. That it was already written was a technicality.' Their reactions also align them with Lili (Anna Paquin), their shared romantic interest who flirts with Walt by revealing how she plagiarised Lou Reed lyrics for her poetry class. This too is reflected in the film's music, since it closes to Reed's distinctive vocals singing 'Street Hassle'; the song lyrics are similar to the writing that Lili reads out as her own work in a scene in Bernard's class.

In addition to being central to the narrative as a whole, Baumbach's use of 'Hey You' increases the importance of specific lines of dialogue. From a structural point of view, any pre-existing song could have filled the song's narrative role (as a song Walt tries to pass off as his own), but much of the song's impact comes from the focus on its closing line, which resonates with the film's opening line and the central premise of a cultured and creative family at war. Consequently, the song's effectiveness somewhat depends on audience members singling out one line and drawing the parallel with the narrative as a whole. In terms of the song's significance, Baumbach himself notes that over time 'it started to feel like it was written for the film' (cited in Levy 2005), yet he also admits that Pink Floyd are one of his favourite bands. The choice is therefore in keeping with Gorbman's description of auteur music as a marker of the filmmaker's personal taste. But, regardless of Baumbach's personal attachment to the band, the song is also entwined with the dialogue design, something that is in keeping with the close attention he generally pays to unifying the dialogue with the soundtrack as a whole.

In Baumbach's later film, *Greenberg*, Roger (Ben Stiller) expresses his feelings for Florence (Greta Gerwig) obliquely by playing her music, which he contextualises verbally, and later by making her a mix-CD that she sings along to while drinking.[11] From the perspective of identification, when a character is shown to play a song and verbally frame its relevance, we are aligned with them not just from the perspective of their thoughts and feelings about the song they discuss, but also through the action of playing it – when, where and on what device. If a character knows the lyrics and sings along (as Florence does) or uses the words of the song as dialogue (as happens in Linklater's *School of Rock*), then the significance of the song is automatically increased. Dialogue can make source music an integral part of characterisation, as when Roger's and Florence's differing relationships with music mirror their characters' dialogue throughout. He is overly controlling and dismissive of others' opinions, while she is polite and modest. She is self-deprecating about the CDs in her car, while Roger is confident that he knows the perfect song for every situation. Florence warmly invites him to watch her sing, but Roger plans a letter of complaint as he listens.[12]

Music is equally important to Baumbach's *Frances Ha*, a film co-written with Gerwig, which includes a memorable sequence in which her title character dances down a New York street to the sound of David Bowie's 'Modern Love'. In interview, Gerwig reveals just how musically driven the film was, in terms of its conception, when she notes that they wanted it to 'feel like a pop song', in the sense of repeatability: 'When it's over, there's a feeling of, "Put it on again"' ('WNYC' 2013).

Understanding the role that characters' comments on song selections plays in 'melomania' becomes clearer when you consider Gorbman's summary of developments in film music:

> The strictures and underlying aesthetic of the classical rules of film music simply no longer hold. Melodies are no longer unheard, song lyrics are perceived to add to rather than detract from audio-viewing, and the sky's the limit with respect to the possible relations between music and image and story. (Gorbman 2007: 151)

Gorbman responds here to criticism of her central argument in *Unheard Melodies* (1987), that film music is not meant to be heard, but works subconsciously to influence the audience's emotional reactions.[13] By framing the audience's context for how to interpret a particular song, characters' explicit commentary on music can encourage us to pay the musical choices more attention than we may ordinarily. Furthermore, just as Gorbman suggests that melomania allows an auteur to express individuality through musical choices, characters who appear to control the soundtrack develop a greater sense of individuality. The strategy leads to music that is connected to (rather than merely associated with) a character, and thus has the potential to increase an audience's identification with a character.

If the norm of non-diegetic music is taken as a familiar but contrived Hollywood convention, then a compilation score where the songs are chosen and discussed by the characters is one way that indie soundtracks can be rendered more 'realistic'. We can also think of soundtrack realism or naturalism in terms of the way that Baumbach's and Jarmusch's dialogue can be de-emphasised on the sound mix.

Not Every Word is Important: Designing Inaudible Dialogue

Advice on dialogue in technical filmmaking manuals tends to be in contrast with early film theorists' insistence that meaning in cinema should not originate in the speech. Consider sound editor Dominic Tavella's (2007: ix; emphasis in the original) mantra that 'in any kind of project, *every word is important* ... The job of the dialogue editor is to make every single word as clear as possible'.[14] Indeed, in keeping with such an aim, performance scholar Donna Peberdy (2007) describes how dialogue recording and editing tends to be treated as 'a sanitising process' that removes 'blemishes and imperfections' from the voice. Writing on dialogue intelligibility (both theoretical and practical) also reveals that, although microphone technology initially limited creative freedom when combining sound and image scale, by the late 1930s a preference for spatial realism was replaced by one for close-up sound.

Rick Altman (1992) chronicles this change through the work of early sound designers from the period like J. P. Maxfield. He notes that sound technicians internalised a new standard for close-up sound because they were praised for dialogue clarity rather than spatial realism (46–9). Crucially for our consideration of audience engagement, Altman explains how close-up sound draws the audience into the narrative and gives them the impression that they are *not* eavesdropping since 'it identifies the sound we want to hear as sound that is made for us' (61–2). Close-up sound also parallels Boon's discussion of dialogue that is 'didactic' in terms of content (telling an audience what they need to know), since both close-up sound and didactic speech are designed to aid comprehension for those outside of the diegetic world. Boon's discussion of 'active dialogue' deals solely with the content and phrasing and ignores how dialogue is recorded and performed. Altman, on the other hand, is not concerned with the content of the dialogue. But the two elements can complement each other, particularly in Jarmusch's and Baumbach's work.

Since the 1980s, Jarmusch has spoken openly about his aim to maintain a realistic scale in terms of sound to visuals – as when boom microphones are used 'in perspective', so that the voices of characters in the foreground are louder than those in the background (Von Bagh and Kaurismäki 1987: 78).[15] This means that we may have to strain to hear portions of the dialogue, with Jarmusch's performers contributing further to the inaudibility of his speech. In *Stranger Than Paradise*, Willie provides a catalogue of vocal sound effects. Some, like sighs, are a reasonably common addition to soundtracks, but actor John Lurie reveals his real-life persona as a jazz musician when his mouth becomes an instrument that randomly whistles, hisses and clicks. His words are also muffled since he often speaks with a cigarette in his mouth. Chion (1994: 85) classifies speech of this kind as 'emanation speech', which he argues consti- tutes a character's sound silhouette. Given the standard practice for dialogue in cinema to be clear and intelligible, Chion asserts that such unclear dialogue is the most cinematically interesting (ibid). Kracauer (1997 [1960]) argued simi- larly three decades earlier, when he praised René Clair's de-emphasised speech for demonstrating that 'the spoken word is most cinematic if the messages it conveys elude our grasp' (107).

Be that as it may, critical reaction to Baumbach's departures from perfectly audible speech reveals the resistance that filmmakers face when taking this approach. Several reviewers of Baumbach's *Margot at the Wedding* com- plained that 'the characters talk quietly and often mumble with no boost in audio level to compensate' (Disher 2008).[16] This effect was intentional, as confirmed by a scan of Baumbach's published screenplay, which includes more than a dozen references to muttered speech and expressive breathing. Claude (Zane Pais) 'blushes and mumbles' when he sits sit beside a stranger; Malcolm (Jack Black) fills an awkward silence when he 'mumbles a tune'; Margot (Nicole Kidman) 'whispers' and speaks 'under her breath'; Pauline (Jennifer Jason Leigh) 'exhales a deep, anxious breath' (2007: 1; 57; 68; 25; 16).

One possible motivation for Baumbach and Jarmusch's use of these tech- niques is to create an increased sense of realism, one at odds with the norms of mainstream Hollywood sound mixing. In his examination of John Cassavetes' dialogue, Berliner (1999) sums up the irony of what generally passes for dialogue realism. As he explains – as part of a strategy to contrast the 'real realism' of Cassavetes' dialogue with Hollywood's approach to verbal realism – transcripts of 'real-life conversation' are able to 'illustrate not only how unlike real speech movie dialogue really is but also how odd real dialogue would sound in a movie' (4). Although writing on verbal hesitations and digressions rather than less audible speech, Berliner's point is further demon- strated by the negative reaction to intentionally unclear dialogue. By masking portions of the speech, Baumbach and Jarmusch's strategy helps to highlight the absurdity of speech that is foregrounded on the soundtrack, as well as the disguised manipulation required to ensure that every word is heard. Indeed, this attention to the sound mix adds extra credence to Tobias's comment that *Margot at the Wedding* 'has a kitchen-sink realism that's genuinely unsettling, like a John Cassavetes movie populated by the hyper-articulate' (2007). When we can fully hear them then they may sound hyper-articulate, but that is not always the case.

At points, Wes Anderson also includes moments of inaudibility that similarly highlight this absurdity, but these moments are less 'realistic' in their design. In a factory scene in *Rushmore*, rather than lowering background noise, Anderson makes a feature of the characters' exaggerated attempts to be heard over the sound of machinery. Max shouts over clanking machines and Herman puts his head down a pipe when he asks a question – his voice booming as a result. Anderson's awareness of the standard soundtrack hierarchy (with dialogue at the top) is more obvious still in a short scene that takes place, for no apparent reason, on the rooftop of a noisy urban location. As Max begins to 'get to the point' (a literal request made by the woman to whom he is speaking), the sound of approaching sirens takes over the soundtrack. The sequence appears to be in homage to the soundtrack to *Made in U.S.A.* (Godard 1966). Throughout the film, the name of the man that Paula (Anna Karina) is looking for is deliberately drowned out by the sound of passing planes or cars. Like with Baumbach's *Margot at the Wedding*, the critical response to Godard's technique was negative with Roud (1970: 97) describing his deliberately inaudible dialogue as 'painful' and enraging.

Stillman also avoids lowering background noise each time that a character speaks.[17] In *The Last Days of Disco*, characters strain their voices to be heard over the loud disco music and, if far enough from the camera, their words are not heard at all. Even *Metropolitan*'s (1990) screenplay offers evidence that a realistic sound-to-image scale is important to Stillman, when, mid-sentence, there is a note directing that the character should raise his voice when 'the music starts' (Stillman 1995: 163). Here, Stillman is not concerned that the audience will miss something or, rather, moments such as these – in which the cinematic verbalists' dialogue is unheard or unclear – are factored in early as aesthetic effects. A comparison can be drawn between this technique and Howard Hawks's use of overlapping dialogue to create *the impression* that an audioviewer is missing out on hearing something. However, as François Thomas notes, 'nothing important [is] lost' since Hawks's overlapping speech tends only to cut off 'the needless ends of sentences' (127).[18]

In terms of audience engagement, these unconventional approaches to dialogue volume can be related to Gianluca Sergi's (2001) discussion of audio spectatorship. Sergi describes developments in sound technology as helping to create 'a "sonic playground" in which the spectator actively participates, making sense of what is around him or her' (121). As Sergi rightly notes, when an audience member is required to single out and locate elements of the soundtrack then an 'active and discerning listener' is the result (126).[19] Using speech that is not aurally prominent is one way through which these indie filmmakers create a 'sonic playground' for their audiences. Such speech also indicates their awareness that we can correctly perceive the words without the sound mix being manipulated so that dialogue is notably prominent. Because, as cognitivist Joseph Anderson (1998: 28) explains in his discussion of the human auditory system, 'a major capacity of [it] is its ability to sort out the many competing sounds in the environment'.

More specifically, the human ability to focus attention on a single talker in a noisy environment has been termed the 'cocktail party effect'. As Barry Arons (1992: 35–6) notes of the phenomenon, '[f]rom a listener's point of view, the task is intuitive and simple', even though the effect is complex when considered from a psychological and physiological perspective. The cocktail party effect means that, despite the norm of foregrounding dialogue on the soundtrack so that every word is clear, if the music remains loud (or the actor's voice quiet), audience members should be able to distinguish between competing sounds, as in everyday life. Unlike in reality, we cannot move closer to the talker in order to hear better, or ask them to repeat something. But, provided the recording and screening environment is of a reasonable standard, then this should not pose too great a problem. In the case of independent filmmakers, the expectation that they will direct their own screenplays, and oversee the treatment of dialogue in post-production, likely encourages them to incorporate less audible (or inaudible) dialogue during the writing stage. These experiments with the material properties of speech extend far beyond its audibility, however.

SOUNDTRACK AMBIGUITIES:
DIALOGUE/SOUND EFFECTS AND DIALOGUE/MUSIC

The creation of ambiguous regions of the soundscape, where the lines between dialogue and sound effects, and dialogue and music, are unclear, is another way that these writer-directors use their dual roles to design a highly integrated soundtrack. Baumbach, for instance, uses sound design to equate characters being competitive at sport and in conversation. In *The Squid and the Whale*, tennis and table tennis matches recur throughout, with the sound of the ball going back and forth equivalent to the to-and-fro of their speech. The technique is in keeping with Sergi's (1999: 135) use of the term 'supporting sound', in reference to enhancements made to a line's delivery through the arrangement of music or sound effects. As he notes, words can be 'protected' by dimming obtrusive background noises, or made more resonant with the addition of complementary music. *The Squid and the Whale* also creates a complementary relationship between verbal and physical sparring when, each with a boxing glove, Frank defends their mum and Walt defends their dad (Figure 3.1). As their argument escalates so too does the boxing, with Frank instinctively hitting Walt harder when he calls Joan a liar. The loud smack of

Figure 3.1   The sounds of boxing gloves support verbal sparring in *The Squid and the Whale* (Baumbach 2005). (Source: screenshot by author)

the glove hitting Walt 'supports' the verbal sparring by providing a finality and punctuation to the scene.

Anderson takes quite a different approach to 'supporting sound' in *Bottle Rocket*, as when Dignan's (Owen Wilson) dialogue includes moments when he verbalises what would normally be a sound effect. Toasting to the success of his robbery with Anthony (Luke Wilson) and Bob (Robert Musgrave), Dignan says, 'Great work, great work, both of you,' and, over the sound of their glasses touching, he adds a redundant, 'Clink, clink.' During the robbery itself, he also speaks a bird sound ('cuckaw, cuckaw') while using his hand to mime a beak.[20] These spoken noises strengthen the impression conveyed by the dialogue of Dignan as childlike and enthusiastic. The character also develops the bird trope verbally when he describes how Bob 'flew the coop' after he abandons them. Elsewhere in the film, Anthony seems to respond to a sound effect when he says that 'crime does not pay', since a leitmotif of tambourines is used non-diegetically throughout, to render musically the sound of money being shaken. In addition to serving as music, the non-diegetic sound of the money/tambourine is thus integrated with the dialogue to create ironic contrasts between the money as a sound effect and its functions as music. In comparison with Hollywood cinema, these kinds of hyper-stylised relationships between soundtrack elements seem somewhat 'excessive'.

Like Baumbach and Anderson, Hartley can also spread meaning across the components of the soundtrack in a thoughtful and efficient way. His attention to sound design is apparent from his published screenplays, with sound effects summed up in the screenplay for *Trust* as 'the brutal sounds of fighting', such as 'dishes smashing, furniture breaking' (Hartley 1992: 170). In fact, since Hartley's dialogue is often delivered in a flat, emotionless style, then his sound effects at times convey a tone that is absent from the speech. An illustrative example of the transfer of emotion from dialogue to sound effect can be found in *Trust*. Maria's mother, Jean (Rebecca Nelson), orchestrates for Maria to discover her boyfriend (drugged by Jean) in bed with Maria's sister. Jean asks Maria to get something from the bedroom and the camera stays on her in the kitchen as she waits to hear Maria react. Hartley rarely diverges from his screenplays on set, with the sounds – detailed below – executed as described:

> On the stove, the kettle starts to whistle.
> JEAN doesn't react. She breathes in deep, waiting.
> The kettle whistles ...
> INT. STAIRWAY. NIGHT – SAME TIME.
> The empty stairway. From the kitchen we hear the kettle's shrill, relentless whistle.
> INT. MARIA'S KITCHEN. NIGHT – SAME TIME.
> JEAN at the table, not moving; stiff as a board, waiting. The kettle is deafening.
> ...
> The whistling stops.
> JEAN looks up, startled.
> MARIA is standing there, her hand still on the stove's burn knob.
> MARIA: Here you go. I'm going to bed. Good night. (Hartley 1992: 164–5)

In the scene, Hartley seems to play with both Jean's and the audience's expectations that the rising sound of the kettle is going to turn into a similarly 'deafening' scream when Maria finds Jean and Matthew in bed. Instead, Maria cuts off the sound of the kettle, while her calm words defuse the tension altogether: a single sound effect is used to capture the dramatic tension, and a single line of dialogue is used to deflate it. In keeping with this interpretation, Hartley describes his role as a director as 'finding the essential' by removing redundancy so that 'the acting, the sound recording, the editing, the music, and the dialogue ... [are all] working in concert' (Fuller 1992: xxix). In terms of the dialogue's relationship with the sound effects, when the latter captures the dramatic tone then the actors' delivery need not.[21]

Lyrical Speech: Polyglot Cinema and Repetition

The aforementioned discussion of spoken sound effects begins to consider American independent cinema's use of speech as an aesthetic – as opposed to narrative – feature, a topic that we will now turn to in more detail. Writing in 1960, Siegfied Kracauer called for the content of film dialogue to be secondary to its material qualities, with several subsequent scholars – including Nelmes (2011) and sound specialist David Sonnenschein (2001) – drawing attention to the ways that dialogue can be partially disconnected from its semantic meaning.[22] As Nelmes (2011: 236) explains, the construction of film dialogue 'is a complex mix of the everyday and the poetic; it creates the illusion of being natural by using colloquial words yet its actual language construction is anything but'. Since the dialogue of our group of filmmakers is used to convey more than just semantic meaning then the term 'poetic' can certainly be applied. Yet unlike the type of dialogue to which Nelmes refers (and excluding the earlier discussion of moments when dialogue clarity is deliberately sacrificed), such uses of language do not necessarily aspire to 'seem real'.

The listing of words in a free-association style is one such example. As the following instances reveal, when characters in their work disrupt exchanges with collections of only vaguely related words, they can partially disconnect speech from its semantic meaning:

> Indian River, Face the Music, Inside Dope, Off the Wall, Cat Fight, Late Spring, Passing Fancy ...
> – Eddie in *Stranger Than Paradise* (Jarmusch 1984)

> Guarantee. Promises. Expectation. Consideration. Sincerity. Selflessness. Intimacy. Attraction. Gentleness. Understanding. An understanding without words. Dependence without resentment. Affection. To belong. Possession. Loss.
> – 'Sheriff' in *Simple Men* (Hartley 1992)

> Barracuda, stingrays, electric eels, trout, hammerheads, piranha, giant squid, octopi [*sic*]...
> – Max in *Rushmore* (Anderson 1998)

Aside from being poetic, streams of loosely connected words are an ideal form of engaging or 'active' dialogue, since they require the audience to bridge the gaps between often unrelated expressions or objects. The use of such lists can again be traced back to the *Nouvelle Vague*, with an overt example found in *Jules and Jim* (*Jules et Jim*) (Truffaut 1962) when Catherine (Jeanne Moreau) lists nearly twenty wine regions. When neither Jules (Oscar Werner) nor Jim (Henri Serre) responds to her digression it reinforces the idea that the list's real function is to draw attention to the names of the regions and the contrived nature of scripted speech. American independent cinema can use lists for a similarly digressive effect.[23] In *Stranger Than Paradise*, Eddie (Richard Edson) reads Willie two lists of racing horses in quick succession, with neither serving any narrative purpose. In Hartley's *Simple Men*, the Sheriff (Damian Young) confuses two relative strangers when he launches into an oblique and unmotivated monologue about what seem to be components of a romantic relationship (including: 'Sincerity. Selfishness. Intimacy.'). These lists can become a source of absurd humour – as with the *Rushmore* list of exotically named sea creatures – while permitting the inclusion of words that are aurally interesting, but would not ordinarily be grouped together.

Lists also have the potential to deconstruct mainstream dialogue norms, as in Hartley's *Simple Men* when Martin (Martin Donovan) ends a debate about Madonna (that he failed to contribute to), by reading out a selection of twenty-two musical artists, many with their names abbreviated or altered in an act of poetic license.[24] This list seems to mock lines that provide a clear sense of closure to a scene – the kind of 'toppers' that Kozloff (2000: 75) describes as 'retorts that attempt to close off a conversational topic by their finality or nastiness'. If Martin's list is an answer, then we are left to determine the unasked question. More generally, when a character enters into a stream-of-conscious list, it is virtually impossible to predict what words will come next, let alone how other characters will respond. In allowing a character to drag a conversation away from an apparent narrative function, the verbal form therefore departs from more formulaic mainstream dialogue.

The inclusion of multiple languages is another technique that indie writer-directors use to incorporate the sound properties of speech, a property previously noted by Kracauer (1997 [1960]: 109) and Sonnenschein (2001: 70–80).[25] In Jaeckle's (2013a: 157) analysis of the shared dialogue techniques of Preston Sturges and Anderson, he outlines how both use dialects and languages other than English.[26] Jaeckle explains that while Sturges does this purely for comedic effect, Anderson's use of multilingualism 'prompt[s] deeper considerations of language as language' (167). Jarmusch, Hartley and Linklater equally use multilingualism to raise audience awareness of broader issues of language, when incorporating a range of predominantly European languages (including Italian, French, Hungarian, Finnish and Portuguese). Since they often withhold subtitles, Anglophone audience members are encouraged to listen to a variety of aural qualities, rather than focusing on the meaning of the words.

The incorporation of multiple languages also serves a narrative purpose by advancing the theme of miscommunication. If the dialogue does contain important information then another character generally translates or pieces fragments of meaning together. This too provides opportunities for the dialogue to convey a deeper message, while adding novelty by using less familiar sounds. Such cinema can thus be categorised alongside other 'polyglot' films that, according to Tessa Dwyer (2005: 296), include two or more languages at the level of dialogue *and* narrative. Writing from the perspective of translation studies, Dwyer captures the strengths of polyglot films that 'approach translation in a radically upfront manner' (305). As the examples to follow demonstrate, the cinematic verbalists' use of multilingualism is 'upfront' and maximises the potential of languages other than English to emphasise issues of 'untranslatability, cultural disjunction and gaps in meaning' that Dwyer identifies as important (ibid.). This incorporation of multiple languages again channels the verbal style of the French New Wave, whose filmmakers occasionally made a feature of English and the accents of non-native French speakers. Godard (cited in Roud 2010 [1970]: 11) explains that a foreign character speaking French gave 'to ordinary words a certain freshness and value that they normally have lost'. [27]

Miscommunication based on foreign dialogue is particularly common in Jarmusch's work, with Suárez (2007: 66) noting that 'it is characters with foreign accents or even non-English speakers who tend to hold the floor'. Roberto Benigni plays a confused Italian in *Down by Law* and one of the shorts in *Coffee and Cigarettes*. In his discussion of *Down by Law*, Suárez identifies how much of the film's humour stems from Bob's/Benigni's 'accent and his way of slightly distorting set phrases' (ibid.). Roberto's accent also allows Steven (Steven Wright), his American interlocutor, opportunities to misunderstand:

> ROBERTO: Do you, when do you leave?
> STEVEN: United States.
> ROBERTO: No, here.
> STEVEN: Oh, I've to leave soon.

This exchange takes advantage of speech's sound properties since depending on the pronunciation 'where do you live' and 'when do you leave' sound similar. Basic English also forces Roberto to rely on tone rather than content. This leads him to respond positively to Steven's logically flawed ideas (such as caffeine popsicles for children) since they are delivered in a neutral inflection with no tonal indication that the content is absurd. [28] There are abundant other examples throughout Jarmusch's work. In the opening minutes of *Mystery Train*, we experience two Japanese teenagers test out their basic English in a Memphis train station. In *Stranger Than Paradise*, Willie's assimilation in the United States is explored almost entirely through his relationship to Hungarian. With Willie unwilling to speak Hungarian, he tries to force his cousin and aunt to speak English, and refuses to answer to Bela, his birth name. [29]

Like Roberto and Steven's exchange in *Stranger Than Paradise*, Linklater's *Before Sunrise* (1995) draws attention to how the words sound rather than to their meaning. Jesse (Ethan Hawke) struggles to understand Céline's (Julie Delpy) French and equates the sounds of the words with those familiar to him from English. In the screenplay, the use of numbers and phonetic spelling captures these nuances of translation:

CÉLINE: Tell him to pick you up at *quai Henri IV*.
JESSE: Arri cat?
CÉLINE: Quai Henri IV.
JESSE: An-ri-cat?
CÉLINE: Henri IV.
JESSE: Oh, like Henry 4. (Linklater and Krizan 2005: 178–9)

Translation is also an important trope in the sequels, *Before Sunset* (2004) and *Before Midnight* (2013). At one point, Jesse even states that when Americans are travelling abroad those who they meet tend to expect them only to speak English.[30] More generally, and recalling the centrality of irony to Sconce's conception of the smart film, characters who speak different languages enable the narrative significance of miscommunication to be laboured ironically to engage the audience.

Historically, non-English dialogue has proven significant to distribution patterns, often determining whether a film is screened in a multiplex or an arthouse cinema.[31] Elsaesser (2005: 76) argues that European productions that successfully reach mainstream international audiences 'have to disguise themselves to look and sound like they [are] American'. Revisiting European national cinemas in respect of contemporary filmmaking, Elsaesser (2013) subsequently describes Lars Von Trier as a 'master of the national camouflage', partly because he includes American actors, but also because he uses English dialogue. Claire Denis's minimal dialogue instead 'slip[s] beneath the language barrier so to speak, rather than vaulting it [as does Von Trier's]'. The cinematic verbalists stand in sharp contrast to the likes of Von Trier and Denis: by intentionally creating a (partial) language barrier for Anglophone audiences they instead push back against the monopoly that English holds on US cinema. In doing so, they (unnecessarily) recreate the problem that European filmmakers often face when exporting to Anglophone countries. Because just as the idiosyncratic dialects used in films like *Breathless* (*À bout de souffle*) (Godard 1960) and *Zazie Dans Le Métro* (Malle 1960) were 'a nightmare for subtitlers' (Wiegand 2012: 66), the cinematic verbalists' incorporation of language's phonetic properties similarly resists translation. The filmmakers should certainly be praised for this strategy, one that better reflects the actual mixture of cultures and languages in the United States.[32] Indeed, Jarmusch has explained that the un-subtitled Native American speech in *Dead Man* (Jarmusch 1995) is for the benefit of those familiar with Native American cultures, even though this means that the dialogue is out of reach for the vast majority of the audience (Rosenbaum 1996: 158–9).

This discussion of multilingualism indicates the difficulty of categorising elements of independent cinema's dialogue design as having either a narrative or aesthetic function. This is also the case with verbal repetition, another notable feature of their verbal style, and one that aligns with Fawell's (1989: 45) discussion of repeated lines 'com[ing] to assume, like a musical refrain, a greater savor and significance'. In their studies of Hartley, both Berrettini and Rawle identify repeated dialogue as central to Hartley's verbal style. As Berrettini (2011: 4) rightly notes, when Hartley's characters appear 'stuck' in circular conversation, the stylised language serves to underline the amusing problems that can arise during communication. Hartley's repetition also serves other functions, including highlighting the contrived nature of film dialogue. Ned's (Jeffrey Howard) declaration in *Simple Men* (that 'there's nothing like a machine to make a man feel insignificant') is what comes to mind when Ned repeats 'there's nothing but trouble and desire' eight times. By giving the impression that characters have also been programmed to repeat a limited number of things, Hartley's repetition emphasises the contrived nature of the speech.

In discussing Quentin Tarantino's highly integrated soundtracks, Lisa Coulthard (2012: 172) describes his use of short and memorable repetitive and rhyming dialogue (including alliteration, consonance and assonance) as memorable 'single-level structures designed for immediate cognition'. The same could be said of Anderson's, Baumbach's, Hartley's, Jarmusch's and Stillman's dialogue when they incorporate alliteration, consonance and assonance, or when the same words are fired back and forth in a single exchange. But, in addition to these single-level structures designed for immediate cognition, they include repetition that could be described as having a *multiple* level structure. Repetition of this nature calls on audiences to recall how certain words or phrases are used at various points in the film. When a certain line or word is repeated throughout, our role in constructing the overall significance of the speech depends on the change in context. If there is little to no change, for example, if the same character keeps repeating the same phrase in new but similar situations, then we have relatively little to 'do', cognitively speaking. Such repetition is common in mainstream comedies and its obviousness can be tedious. As Kozloff (2000: 85) notes, screenwriters often deliberately coin a line or exchange that recurs in a 'highly noticeable' way. But when a word or phrase (or a close variation of either) is used by different characters – or the same character in a radically different context – we are called on to reinterpret its meaning, often to reveal subtle irony or a nuance of character. Indeed, Linklater's own awareness of this is indicated by a card in *Slacker* that reads 'repetition is a form of change'.

Repetition of this nature can be illustrated by an example from Hartley's *Trust*, in which Matthew becomes associated with the words 'fix' and 'fixed', and this gives way to a moment crucial for revealing his depth of feelings. While Matthew's father describes how 'he can fix anything', Matthew's view is that 'some things shouldn't be fixed', including TVs, as when he refuses a job when his terms ('I'll fix radios, phone answering machines, calculators') aren't met ('but TVs is what we fix'). In a later scene, Matthew is in the waiting room at an abortion clinic, when a stranger uses the word 'fix' in respect of Maria's baby: 'You come in here the first time, your whole life's a mess. All this tension and stuff. Then she goes in there and when she comes out everything's fixed.' At this point Matthew grabs the man and throws him to the floor because, as Matthew says previously, 'Some things shouldn't be fixed.' Since he wanted Maria to keep the baby then this is presumably one of them. Although Matthew's aggressive reaction may seem unprovoked, it is the repetition of variations on the mundane word 'fix' that explains his behaviour. This subtlety is in contrast to the kind of tag lines that Kozloff discusses that, because they recur in their entirety, depend on the viewer's overt familiarity to giving them resonance. Thus, although the cinematic verbalists' use of repetition can at times be pleasurable in a passive way (when designed for immediate cognition), verbal echoes can also require audiences to compare the various instances in which a word or phrase (or close variations on them) is used.

In fact, in several of Jarmusch's, Hartley's and Anderson's films, dialogue repetition extends beyond one diegetic world to several of their films. In Jarmusch's *Coffee and Cigarettes*, characters in different short films discuss the same things, sometimes almost verbatim.[33] Repetition between separate film worlds is complicated further in *Broken Flowers* (Jarmusch 2005), since words appear to 'spill over' from the television. The film opens with Don (Bill Murray) watching *The Private Life of Don Juan* (Korda 1934) and its dialogue about Juan's womanising is continued when his girlfriend Sherry (Julie Delpy) enters, announces she is leaving and describes Don as an 'over-the-hill Don Juan'. Although Sherry quickly leaves, the disillusioned female characters on Don's screen continue to speak for her. Such highly coincidental repetition could be seen as another dimension to the kind of coincidental worlds described in Sconce's conception of the smart film.

Overall, the impact of these kinds of repetition exemplifies Bruce F. Kawin's (1972) argument in *Telling It Again and Again: Repetition in Literature and Film*. Kawin makes a crucial distinction between repetitive and repetitious, noting that while each depends on something occurring multiple times, the latter recurs with less impact or to no particular end, while the former repeats with an equal or greater impact (4). For the most part, these writer-directors repeat language using what Kawin terms as 'artful variations', which can create a poetic effect (37–8). With dialogue, as with song lyrics, their repetitive word choices take on new meaning in a new time and context, highlighting why verbal repetition in cinema should not automatically be criticised as derivative or repetitious. The concept of temporality is the final aspect of their carefully integrated soundtracks to consider.

LANGUAGE AND MUSIC AS MARKERS OF TIME

Like musical genres, styles of speech evolve over time and American independent cinema often experiments with the temporal nature of both, using the treatment of one time-stamped soundtrack component to reinforce that of another. In Linklater's *Boyhood*, music plays a particularly strong role in marking time. The film spans a twelve-year period and, rather than using expositional dialogue or intertitles to signal different years, Linklater uses popular music, including songs by Coldplay, Gotye and Arcade Fire. More generally, these filmmakers tend to use diegetic music that predates each film's release (and, sometimes, setting) by several decades. By also incorporating dated sound effects and dialogue, they are able to reinforce the sense that characters are preoccupied with an idealised past, often their own.

While the word 'nostalgic' applies well to the general style of the cinematic verbalists' music, the term 'anachronistic' is more fitting to their soundtracks as a whole since it can incorporate how language is chronologically specific. David T. Johnson (2012: 29–30) picks up on this in his book on Linklater: '*Dazed and Confused* [1993] attempts to capture the rhythms of late-twentieth-century adolescent speech, at once both inventive and derivative'. Linklater's incorporation of the vernacular of the early nineties aligns well with Johnson's central argument that the filmmaker is preoccupied with temporality since language serves 'as a constantly updated dynamic oral history' (30). The meandering speech of characters in this and other Linklater films would be difficult to recreate verbatim, thus allowing them to capture how speech is transient. From this perspective, the character of 'Old Man Recording Thoughts'[34] in *Slacker* gains particular importance. Speaking into his dictaphone as he walks down the street, the man is a reminder that words are ephemeral. If they are not recorded in the moment then they can never be either spoken or heard again. Although this occurs constantly in reality, it takes Linklater (or any filmmaker) recording language to capture and preserve its transience. Rob Stone's discussion of dialogue in *Before Sunset* (2004) also connects Linklater's speech with time. As Stone (2013: 131) notes, since the film is set in 'real-time' then speech 'is rendered as an even more urgent activity' than in *Before Sunrise* (1995). In other words, because Céline and Jesse only have a limited number of hours with each other (as well as with the audience), then everything they say prevents them from saying something else. Thus, like pre-existing music, dialogue is a marker of time.

Stillman also integrates dialogue and music to create a highly stylised sense of anachronism. According to Mark C. Henrie (2001: xiv), 'a wistful nostalgia colors everything' in Stillman's films. This is immediately evident in Stillman's choice of music, with *Barcelona* (1994) and *The Last Days of Disco* reflecting his interest in disco. The interest began when Stillman lived in Spain and continued in New York, where he was a regular at Studio 54 in the late 1970s and early 1980s (Cunha 1998). Combined with his love of dance, Stillman's films can be viewed as contemporary updates of classical musicals in which music frames the action and is what urges the character both to talk and to stop.[35] In *Metropolitan,* cha-cha music is first heard off-screen and gives way to a debate about the dance, followed by characters actually dancing. The inclusion of dated sound effects is another element of Stillman's stylised nostalgia, as revealed in the screenplay direction for *Metropolitan*: 'During his speech, an archaic buzzer sounds – the house intercom connecting the lobby to an antique apparatus hidden away in the kitchen' (Stillman 1995: 254).

Stillman's verbal style is equally nostalgic. Characters tend to speak in a formal and outdated vernacular, as though their words have spilled off the pages of the Shakespeare and Jane Austen texts from which they quote. In *The Last Days of Disco*, Charlotte (Kate Beckinsale) transforms stock phrases into nonsense by applying them to her limited experiences. Indeed, the tendency for clichés to be appropriated for humorous effect is also noted by scholars of Austen (Johnson 1990: 30; Waldron 1999: 23–4).[36] Hymns, both spoken and sung, are another unconventional and dated aspect of Stillman's soundtracks. David Whalen (2001: 119–21) alludes to this when he notes that Stillman's paradoxical humour includes a contrast between his incorporation of both traditional hymns and disco music. He explains that disco is 'ridiculed for its musical vapidity', while discos themselves were associated with 'vanity, excess, [and] hedonism' (ibid.). However, in *The Last Days of Disco*, it is Charlotte (the most superficial and judgemental character) who ends up defending hymns and singing 'Amazing Grace' on the street. With dialogue that is all surface and no depth, Charlotte initially seems like the perfect ambassador for disco. Since Stillman holds disco in higher regard than those who consider it to be vapid, it is therefore fitting that he would subvert audience expectations of Charlotte, revealing her depth and disco's simultaneously.

Anderson's use of music to convey nostalgia has also received attention. Elena Boschi and Tim McNelis (2012: 30–2) link Anderson's use of male singers and rock bands from the 1960s and 1970s to his narratives that are 'driven by a desire to restore past glory'. Although Boschi and McNelis acknowledge that Anderson's films display 'a carefully crafted symbiotic relationship between songs, visuals and dialogue' (29), they only comment on speech when it cues a song directly. Yet the formal structure of the characters' speech can be seen to prime an audience to travel back – musically and narratively – in time. A fatalistic pessimism about passing time is especially evident in *The Royal Tenenbaums*. The film opens with an external narrator

(Alec Baldwin) chronicling events in the characters' lives in authoritative style: Margot (Gwyneth Paltrow) was adopted 'at age two' and in 'the ninth grade' she won a grant 'of fifty thousand dollars'. She disappeared 'four years later', and was gone 'for two weeks'. Specific milestones are also laid out for the other children, after which the narrator departs until the closing scene. But, in his absence, the characters carry on the same type of numerically precise documentation. For instance, when Royal takes Margot to a restaurant she tells him, 'I only have five minutes.' Then, when Margot discovers a faded pack of cigarettes hidden behind a brick, Richie (Luke Wilson) asks her how old she thinks they are; after one puff she replies, 'About ten years.'

So although Jaeckle (2013a) rightly identifies Anderson's formalist approach to dialogue in terms of his use of rhyming and alliteration, we can add to this the formal use of temporal measurements. Unnaturally specific dialogue of this kind indicates how Anderson's characters are obsessed with (or misplaced in) time. It can also be considered the verbal equivalent of Anderson's intensely detailed visual aesthetic. In this way, when a feature is made of numbers in Anderson and Baumbach's co-authored screenplays it is most likely Anderson's contribution.[37] Because although Baumbach's characters use language precisely, they tend to question one another's word choices rather than speaking with an artificial level of detail. Anderson's overt foregrounding of numbers is another example of 'excessive' dialogue since, in keeping with Thompson's (1977: 57) description of excess, it serves both 'to contribute to the narrative and to distract our perception from it'. For the most part, the precise week, month or year in which things happen to Anderson's characters does not matter.[38] The technique therefore draws our attention to the artifice of the diegetic world and the way backstory is often incorporated, as though natural, in more mainstream dialogue.

Only Language Left Alive

Jarmusch's *Only Lovers Left Alive* (2013) offers a particularly interesting example of verbal anachronism in practice. Based on summary alone, a romantic vampire film appears at odds with Jarmusch's body of work. But this move towards genre cinema seems to be partly motivated by a desire to reveal something generally overlooked in the spate of vampire films emerging in the twenty-first century: such characters would experience vast changes in language, accumulating extensive vocabularies and knowledge over the course of their long lives. With *Only Lovers Left Alive*, the central figures of Adam (Tom Hiddleston) and Eve (Tilda Swinton) are presented as a set of human encyclopaedias, woven together with the thread of human subjectivity. History, and their experience of it, results in casual conversations laced with references to familiar people: understanding the vampires' long lives depends on audiences picking up on, and being familiar with, the predominantly European events to which they refer, mostly cultural and scientific.

These particular vampires seem to have originated from medieval England, with their vocabulary inflected at times with traits of Middle English or Early Modern English. At one point, while Eve tries to raise Adam's spirit by recounting events from the past, she refers to him as 'my liege lord'. The phrase, which dates back to the feudal customs of medieval Europe, signifies her long-standing allegiance to Adam. Eve also uses the term 'weskit' to refer to an item of clothing belonging to the character of Christopher Marlowe (John Hurt).[39] This informal word for a waistcoat is never explained, but the term is temporally situated by Marlowe's response, 'I was given this in 1586, and it's one of my favourite garments.' Like with the frequent and precise references to time in Anderson's work, the vampires' ability to provide specific dates supports the impression that they are misplaced in time, linguistically and more generally. Similar to Margot in *The Royal Tenenbaums*, Eve can generally tell how old things are just by touching them, such as Adam's dressing gown that is 'at least a century older' than his new (old) guitar.

As long-standing citizens of the world, the vampires have also accumulated knowledge of various languages. As such, they ironically become realistic ambassadors for Jarmusch's tendency to combine multiple languages to create polyglot cinema. An early example of this, in which Adam suggests types of hardwood that would be suitable for a wooden bullet, combines the Latin of scientific taxonomy with the kind of poetic listing previously identified in cinematic verbalists' screenplays: 'I'd suggest ironwood, lignum vitae; maybe snakewood, Piratinera guianensis; or possibly African blackwood, Dalbergia melanoxylon.' Adam/Hiddleston moves swiftly through the names, listing the complicated Latin terms with as much ease as their English equivalents. The decision to include these more aurally interesting versions is in alignment with Jarmusch's consistent incorporation of lyrical dialogue, and yet the terms are also technically correct – and so is evidence of Adam's considerable knowledge, as a result of living (as an undead) for so long, as well as Jarmusch's enduring interest in both the history of science and of language. In relation to the former, this was already apparent from references to Nikola Tesla, the early twentieth-century inventor, in *Coffee and Cigarettes*, when two characters explain how he considered Earth 'a conductor of acoustical resonance'. Tesla's ideas are discussed again in *Only Lovers Left Alive*, as part of Adam and Eve's lamentation over the mistreatment of various scientists whom they once knew: 'Tesla, destroyed – his beautiful possibilities completely ignored.'

The vampires' multilingualism is signalled as something of an inhuman power. When packing in Tangier in preparation for her trip to visit Adam in Detroit, Eve is shown packing up books, a number of which she skim reads, appearing to absorb their content by tracing over the words with her finger.

This apparent ability to be all-knowing, in terms of language, is later revealed as a life-sustaining trait: in the closing sequence, desperate for blood, the pair approach a couple in Tangier, with Eve politely addressing them in their native language – *excusez moi* (excuse me) – before revealing her fangs. Jarmusch thus renders Adam and Eve as refined, intellectual vampires, who attempt to replenish their minds with knowledge (cultural, linguistic and technologic) as often as they replenish their undead bodies with blood (which they generally procure on the black market). This impression is heightened by the arrival of Eva's sister Ava (Mia Wasikowska). Ava's behaviour and language is less refined, leading her to obtain blood the old-fashioned way: draining it impulsively from a man to whom she is attracted.

As with many of the other examples from the cinematic verbalists' work, music (including explicit discussion of music) contributes to the impression that characters' language is mistakenly placed in a time to which it does not belong. Music is central to Adam's identity: his relocation to Detroit is presumably tied to his work as a musician. Like with the setting of *Mystery Train* in Memphis, setting much of *Only Lovers Left Alive* in Detroit provides Jarmusch's characters with natural opportunities to discuss rich moments in musical heritage, past and present. The twist here, of course, is that the vampires have experienced much of this music first hand, leading to some amusing exchanges. Eve counters Adam's suggestion of going to visit the Motown museum by noting, 'I'm more of a Stax girl myself.' She is, however, excited to see the home of Jack White, the Detroit-born rock musician. Given that White appeared in Jarmusch's *Coffee and Cigarettes*, the discussion of White (including that he was 'his mother's seventh son') is both absurd and playfully intertextual.

After Adam boasts to his young American friend Ian (Anton Yelchin) that he once saw Eddie Cochrane (who died in 1960) play the kind of guitar he now has, Adam responds to Ian's amazement by adding that he only saw Cochrane play 'on YouTube'. The vampires' embracing of digital technologies becomes a playful verbal-visual motif throughout – most notably Adam and Eve's use of Apple devices, with the fruit logo notably present in certain shots, and so adding to the confusing timeline of names and symbols that were present in the mythological Garden of Eden, right up until the present day. Adam is up to date with the vernacular of digital platforms and social media, referring to the humans of the twenty-first century as 'zombies'; a slang word often used by the popular media to describe humans' increasing willingness to sleep-walk through life paying more attention to phones and tablets than to what is around them (see Davis 2013). At the same time, a platform like YouTube becomes a convenient excuse – when they accidentally make comments that reveal their advanced age – as well as a convenient database that allows them to re-experience their lengthy lives.

Unified Soundtracks

Taking these findings together it becomes apparent that, from the early stage of the writing through to post-production, the independent filmmakers considered here treat the soundtrack as a cohesive unit. Its three elements (dialogue, music and sound effects) are combined in creative and reinforcing ways. Unlike Simon (James Urbaniak) in Hartley's *Henry Fool* (1997) – who is decreed by his publisher to have 'an innate sense of the musicality of language, a good ear maybe', but who does 'nothing significant with it'[40] – the cinematic verbalists use their innate sense of language musicality to carefully integrate their soundtracks. When compared to non-diegetic music, the active role of audience members is increased when characters play, and comment on, their own music. And, given the attention the cinematic verbalists pay to what their characters say, it is not surprising that lyrical content can influence their choices for what music will be used. But their films also take advantage of cinema's ability to capture speech's creative but generally latent aural properties. When the rhythm of their speech turns it into a sound effect, or when a character vocalises a noise that would normally be a sound effect, then language is also partly separated from its semantic meaning.

Overall, through their musical uses of dialogue, the cinematic verbalists ignore many of the verbal 'codes of realism' that Nelmes (2011: 217) argues lead to the construction of speech 'to appear natural'. And yet, at times, they can attempt to create a sense of realism when they choose not to foreground dialogue clearly on the sound mix, or to muffle the clarity of the words (either when performed or through their recording). Their design of inaudible dialogue provides a counterpoint to Altman's discussion of 'close-up' sound that gives the audience the impression they are *not* eavesdropping. Unlike sound that seems constructed purely for the audience, they *create* a sense of eavesdropping and – in the case of Anderson's playful blocking out of speech – this draws our attention to the privileged listening position that we generally occupy. The sound mix thus helps these filmmakers with their general strategy of using dialogue design to exclude audiences, with the use of multilingual speech further subverting the expectation that dialogue should always be clear and easily understood. This tendency to include non-Anglophone scenes, often without subtitles, is another form of exclusion by design that characterises these films in terms of 'overhearing' rather than 'side-participation'. Since these scenes also make a thematic feature of miscommunication between characters, such dialogue serves both a narrative and aesthetic function, and so further establishes the importance of dialogue design to American independent cinema.

Notes

1. A notable exception to this is Liz Greene and Danijela Kulezic-Wilson's recent edited collection, *The Palgrave Handbook of Sound Design and Music in Screen Media: Integrated Soundtracks* (2016). The collection, like this chapter, highlights the 'blurred boundaries' between the various aspects of the soundtrack.

2. A few notable examples of the substantial literature on film music include: Claudia Gorbman's *Unheard Melodies* (1987), Pauline Reay's *Music in Film: Soundtracks and Synergy* (2004) and Matthew Caley's and Steve Lannin's *Pop Fiction: The Song in Cinema* (2005). The tendency for dialogue to be relatively overlooked in studies of the soundtrack is illustrated by *The Oxford Handbook of New Audiovisual Aesthetics* (eds Richardson, Gorbman and Vernallis, 2013). The collection is extensive, with contributions from forty-one prominent scholars of audiovisual media, however there is just a single reference to dialogue in the index.

3. Reay's (2004: 77) examples of collaborations between indie film and cinema include: J. Mascis from Dinosaur Jr's music for *Gas, Food, Lodging* (Anders 1992); Thurston Moore from Sonic Youth's music for *Heavy* (Mangold 1995) and *Things Behind the Sun* (Anders 2001); and Belle and Sebastian's music for *Storytelling* (Solondz 2001).

4. Poster has worked as the music supervisor on the vast majority of Anderson's film, along with four of Linklater's and Baumbach's *The Squid and the Whale*.

5. Hartley uses the pseudonym, Ned Rifle, also a character name in several of his films, including in his most recent film, *Ned Rifle* (2014).

6. Tarantino is another filmmaker whose characters shape their own sonic environment. As Coulthard (2012: 165) notes, 'songs figure prominently both for [Tarantino's] audioviewers and for the characters themselves, who discuss, select, play, sing, and dance to diegetic music'.

7. Elena Boschi and Tim McNelis (2012: 40–2) also discuss how shots of transistor radios and phonographs are particularly important in Anderson's films when the technology has nostalgic connotations.

8. As Murphy (2007: 36) notes in his discussion of Jarmusch's screenplay, given that Eva has picked up the insult from Willie, the American slang is particularly appropriate.

9. Citing *Magnolia* (P. T. Anderson 1999) as an exception, Reay (2004: 56) also notes that few films are inspired by, or built around, songs.

10. In a similar vein, Linklater has described how *Dazed and Confused* was inspired by an early ZZ Top song that came on while he was driving and led him to picture a scene (D. T. Johnson 2012: 26).

11. For Baumbach's discussion of this in relation to characterization, see Martens' (2010) *LA Times* piece on 'Greenberg's Noah Baumbach on his music-obsessed films'.

12. Elsewhere, I have considered *Greenberg*'s development of a subjective, character-oriented sound design as part of a broader study on point-of-audition sound and audience identification. Hartley's *The Unbelievable Truth* is also used as a case study of films that include characters who display 'hyperacousia' – a hypersensitivity to sound (O'Meara 2014c).

13. Similarly, Perkins (2012: 110) suggests the classical principle of film music that compilation soundtracks most clearly contest is that of inaudibility.

14. Consider, for example, the controversy around unclear dialogue on the BBC drama *Jamaica Inn* (2014), which created public debate and defensiveness from sound engineers after the BBC received more than 100 complaints regarding the audibility of the dialogue (Burrell 2014). The sound branch of the broadcast union,

the Broadcasting, Entertainment, Communications and Theatre Union (BECTU), contended that sound engineers have been unfairly stigmatised for what BECTU representative Ian Branch referred to as 'an artistic issue' between the directors and actors (ibid.).

15. Jarmusch is aware that the sound quality in his work will never be 'the best in the field', but says it is more important to him that sound is 'always in perspective from the point of shooting' (Jarmusch cited in Von Bagh and Kaurismäki 1987: 78).

16. Similarly, in his blog review of the film, Johnny Betts (n.d.) complains that it is 'nothing more than a home movie of unpleasant, miserable, despicable people mumbling through drab conversations'.

17. Johnson (2012: 22–3) notes this of Linklater's *Slacker*, in which cars pass characters and engines rise 'without regard to the dialogue'.

18. Although Thomas focuses on Orson Welles's use of overlapping dialogue, he briefly compares Welles's use to that of Hawks. For a further discussion of overlapping dialogue see Michael Toolan's (2011) '"I don't know what they're saying half the time, but I'm hooked on the series" – Incomprehensible dialogue and integrated multimodal characterisation in *The Wire*', in R. Piazza, M. Bednarek and F. Rossi (eds) *Telecinematic Discourse: Approaches to the Language of Films and Television Series*, Amsterdam/Philadelphia: John Benjamins Publishing. Toolan notes that, although *The Wire*'s dialogue is difficult to hear, it is combined with visual information in order to facilitate audience comprehension. This suggests that such dialogue is also medium-specific, since it takes advantage of television as a bi-modal medium.

19. It should be noted that Sergi is referring to Hollywood rather than independent cinema when he describes the increased aural sophistication.

20. In *Ghost Dog: The Way of the Samurai*, Jarmusch also has a character make the sound effect of an elk.

21. Murphy (2007: 100) instead describes this scene in the screenplay as 'a good example of the Bressonian strategy of paring down a scene to its most basic cinematic elements'. Similar to my interpretation, he explains, 'The emotional turbulence is not conveyed through performance, but becomes evident instead from the cinematic details Hartley chooses' (102).

22. Sonnenschein (2001: 137–8), for instance, refers to speech's 'pure acoustical characteristics', and suggests that foreign accents, nonsense sounds and technical jargon can be used 'to release the analytic mind-set into a more feeling mode'.

23. In his study of independent screenplays, Murphy (2007) dedicates a chapter to the use of 'free association' in *Gummo* (Korine 1997).

24. Martin's list is as follows: 'Hendrix. Clapton. Allman Brothers. Zeppelin. Tull. BTO. Stones. Grand Funk Railroad. James Gang. T. Rex. MC5. Skynyrd. Lesley West. Blackmore. The Who. The old Who. Ten Years After. Santana. Thin Lizzy. Aerosmith. Hot fucking Tuna.'

25. However, Kracauer notes this in relation to Cockney rather than another language per se. Kozloff (2000: 80–4) also provides a good overview of the potential benefits of, and care needed when including, multiple languages and dialects.

26. Jaeckle refers to accents and foreign language as one of four 'verbal embroideries' present in both filmmakers' work. The other three (overlapping) techniques that Jaeckle identifies are: 1) wordplay, 2) meta-language (typically exchanges about language) and 3) dialogue that is explicitly scripted, as indicated by voice-overs, printed texts, and scenes in which characters read. I touch on each of these in relation to the six cinematic verbalists over the course of this book.

27. As Dwyer (2005: 299) notes, 'Godard sought to make a film that was impossible to dub. If all characters speak the same language, the figure of the translator becomes

redundant and the entire meaning of the film is forsaken.' In the same way, when the cinematic verbalists foreground acts of translation they make their films very difficult to dub.

28. Richard Raskin (2002: 47) commends this segment of *Coffee and Cigarettes* for its refrain-like dialogue, although he limits this to Roberto referring to Steven (Steven Wright) as Steve throughout.

29. Murphy (2007: 29–38) describes Willie's conflicted relationship to Hungary in more detail (as well as some dialogue subtleties) in his study of *Stranger Than Paradise*.

30. In *Barcelona*, Stillman shows awareness of – but refuses to endorse – this cultural stereotype. As Americans working abroad, Ted and Fred (Chris Eigeman) speak both Spanish and Catalan. Fred even uses low expectations of him to an advantage in certain social situations: 'I'm only speaking English here. I don't want them to know good my Spanish is.'

31. In Wilinsky's study of art-house cinema, she draws on a 1956 interview with a distributor, Thomas J. Brandon, who explains that producers and distributors believe that if they erase the foreign speech then the films will appeal to a broader market (Brandon 1956: 16). Furthermore, Wilinsky (2001: 31) explains that being considered 'foreign' was a marker of prestige, and surveyed 1940s filmgoers did not consider British films as 'foreign' since their dialogue was in English.

32. This is not to suggest that independent American writer-directors are alone in their use of multiple languages. Although polyglot films have existed in a small number since the introduction of sound to cinema, critics like Dwyer (2005) and Carol O'Sullivan (2008) have noted an increase in their numbers in recent years. In 'Multilingualism at the Multiplex: A New Audience for Screen Translation?', O'Sullivan details this trend and considers the aesthetic and political effects of incorporating subtitles into US productions.

33. In *Coffee and Cigarettes*, two characters explain how Nikola Tesla, the early twentieth-century inventor, considered the earth 'a conductor of acoustical resonance'. As Suárez (2007: 87) notes, perhaps this is Jarmusch's explanation for why bits of conversation echo throughout.

34. As is discussed in Chapter 4, characters in *Waking Life* and *Slacker* are not given names, but are cited in the credits with short descriptions of what they said or did in the film.

35. In *Damsels in Distress*, for instance, considerable narrative attention is dedicated to the central character's aim to start what she refers to as 'The Sambola! International Dance Craze!'

36. The influence of Jane Austen on Stillman's verbal style is discussed further in Chapter 7.

37. For example, in *The Life Aquatic*, Steve discusses their route on the map in terms of inches ('four' versus 'an inch and a half') and, in *Fantastic Mr. Fox*, Bean asks for 'three shovels, two pick-axes, [and] 500 rounds of ammunition'.

38. Time also becomes central to narrative development in the film since Royal pretends he only has six weeks to live so that his family will reconnect with him.

39. The character of Christopher Marlowe is subtly suggested to be the actual Elizabethan author of the same name, whose work is believed to have strongly influenced that of Shakespeare. *Only Lovers Left Alive* incorporates a number of comments in support of the rumour that Marlowe faked his own death and continued to write under the assumed name of William Shakespeare.

40. This criticism is offered by Angus, a book publisher, to the film's protagonist, who accidentally writes a manuscript in iambic pentameter.

4. DIALOGUE AND CHARACTER CONSTRUCTION

In American independent cinema, speech can be crucial both to individual character construction and to the development of group character dynamics. Dialogue is often used to individuate a character through a personalised speaking style, and nuanced choices of words and phrasing can influence how we perceive and understand characters. A character's personal development can be indicated, for example, by a communication style that evolves over the course of a film. In keeping with the tendency for indie cinema to capture the mundanity of everyday life, dialogue can also be used to create the illusion that characters exist independent of the film world – that they have lives beyond the text. The 'liveness' of such dialogue could be positioned as an alternative to action, but, by demonstrating the various ways in which these filmmakers foreground verbal games and debates as a *form* of action, this chapter reveals this to be an overly simplified relationship. Film-specific idioms and repeated words or lines of dialogue can create a complex cross-network of verbal meaning that establishes individual and groups of characters. And though this chapter focuses on the cinematic verbalists' films, paying particular attention to Linklater's and Stillman's work in relation to verbal impressions of character autonomy and their use of idioms to represent a group of characters as a particular subculture, the analysis aims to increase our understanding of dialogue's role in characterisation more generally.

The relationship between speech and characterisation has already received a certain amount of attention. Kozloff (2000) devotes a brief section of *Overhearing Film Dialogue* to dialogue's function as character revelation.

She notes how speech helps us distinguish one character from another and to make characters more substantial by hinting at an inner life (43). In Jaeckle's (2013b: 4) 'primer' on film dialogue, he uses *Psycho* (Hitchcock 1960) as an example to help explain how analysis of characters' dialogue can help scholars to appreciate how verbal nuances complicate fictional personalities.[1] In those rare instances when analyses of characterisation are grounded in dialogue, the findings can be illuminating. Hannah Patterson (2007) outlines the significance of the central characters' different communication styles to the narrative of *Badlands* (Malick 1973). She notes how Holly's (Sissy Spacek) impressionability is conveyed by monosyllabic responses, contrasted with the 'comparative abundance' of Kit's (Martin Sheen) speech (31). Indeed, she suggests that much of the dramatic ambiguity in the film's central relationship plays out via Kit's and Holly's respective styles of speech.

The study of character is increasingly receiving attention from scholars of independent and Indiewood cinema, as well as from cognitive film theorists. Yannis Tzioumakis (2006: 174–84) links the association between independent cinema and character-driven films (as opposed to plot-driven films) to John Cassavetes's call for a cinema 'about people'.[2] In *Indie*, Michael Z. Newman (2011: 90–1) identifies the problem of trying to measure characters in terms of 'comparative interestingness', and suggests interesting characters may be more thought-provoking, lifelike or surprising – something that will be considered here from the perspective of dialogue. In Kim Wilkins's article on 'hyper-dialogue' in selected contemporary cinema, she makes a connection between characters' underlying anxiety and verbose speech that serves as action. Wilkins highlights a number of crucial ways through which dialogue and character are linked:

> [T]he manner in which the characters speak, the rhythms, inflection, and word choices reflect, and at times indicate, the character's motivations, ideologies, aspirations, and beliefs. Thus, by affording them with an expressive voice, characters are imbued with complexity (including wants, desires, emotions) and the textures of realism, while simultaneously encouraging audience identification and alignment. (Wilkins 2013: 410)

Here, Wilkins begins to capture the complexity not just of what the characters say, but also how they say it and how audience members interpret it.[3]

From the perspective of engagement, the analysis in this chapter is informed by Per Persson's (2003) and Murray Smith's (1995) cognitive approaches to character. How we construct character psychology – defined as 'cinema characters' mental states' (158) – is central to Persson's model in *Understanding Cinema: A Psychological Theory of Moving Imagery*. As he explains, while narrative films are 'more "semiotically" dense than reality, the understanding of both fictional characters and real characters [individuals in real life] makes use of a similar set of dispositions and processes' (157). As will become clearer in the close analysis to follow, the inferences we are encouraged to make about characters, based on what they say, can be central to the effectiveness of independent cinema's character-driven narratives. Persson argues that, based on social and personal experience 'we presuppose that certain expressions are more likely to be caused by certain mental states' (160). While he is concerned with characters' visual and verbal character expressions, focusing on the latter allows us to understand how independent writer-directors can script dialogue that cues audience members to infer a variety of things about characters' personalities.

When doing so, it is useful to think of dialogue's relation to character as something of a tiered system, with different components of speech contributing different dimensions. Dialogue can help signify simple and complex character traits, or the relationship between one character and another, as well as between a character and group of characters, or between one or more characters and the functioning of the diegetic world. The last of these includes how dialogue can situate a character in relation to their location and time period, and reflect their alignment with, or subversion of, communication norms, including those linked with class and race. To this end, the chapter will highlight Jim Jarmusch's verbal rendering of people of colour, as well as how the indie writer-directors incorporate the parlance of therapy culture and later digital media. Let us start by thinking about characters' names, the most basic component of characterisation via speech. The cinematic verbalists deal with even these smallest of verbal units in creative and complex ways.

Creative Naming Practices

Generally spoken throughout, character names are a basic yet significant component of a script's structure. As Smith details in *Engaging Characters: Fiction, Emotion and the Cinema* (1995: 130), in order to help the audience attach meaning to characters, the opening scenes of Hollywood films generally labour both characters' proper names and titular ones such as mother and father. He cites *The Man Who Knew Too Much* (Hitchcock 1956), which contrives both clear introductions and a confusion so that Hank's (Christopher Olsen) name can be repeated three times (123). Indeed, Richard Dyer (1998 [1979]: 109) notes similar in his influential analysis of 'stars as signs' when he explains that since names are harder to establish in cinema than literature they depend on characters repeating them. Linklater, Jarmusch and Anderson can take a very different approach to names, and therefore character 'recognition', by avoiding this standard aspect of verbal repetition. For the most part, experimental naming techniques become another means through which the artifice of mainstream film dialogue is exaggerated.

Linklater frees himself from countless introductions by not giving names to *Waking Life*'s and *Slacker*'s multitude of characters. Actors are instead tagged in the credits based on descriptions of what their characters said or did, for instance 'Sidewalk Psychic' and 'Paranoid Paper Reader'. Similarly, in Jarmusch's *The Limits of Control*, 'The Lone Man' interacts with a series of nameless characters who are credited as 'Man with Guitar', 'The Blonde' and 'The American'. Anderson employs a similar technique in *Moonrise Kingdom*, with Tilda Swinton's character referred to only by her occupation, 'Social Services'. In each case, names serve as playful reminders that these are scripted characters and not people.[4] Such an approach also takes advantage of a key difference that Smith (1995: 114) identifies in relation to *film* characters: structuralist literary theory considers proper names to be 'the preeminent textual elements ensuring character continuity'. Recognition in cinema can instead be established based on 'exterior, perceptible traits – the body, the face, and the voice' (ibid.). When Linklater, Jarmusch and Anderson leave out names, or refuse to labour them repeatedly in the script, they indicate awareness of the redundancy of this basic component of film dialogue: knowing a character's name is not crucial since we can recognise them in other ways.

Other forms of creative naming are also used to add interest to one of dialogue's rudimentary elements. Names are integrated in such ways that they help to create misunderstandings between characters, or explore cultural diversity. In the New York segment of Jarmusch's *Night on Earth,* an African American named YoYo (Giancarlo Esposito) tells the German taxi driver, Helmut (Armin Mueller-Stahl), 'That's a fucked up name to be naming your kid ... In English, that be like [*sic*] calling your kid lampshade.' YoYo subsequently introduces the taxi driver to his sister-in-law as 'Helmut Lampshade, or some shit like that'. Although YoYo shows no respect for Helmut's cultural background, he is defensive when Helmut mocks his name as 'a toy for kids'. By naming characters after inanimate objects, Jarmusch again highlights that language can be both highly specific and ambiguous with regard to its referent. A similar dynamic is created in *Paterson* (2016), Jarmusch's latest film, since the title refers both to Adam Driver's central character and the New Jersey city of Paterson in which the character drives a bus.

The norm for names to clarify rather than confuse is also subverted in *Bottle Rocket*, since certain characters are referred to by various names. Bob's brother (Andrew Wilson) introduces himself as John Mapplethorpe in a scene that takes place late in the film, having previously been referred to as Future Man by other characters. Anderson takes the absurdity of repeating names to the other extreme when characters in the film constantly introduce and reintroduce one another, sometimes with highly alliterative names: 'Anthony, I'd like to introduce you to Applejack. Applejack, this is Anthony.'[5]

In another instance of dialogue being used to advance the irony of smart cinema, both Jarmusch and Hartley integrate the same character name (Nobody) in distinctly ironic ways. At various points in *Dead Man* the dialogue takes advantage of the literal meaning of Nobody's (Gary Farmer) name, as when Bill (Johnny Depp) is asked with whom he is travelling and he answers 'Nobody'. Attention is drawn to discrepancies between the way that a word sounds and the way that it looks in text, since the viewer knows he is referring to a person, with a capitalised 'N', while the other character takes this to mean that he is travelling alone. The audience is also invited to note the difference between 'nobody', the concept, and 'Nobody', the name of the female alien in Hartley's *The Girl from Monday*. When Cecile finds Nobody in Jack's apartment and asks who she is, the response ('Nobody') works on two levels: Cecile assumes that the woman is trying to downplay her presence with an evasive answer. In play here is the kind of ironic double meaning that Sconce discusses as bifurcating an audience into those who 'get it' and those who do not. In the case of both characters named 'Nobody', the characters don't get it while the audience is placed in a position from which to appreciate the irony – provided attention is paid to the way names are integrated with the broader script.

Hartley also uses surnames (Matthew Slaughter; Ned Rifle; Simon Grim) to give an ironic sense of predestination to the characters' violent and difficult stories.[6] Such typifying names exaggerate the tendency Dyer (1998 [1979]: 109) identifies for character names that are used to suggest personality traits. Stillman takes a similarly stylised approach in *Damsels in Distress*, with floral names used to unite the clique of Violet, Rose, Heather and Lily. This approach to naming is a further example of the cinematic verbalists' use of 'excessive' forms of dialogue. But, even through this interweaving of names, they continue to alternate between verbal extremes since they also include certain exceptionally naturalistic examples. This is the case when they refuse to conveniently designate characters by titular names, or to repeat names in the script in the standard fashion. In fact, Jarmusch neatly captures the contrived tendency for names to be repeated in *Stranger Than Paradise* when Willie's cousin arrives to stay and introduces herself as 'Eva Molnar', to which he responds, 'Yeah, no kidding': since Willie would obviously know his own cousin's name, his comment highlights the absurd artificiality of many film-character introductions.

Linklater's and Stillman's Verbal Impressions of Character Autonomy

As part of Dyer's (1979: 106–7) analysis of film stars, he identifies a character's speech and the speech of others as two of the cinema's main signs of character. More generally, he includes useful concepts for character construction in film, particularly how such characterisation differs from that of literature. Dyer positions character 'types' against more novelistic characters, with the latter incorporating the qualities of: particularity, interest, autonomy, roundness, development, interiority, motivation, discrete identity and consistency (93–7). By arguing that dialogue has a central role in establishing traits like particularity, autonomy, roundness and discrete identity, here I contend that these independent writer-directors, particularly Linklater and Stillman, use verbal style to create more 'novelistic characters'.

Dyer rightly identifies that the issue of discrete identity – a sense that a character has a life independent of what we see them say and do – is a problem for all narratives forms: logically, they can exist only 'in the detail of the medium' (95). Yet verbal references can complicate this if, when characters are revisited in subsequent films, there are extensive references to the in-between period. Linklater and Stillman both create a sense of 'discrete identity' for characters when they give them small cameo roles in films that are *not* sequels. Two characters from Linklater's *Before Sunrise* appear briefly in animated form in *Waking Life*, and four characters from Stillman's *Metropolitan* are shown from afar in *The Last Days of Disco*. In the latter, Charlotte provides another character (and the audience) with a verbal update on Audrey (Carolyn Farina), the central female character in *Metropolitan*. In Stillman's debut, Audry was obsessed with literary classics and according to Charlotte she is now a book publisher. Stillman explains in interview that he likes to consider the possibilities of film worlds being real, in which case '[i]t would be logical for some people from *Metropolitan* or even from *Barcelona*, when they're in Manhattan, to be attracted to [the club in *The Last Days of Disco*]' (Hogan 2000).

In terms of the demands that Stillman's strategy makes of us, its effectiveness depends on whether or not we are familiar with his body of work and, assuming we are, if we remember sufficient detail from the films to recognise a character and/or pick up on references to their trajectory. Like with Sconce's discussion of irony as bifurcating audiences into those who get it and those who do not, references to a character's life in a former film can be similarly divisive. Significantly given our focus, recognition of characters' cameo appearances can depend heavily on dialogue. In *The Last Days of Disco*, for example, Jimmy (Mackenzie Astin) asks Ted from *Barcelona* (who is unnamed in this context) if he still works for IHSMOCO, which is the name of the car company that Ted works for in *Barcelona*. Assuming that we have watched Stillman's earlier film, then the company's lengthy acronym is potentially more recognisable than the relatively unknown actor (Taylor Nichols) who plays Ted.

By representing characters at a variety of points in their fictional lives, Linklater has also developed ways to challenge the understanding of film characters as diegetically confined. This impression is strong in *Boyhood*, given that the film was shot for a short period each year over twelve years.

His approach extends on that of the *Before Sunrise* series. In the second film, Céline and Jesse allude to things that have happened since they last met, ten years previously in *Before Sunrise*. Similarly, in *Before Midnight*, they allude to things in the period between *Before Sunset* and *Before Midnight*. Obviously this does not grant the characters independence but, given that there *was* nearly a decade between each production, combined with their physical signs of ageing, the impression for the viewer is no less credible than seeing someone from their past in reality: you accept that they have continued to exist, even though you were not there to see it.[7] Although the same could be said of all sequels, when the subsequent film has a new plot to uncover, then little time is generally dedicated to discussion of the interim period. Horror and action film sequels and series provide such examples. Consider Wes Craven's *Scream* series (1996, 1997, 2000, 2011), for instance: despite several characters appearing in multiple films, they tend not to discuss the details of their lives in between. By contrast, character-centred narratives – such as Linklater's *Before Sunrise* trilogy – more often use verbal references to the in-between period to create the impression of a character's discrete identity.

Another way that dialogue can create the illusion that characters are autonomous (as opposed to fictional constructs) is when speech is designed so that characters are argumentative in a pedantic or inconclusive way. Stillman explicitly refers to dialogue and autonomy when he explains his aim of developing characters' speech 'to the point where they seem to be operating autonomously' (Pinkerton 2009). Opposing certain writing conventions, Stillman acknowledges that his method is the opposite of that of the screenwriting guru, Robert McKee: '[McKee] said, you don't find your scenes through dialogue and find your characters that way. He has this very firm rule that you plan out the story, and then you fill in the blanks' (E. Brown 2012). When Stillman writes debates purely to reveal interpersonal dynamics he thus departs from the kind of mainstream dialogue that is inserted to serve a clear narrative purpose in the kind of 'fill in the blanks' dialogue style that he notes in relation to McKee. Instead, Stillman explains how characters in his films are often 'sent in' to point out exceptions to another character's argument, so that the overall effect is 'thesis and antithesis, and we never get to a synthesis' (C. Brown 2012). Stillman goes so far as to discuss his characters as though they have lives of their own, as when he explains how Nick (Chris Eigeman) in *Metropolitan* 'refused to stay in his place and seemed to invent lines for himself', to the point that the character became more important than originally intended (Sussler 1991). Similarly, some of Stillman's blocks of speech are structured to include suspense, since the actual point or punchline is only revealed after a series of anti-climactic twists.

Dangling a Verbal Bait

This kind of constructed spontaneity is also central to the speech of Linklater, Jarmusch and – at times – Hartley, with Murphy (2007: 91) identifying a similar unwillingness for dialogue to 'escalate toward a dramatic climax' in Hartley's work. The tendency for such dialogue *not* to escalate to a dramatic climax is in alignment with Berliner's analysis of the verbal style of Cassavetes. Indeed, in Murphy's (2007: 256; cf. 243) chapter on Linklater's *Slacker* as a 'character-based structure' he concludes that the film creates the same kind of 'tension between real life and performance' as in a Cassavetes film. Because although, in Hartley's case, dialogue can create a conventional 'push and pull' momentum between characters, he 'chooses to flatten rather than to exploit the inherent drama of the situation' (91). By contrast, dialogue in mainstream cinema is generally concerned with advancing plot. If a character makes a remark that would warrant a response in reality, the other character(s) generally do not question it since this could delay or distract from the speech's function of providing expositional information. Instead, by allowing their characters to take the verbal 'bait', the cinematic verbalists subvert the kind of contemporary film dialogue that DiBattista (2001) criticises:

> Wisecracks still ricochet off movie soundtracks, but too often they are severed from their roots in actual harsh or bitter experience ... The smart talkers of today's movies [mimic] the monologism of stand-up comedians or the one-liners of sitcoms ... Their gibes are meant to forestall or foreclose conversation, not quicken, complicate and enliven it. (DiBattista 2001: xi)

With the exception of some of Baumbach's dialogue in his earliest films, *Kicking and Screaming* and *Mr. Jealousy*, these writer-directors generally depart from such speech, since their characters are argumentative in a digressive rather than dramatic fashion.[8]

Unlike the verbal aggressiveness of paired 'toppers', which Kozloff (2000: 75) explains as characters outdoing one another with retorts 'that attempt[s] to close off a conversational topic by their finality or nastiness', characters point out flaws in the initial words (as is considered later in this chapter in relation to 'verbal games'). Although this is a form of 'smart talking', it involves subtle corrections rather than clever comebacks. For instance, in *The Last Days of Disco*, Charlotte counters with an obvious but logical rebuttal: 'Of course it's formulaic; it's a formula.' Such responses are more grounded in 'realism', since it is typically easier to find a small flaw in another's words than to instantly generate something better. This allows the dialogue a sense of action, without reducing it to a stream of witty comebacks. Since the retort often draws on a character's previous comments (again, subtle repetition is key), the impression is that it originates *within* the diegesis, rather than being imposed on characters by a scriptwriter. In other words, going back to DiBattista's (2001: xi) critique, American independent cinema's dynamic use of words as action is partly because it relies *less* on one-liners; because it *does* root words in 'harsh or bitter experience'; and because it *does* include quick back-and-forth exchanges that instead 'quicken, complicate and enliven'.

LINKLATER'S AND STILLMAN'S UNITING OF SUBCULTURES THROUGH IDIOMS

Moving from the level of individual characterisation to that of group dynamics, the use of speech to reflect broader communication norms helps to contribute to independent cinema's nuanced representation of specific subcultures. In particular, these writer-directors often employ idiomatic language to establish the sense that characters belong to, or are excluded from, a distinct social group. I use the term 'idiom' here in the standard sense, to refer to 'the language peculiar to a people or to a district, community, or class',[9] and the tendency for independent cinema to represent distinct social groups has already been explored. Newman (2011: 117) explains how indie films often encourage a reading of the protagonist as an emblem of their social identity:

> The [independent] filmmaker is content to describe a social reality, especially its representative types, as a means of capturing a slice of life in its vividness and specificity. One gets the sense that the filmmaker just wants his or her world, or a particular contemporary subculture he or she finds interesting, to be thrown up on the big screen. (Newman 2011: 32)

Personal attachment to their subjects does seem to be a critical aspect of the cinematic verbalists' work, and their dialogue. Although Newman doesn't look at dialogue, he lists Stillman's *Metropolitan* and Linklater's *Dazed and Confused* as examples of the kind of represented subcultures common in independent cinema.[10] The kind of vivid and specific representations that he highlights can be heavily dependent on vivid and specific language. Stillman's films have even been referred to as 'mock anthropological' studies (Lyon 2001: 154), with dialogue precision seemingly key to audiences' impression that one societal group is being studied in an anthropological way.

In order to demonstrate the existence of diegetic vernacular that unites groups of characters (and simultaneously distinguishes them from character types), it is useful to return to Dyer's discussion of characters, including their reception. Dyer (1998 [1979]: 122) argues that audience members compare characters to stereotypes of the social group to which they belong and, if some of their traits mark a departure from what we expect, they come across as 'more individuated and hence more "real"'. Murray Smith (1995: 116–17) similarly argues that a cognitively 'plausible' character breaks with familiar types, although he qualifies that for certain audiences 'the mark of plausibility will be a high degree of conformity'. Applied to verbal style, the breaking of a common type is captured by Linklater's idiomatic dialogue in *Slacker*, *Dazed and Confused* and, most recently, *Everybody Wants Some!!* (2016)

In each film, the dialogue of characters (mostly teens and young adults) departs in terms of content and phrasing from unrealistically smooth and articulate dialogue in more mainstream teen films and television. The rambling speech that opens *Slacker* is a good example of this in practice. The character (played by Linklater himself and credited as 'Should Have Stayed at the Bus Station') repeats several phrases, or variations on them, a number of times: 'man', 'you know', 'it's like', 'uh' and 'I mean'. In a prime example of the kind of inarticulate speech that recurs in his work, at one point Linklater says almost all of these phrases together ('I mean, it's like uh, you know'). In Chapter 3, we consider the cinematic nature of unclear emanation speech that amounts to, in Chion's description, a character's sound silhouette. I would add that, even when perfectly audible, hesitant and inarticulate speech is a variation of emanation speech. Only rather than alluding to a character's bodily presence (as in Chion's discussion), such speech alludes to their mental presence.

This incorporation of scripted hesitancy is complemented with departures from type based on content, as indicated by Lesley Speed (2007), who positions the literary and philosophical preoccupations of Linklater's characters in opposition to theories of American anti-intellectualism. As she explains, Linklater's characters 'naturaliz[e] reflective discourse, and [depict] intellectual engagement as pleasurable and inclusive' (104). Indeed, considering Linklater's films from a youth genre perspective, she rightly notes that Linklater's 'cool' intellectual teenagers defy what Timothy Shary (2002) refers to as the stereotypical 'option for all nerds: change or perish' (Speed 2007: 102; Shary 2002: 33). Linklater's young characters move swiftly between discussions of sex, culture and philosophy, in exchanges littered with inconsequential cursing.[11] The departure of Linklater's characters from type thus depends on (1) their discussion of uncommon subject matters in (2) an uncommonly hesitant, candid and thus 'realistic' way.

A similar dynamic exists in Stillman's films, with a precise diegetic vernacular helping to create the impression that they are 'mock anthropological studies' (Lyon 2001: 154). In another instance of verbal irony, despite characters in *Damsels in Distress* making explicit references to 'American college slang', characters' formal phrasing and vocabulary are at odds with slang as an *informal* kind of speech. The characters use words like 'immutable', 'laudatory', 'extirpating' and 'excelsior'. Stillman's mannered dialogue seems too contrived to pass for 'real', even if the sub-section being represented is suggested to be an elite one. Indeed, reviewer David Gritten (2012) comments that Stillman's characters in the film 'speak like poets'. Since Stillman's highly articulate speech seems far-removed from the everyday vernacular of contemporary American youth, the impression it creates is almost the opposite of Linklater's use of vernacular. But, like Linklater, Stillman represents 'smart' young people in a positive way, a way that is at odds with American anti-intellectualism (as Speed observes of Linklater's characters).

Stillman's mannered style of idiomatic dialogue shares certain features with that of Anderson. In fact, in a rare example of one of the cinematic verbalists comparing their work to that of another, Stillman refers to *Damsels in Distress* as a female version of *Rushmore* (Gritten 2012). Many of the similarities come in the form of dialogue design. Like Violet and her friends, Max in *Rushmore* speaks in an overly formal and literary style, inserting phrases like 'as per our conversation' into casual conversation. *Rushmore*'s and *Damsels in Distress*'s educational settings also allow for a vernacular localised to a small area. *Damsels in Distress* has a number of recurring, context-specific phrases. These include: 'youth outreach' (dating someone who is 'below' you) and 'nasal shock syndrome' (a strong reaction to unpleasant smells). Throughout, poorly behaved males are referred to as 'confidence tricksters' and 'playboy operators', and such character labels are also an Anderson trademark. Perkins (2012: 35–6) explains how Stillman's self-reflexive approach to characterisation based on type echoes across the films in the form of the rampant stereotyping of others by his characters themselves. In *Metropolitan*, the group of friends create a series of acronyms with which to refer to themselves. The group takes offence to the term 'yuppie' and, after initially taking the name of the member in whose Manhattan apartment they meet (the 'Sally Fowler Rat Pack'), the term 'Urban Haute Bourgeoisie' (or UHB) is employed. The potential of words to be used as weapons is recalled whenever characters are offended by one term or another, or debate the suitability of various labels.[12]

Similar to the verbal games discussed later in the chapter, Stillman foregrounds the politics of language and how it can be used to unite or divide people. By linguistically belittling or disassociating themselves from certain characters (either within their distinct social group, or from those outside it) labelling thus signifies the exertion of power by certain characters over others. To summarise, then, both Linklater and Stillman create idioms particular to their film worlds and, although Stillman typically does so with more impressive vocabulary and diction, Linklater's are similarly contrived even if they appear more 'real'. Furthermore, both filmmakers represent intellectual engagement as pleasurable and inclusive by incorporating philosophical discussion on any number of significant and trivial subjects.

Although the focus here has been on Linklater and Stillman, such idiomatic language is also a notable feature of Jarmusch's and Baumbach's films.

One critic of Baumbach's work even explicitly identifies this when describing his 'unfailing ear for the idioms of the intelligentsia' (Scott 2007). Even in Baumbach's debut, the barrier between being 'inside' or 'outside' of a particular group is presented linguistically. A student named Kate (Cara Buono) tells the central group of guys in *Kicking and Screaming* that 'you all talk the same'. In a later scene, the impression that Kate is not one of them (she is younger and less privileged) is strengthened when Miami (Parker Posey) makes the same point in a more grammatically correct way ('you all talk alike'). A subtle difference in phrasing thus signals one character's inclusion in the clique and another character's exclusion. Overall, then, the cinematic verbalists tend to use a shared vernacular to make the story world coherent, even if such language is not otherwise credible: certain characters are united with one another via language, but distanced from other characters and more generic representations of teenagers and young people.

Contagious Language and Verbal Games

Aside from using idioms to unite a group of characters, or suggest that they are part of a particular subculture, these independent writer-directors frequently design speech to signal bonding and connections between characters. This means that, although their narratives can have little resolution (or introduce few plot points to resolve), their dialogue can instead provide a kind of rewarding catharsis. More broadly, meta-communication complements their incorporation of multiple languages by showing that problems of misunderstanding are common even *within* one language. Personalised definitions of words and the parroting of one character's words by another are two, often overlapping, verbal traits used to increase dialogue's role in character dynamics.

In the first segment of Jarmusch's *Night on Earth*, a teenaged taxi driver named Corky (Winona Ryder) is quizzed about her life aspirations by her passenger, Victoria, played by Gena Rowlands – Cassavetes' regular performer and his wife. The street-smart Corky is irritated by Victoria's uncalled-for comments and several times responds, 'Yes, Mom,' in a sarcastic tone. Despite their initial judgements of each other, the two develop something of a bond over the course of the journey and this is confirmed via dialogue when, after being thanked by Corky for her tip, Victoria replies, 'Sure, Mom.' Victoria thus transforms Corky's insult into an affectionate remark. In another segment of *Night on Earth* dialogue gives a cathartic unity to an otherwise random interaction when, mirroring YoYo's one-sided exchange at the start of the segment, the sequence ends with Helmut talking to himself extensively. Like with Corky and Victoria, a sense of closure comes from a full circle in the dialogue, rather than from the neat tying up of events.

Dialogue is also used to unite or divide characters when they struggle to reach a consensus on words, particularly when they refine or repeat definitions in thought-provoking ways. As one character's subjective interpretation of a word, such definitions can reveal more about the character than the word itself, which may only be of marginal importance to the narrative. Consider Willie's use of 'alright' – the most innocuous of words – in *Stranger Than Paradise*. During scenes in which either Eva or Eddie impress him, Willie tells them that they're 'alright'. The word 'alright' takes on a charged contextual meaning (it reveals Willie's reluctance to offer praise outright) that departs from its literal one. Personalised definitions are particularly significant to Baumbach's work.

In *Margot at the Wedding* Claude asks his mother what 'insufferable' means after she uses the word to describe Maisy (Halley Feiffer). Margot's largely unhelpful response ('it means that I can't suffer her') is in keeping with the distance and impatience she shows for Claude throughout; the definition thus becomes a means of condensing the more general impression made by Margot's speech. In *The Squid and the Whale* it is the *combination* of personalised definitions and the 'parroting' of another character's speech that efficiently distils character dynamics into a few lines of dialogue. Take, for example, Bernard's use of the term 'family conference' to describe a conversation between the four family members: in addition to causing confusion among his sons, by using the formal term to describe a small family meeting, Bernard alludes to his academic background. The word thus captures his prioritisation of work and his general detachment from his sons.

Perkins explains how Walt tries to seduce Sophie with the kind of 'empty literary clichés' that he picks up from his father (66) and she notes the 'tremendous economy' with which a discussion about Charles Dickens in the film signals that Walt is 'morphing into his father' (64). This is one of several instances of what I would term contagious language in the film. After Bernard brands the tennis coach Ivan (William Baldwin) as a 'philistine', Frank repeats Bernard's improvised definition ('a guy who doesn't care about books or interesting films or things') word for word, to Ivan. Perhaps most revealing, however, is Bernard's comparative explanation that 'your mother's brother Ned is also a philistine'. Not only does the description become another way for Bernard to insult Joan, but it also gives Frank further opportunity to side with his mother, when, presumably comparing himself to his uncle, he declares, 'Then I'm a philistine.'[13]

In her discussion of dialogue repetition, Kozloff (2000: 86) notes how a change in the relationship between characters can be solidified when one character repeats something that another has said earlier. Such parroting is crucial to the cinematic verbalists, who use dialogue to verbally signal different kinds of connections, such as compromises and side-taking, as well as disconnection. Although parroting is woven into the cinematic verbalists' dialogue structure in a cohesive and stylised way, the technique is itself grounded in cognitive realism. As Carl Plantinga (2009: 125) explains, humans have a pervasive tendency to mimic one another's vocalisations. As Plantinga notes, this mimicry often occurs subconsciously 'as a kind of automatic response' (ibid.), as seen in *The Squid and the Whale* and a number of other independent films; whenever characters can't seem to stop themselves from repeating what may have been better left unsaid. In this way, such dialogue reveals awareness of the automatic nature of verbal and vocal mimicry, and the potential of this to develop characterisation along both realistic and overtly staged lines.

The Squid and the Whale also includes a sequence in which a character parrots from another film, when Bernard impersonates Michel (Jean-Paul Belmondo) in *Breathless* when he quotes a line of dialogue and expects Joan to recognise the reference. Other intertextual parroting is not signposted as such and thus only serves as a reminder of the quotability of dialogue to those who recognise it independently.[14] Both kinds of mimicry indicate Baumbach's awareness that individuals (real or fictional) can store and recycle the words of others for a long time. Linklater also includes scenes that indicate a certain reflexive awareness of this human tendency. In *Before Midnight*, a minor male character perfectly mouths the words of his wife's story behind her back – humorously revealing his intimate familiarity with both the content and delivery of her speech.

Bickering in their work shows how verbal exchanges are inherently competitive with strategic moves, injured parties and, ultimately, winners and losers. In showing the potentially contagious and scarring effects of speech, particularly familial speech, such parroting can be understood in relation to Kozloff's (2000: 241) examination of melodrama's verbal norms. Given the combative nature of this speech, the most important point to take from Kozloff's analysis of melodrama is that the genre's dialogue typically conveys 'the sense of a "debating society" where the action ... lies in the thrashing out of contesting viewpoints'. The cinematic verbalists depart, however, in the content of the debates. While Kozloff (2000: 241; 243) and Jeanine Basinger (1993: 5) explain how characters in melodrama are rarely granted the kind of 'sensible talk' that could help sort out their emotional drama, characters in Baumbach's, Stillman's, Hartley's and Anderson's films include an abundance – rather than a lack – of 'sense'. Characters deal with personal issues passive-aggressively via pedantic intellectual arguments. Indeed, characters regularly correct one another's word choices rather than addressing the underlying emotional issue. Murray Pomerance (2008: 302) describes kinship in Anderson's *The Royal Tenenbaums* as 'something of an elaborate game', with characters in Baumbach's, Linklater's, Hartley's and Stillman's films adept at *verbal* games, the rules of which audiences are expected to learn.[15]

VERBAL CHARACTER DYNAMICS IN *MISTRESS AMERICA*

Baumbach's *Mistress America* (2015), co-written by Greta Gerwig, is driven by many of the verbal character dynamics identified so far. The film focuses on the developing relationship between college freshman Tracy (Lola Kirke) and her zany future stepsister, Brooke (played by Gerwig). Despite sharing some demographic traits (both are young, white, cultured), their differing personalities are quickly signalled through contrasts in communication style. Brooke is notably candid, zealously jumping from one idea to the next. She is unapologetic and much more self-possessed than Tracy, who takes some time to adjust to her forthright nature. As is typical in Baumbach's films, the screenplay incorporates mundane moments that give way to unexpected dialogue, such as when Brooke asks Tracy to start the coffee machine and does not except her excuse, 'I don't know how.' Brooke's self-sufficiency and slightly startling intolerance are revealed: 'Yes, you do. Don't be incompetent. If you spent two seconds with a coffee maker you'd figure it out. You just aren't trying hard enough.' The scene thus builds on an earlier one, in which Brooke tells Tracy (a Barnard College student) that she is 'an autodidact', someone who teaches themself, going on to explain how 'that word is one of the things I self-taught myself'. In subtle ways, then, Brooke's impatience with Tracy over the coffee machine seems to stem from her self-proclaimed status as an autodidact: if she can teach herself any number of things, then why can't Tracy figure out a coffee machine?

Although, at this point, Tracy is somewhat perturbed by Brooke's blunt impatience, she generally responds well to such candour and begins to adopt elements of it herself. The script neatly signposts this gradual verbal transformation, beginning when Tracy agrees with Brooke that feeling inferior to girls attending Columbia is 'stupid' – she parrots back Brooke's comment ('You're right, that is stupid'). Brooke's growing assertiveness is also established when she revisits an earlier situation, in which she was too reserved to provide feedback on her friend Tony's (Matthew Shear) story, despite him have no problem critiquing hers. Later in the film, she allows Tony to read her next story, adding, 'I don't want notes – but I thought about it and I actually do have notes for you.' Tracy's comments to Tony are both frank and extensive – precisely the kind of remarks that she has learned to express (and to accept when directed towards her) from Brooke:

> You write like you are imitating someone who is free and wild and it is so weird because you aren't at all and it made me uncomfortable and I think it would make everyone uncomfortable. And also, stop trying to be funny because you aren't funny so it just adds to the awkwardness. And it could be 30 per cent shorter, easy.

As with many of Baumbach's writer-characters, Tracy's feedback blurs the line between constructive criticism and character assassination. This, and other, critiques of someone's writing, ultimately becomes a passive-aggressive attack, but, in Tracy's case, it can equally be read as a moment of self-empowerment – one facilitated by Brooke. The film thus provides a sustained study in the contagious nature of language, and how this can be particularly common in families: given that, initially, Tracy only arranges to meet Brooke since her mother is engaged to Brooke's father, her gradual adoption of Brooke's communication style could be seen as an attempt to (verbally) bridge the two families. Their sharing of a verbal common ground comes to fruition towards the film's close, when Tracy helps Brooke to pitch her restaurant idea to potential investors. After watching the normally persuasive Brooke lose her articulacy under pressure, Tracy begins to finish her sentences using the kind of forceful, persuasive style that Brooke generally maintains.

Mistress America also includes some reflexive commentary on the idiomatic language use of various groups. Brooke responds very strongly when Tony's girlfriend employs the word 'adultery' in reference to her own experiences. Brooke loudly and incredulously repeats the term back before explaining why such language does not seem appropriate to this cohort: 'You are all eighteen! Where is this old-person morality coming from? There is no "cheating" when you're eighteen. You should all be touching each other all the time.' Although, in this sequence, Brooke (who is thirty) distinguishes herself from the group of college students, she will later object to a comment that implies she is markedly older. While visiting a psychic with Tracy, he refers to Tracy as 'the young one', with Brooke snapping that 'she's not that young. Ten ... ten to twelve years younger, we are contemporaries, okay?' Brooke's use of the term 'contemporaries' comes across as both technically correct and a defensive self-delusion. In the grand scheme of things, the women are relatively close in age – and both are 'millenials' (a term that is never used) – and yet Brooke's unwillingness to be considered older is at odds with: (1) her tendency to impart wisdom to the students; (2) the way she addresses her future stepsister ('hey, baby Tracy'); and (3) her insistence that they are too young to use the words 'adultery' and 'cheating'.

But Brooke's use of the term 'contemporaries' is in keeping with the way that Stillman's characters self-label when they decide on a precise set of words to describe their individual and group identity. *Mistress America* also verbally highlights the kind of creative naming practices discussed at the start of the chapter in relation to the cinematic verbalists more generally. When Brooke explains the potential titles of her future creative projects – a cabaret called 'High Standards' and a television show called 'Mistress America' – the process of naming is revealed as one that can confuse as much as it clarifies. Tracy guesses that Brooke will sing the cabaret standards in a higher pitch, while

Brooke intends for it to be a show about the integrity of being single as a result of high standards. The title of 'Mistress America' also causes misunderstanding, with Brooke using the name to capture the self-invented female superhero she intends to create, while Tracy associates the term 'mistress' with marital infidelity, explaining how 'that sounds like she's America's girl on the side'. With both examples, we again see how the film is in keeping with the cinematic verbalists' willingness to playfully destabilise the norm for names to clarify situations and plot points.

Talking Technology and Therapy

In *Mistress America*, Brooke's unbridled enthusiasm for life includes an embracing of social-media platforms: 'You have to market yourself. If you don't know what you're selling, no one will know how to buy it.' Brooke's flowery assertion captures the kind of inspirational quote-cum-jargon on which digital marketing thrives. This is a prime example of the way that the cinematic verbalists have consistently scripted commentary on contemporary communication norms, with those related to digital media extending on an earlier trend for them to include the parlance of therapy culture. Twitter, in particular, takes on an important role as a kind of third participant in several conversations between Tracy and Brooke. First, Brooke uses Twitter as a way to demonstrate her willingness to confide in Tracy. After explaining that she shares many of her ideas on the social-media platform, Brooke prefaces a discussion of her creative plans by clarifying that 'here are two ideas that are not on the internet'.

In a later sequence, Brooke expresses agreement with Tracy's insights about high-school students by telling her, 'I'm going to shorten that, punch it up, and turn it into a tweet.' This reaction gets to the heart of debates about the impact of digital technologies on everyday communication: rather than responding to Tracy's words, Brooke chooses to use them to engage with other people who are not present, and to present Tracy's words as her own. At this time, Tracy does not have a problem with this (although she will later use it to defend herself when Brooke accuses Tracy of appropriating her life for a story), but the idea of sharing someone's casual comments with a much larger digital audience can be read as both validating and frustrating for Tracy. Her meandering insights will need to be 'punch[ed] up' as well as shortened in order to conform to Twitter's 140-character policy. Although Brooke does not see any problem with this, at another point in the film she objects to someone taking a photo of her kissing a man in a group setting. Her reaction – 'Must we all document ourselves all the time? Must we?!' – reveals her ability to see through the façade of living life through an iPhone screen. Indeed, the screenplay directions specify this brand of device (Baumbach and Gerwig n.d.: 19), and yet such a position comes across as slightly hypocritical – given that she happily documents her own ideas, as well as Tracy's, via Twitter.

At other points in the film, characters use or amend the vocabulary of digital media in ways that demonstrate how these words have entered the vernacular of twenty-first-century English, whether we like it or not. When Brooke uses the term 'twittering' rather 'tweeting' in reference to Twitter, it becomes a further example of her personalised approach to vocabulary (as with the aforementioned example, when she uses the word 'contemporaries' to align herself with Tracy). More generally, *Mistress America* engages with the question of how to incorporate Internet-speak into everyday conversation, or whether there is something unnatural about verbalising familiar terms and abbreviations that are usually communicated only via computer keyboards and phone keypads. This is presented as a form of 'code switching', when individuals move back and forth between two languages, or between two dialects or registers of the same language: in this case, English and Internet-speak. Although characters do not go so far as to verbalise terms like 'LOL' and 'hashtag', a group of characters who barely know one another nonetheless muse and become pedantic about the suitability of 'BCC'ing something versus 'CC'ing them:

> KAREN: I'll give you my email and you can BCC me.
> NICOLETTE: She could just CC you.
> TONY: Nic's right, because we'd already know that you're getting it …
> KAREN: Sure, CC me.
> HAROLD: Technology can be complicated.
> DYLAN: I know! I just learned what "case sensitive" meant, seriously, yesterday.

Here the exchange assumes that everyone present understands that 'BCC' refers to blind carbon copy, with Karen, the older lawyer character, ironically corrected by the college students: presumably, Karen's professional life would require her to both 'CC' and 'BCC' more often than the students, and yet she seems to have momentarily forgotten the difference between the two. Alternatively, this small gaff in email protocol may be interpreted as a sign that Karen's default choice is to be 'BCCed', thus allowing her to observe surreptitiously while decreasing the transparency of the exchange. Dylan's comment, acknowledging that he only recently learned what 'case sensitive' means, seems to equally provide a commentary on the relationship between digital communication and verbal 'real-life' communication. Because although uppercase and lowercase letters are crucial to the passwords that attempt to safeguard individuals' identities online, the term (and the corresponding safety device) has little relevance in everyday conversations. We are all expected to know what it means, and to follow its directive, but the term itself is largely contained to the (increasingly) digital portion of everyday life. Here, Dylan admits his failure to master Internet jargon, and in front of the younger millennials – for whom the familiar term would probably be taken for granted. In this same extended scene, Tracy voices her distaste for the way Brooke openly discusses her Twitter account, issuing a rare order that she 'stop talking about Twitter, it's so awkward!' Tracy's reaction suggests a certain discomfort for code switching between everyday English and specialised Internet-speak: using Twitter is normal and acceptable, but constantly talking about how you're using Twitter is not.

Such references to Twitter, as well as to YouTube – for example, in Jarmusch's *Only Lovers Left Alive* and *Paterson* – can be seen as a continuance of earlier characters' references to therapy as a 'talking cure'. Writing on everyday life, Frank Füredi (2004: 1) explains how 'the vocabulary of therapeutics' is no longer reserved for trained psychologists, but has infiltrated 'the normal episodes of daily life'. He cites the character of Tony Soprano (James Gandolfini) in *The Sopranos* (HBO 1999–2007) as an example, noting that most viewers did not think it strange for a Mafia man to make sense of his life through therapy (ibid.). With the exception of Jarmusch's work, this vocabulary is also evident throughout the cinematic verbalists' films. Baumbach incorporates scenes of individual or group therapy into *Mr. Jealousy* and *The Squid and the Whale*, while therapy is referred to directly in his other films.

In *The Squid and the Whale*, the content and the speed with which Walt's revelations take place almost parodies the process of treatment. In *Mr. Jealousy*, on the other hand, Vince (Carlos Jacott) refers to himself as 'half a diagnosis, half a man'. The power of the therapist figure is also ridiculed in *Kicking and Screaming* when Jane worries she will let hers down by going to see him after drinking. Another female character in the film explains that she does not have a room-mate because her uncle, a therapist, told the college (falsely) that she is mentally unstable. Again, Baumbach appears to comment cynically on therapists' power and the potential misuse of this power. The effectiveness of therapy is also satirised in *Greenberg* each time a character quotes their therapist, or when Roger repeats Florence's words ('hurt people, hurt people') back to her, forgetting it was she who told him in the first place.[16] Baumbach's references to therapy are one of the strongest overlaps between his work and that of Woody Allen. In films like *Manhattan*, Allen uses mantras similarly to reveal characters' dependence on the figure of the psychotherapist.[17] Characters' repetition of mantras also evokes the one-sided therapist–patient dynamic.

At times, dialogue in the other cinematic verbalists' films can also emulate the very format of contemporary therapy sessions; the patient dominates conversation, while the therapist is predominantly assigned the role of listener. Consider characters' one-sided monologues, which Murphy (2007: 253; emphasis in the original) describes as 'decidedly one-sided tirades' in relation to *Slacker* when characters 'talk *at* each other rather than *to* each other'.[18] As Gerrig and Prentice discuss in their use of the term 'side-participant', the real addressee of one character's speech is often the audioviewer (as much as the character addressee, present in a given scene to serve as the audioviewer's substitute). However, the audioviewer's role is rarely acknowledged. Instead, when Hartley and Linklater use overtly one-sided dialogue – when characters talk 'at' rather than talk 'to' another character – it draws our attention to this norm. Crucially, it does so *without* masking the audioviewer's status as an addressee by having another character respond. A representative example occurs in *Trust,* when Maria recounts seventeen lines of dialogue about her relationship to a stranger. In such one-sided tirades, the audioviewer and the other character are *both* positioned in the role of the silent, listening therapist.

Selective and Racial Silencing

In dialogue-rich films, moments of unexpected silence can be pregnant with meaning.[19] And just as this independent cinema presents a tension between articulacy and inarticulacy, it often creates a strong contrast between verbosity and what is left unsaid. At times, verbose characters are put into relief by contrasting them with a character who says next to nothing, as when Stillman employs a near-silent supporting character in *The Last Days of Disco.* Although Holly (Tara Subkoff) makes the occasional comment, more often we hear the other female characters allude to things she has said off-camera, with a causal relationship indicated between her silence and their concern that she is not very bright. Holly's speech tends to be clumsily phrased – noticeably different from Stillman's other characters – as though justifying why she is not allowed to say more. Her presence can also be considered an acknowledgement on Stillman's part of how his highly verbal characters 'crowd others out' of the soundtrack, in a departure from screenplays that apportion dialogue among characters using a relatively equal ratio.

Hartley also uses silence to subvert audience expectations of how film dialogue is typically structured into what Berliner (1999: 4) describes – in his analysis of Cassavetes' dialogue – as 'a clear line', with back-and-forth exchanges. In *Henry Fool,* Simon is associated with listening rather than speaking, and although the camera is focused on him from the opening shot, it is more than eight minutes before he says anything. Simon eavesdrops on other characters, and does not respond to orders given to him. When Simon is eventually asked a question – where Henry (Thomas Jay Ryan) can buy beer – the camera cuts to a sign of a grocery store, which conveniently relieves Simon of the need to speak. In the next, equally contrived scene, Hartley reveals his intention to keep Simon silent by playfully undermining dialogue norms. Inside the store a girl shouts, 'Say something!' The shot widens to reveal her target (a woman behind the counter), while an off-screen male voice says, 'She's mute.' Not only does the girl say what we may be thinking in relation to Simon, but, if we assume that because the camera has moved inside Simon must have too, then the off-screen voice should in fact be his. *Henry Fool* is also somewhat representative of the cinematic verbalists' tendency to begin or end films with wordless sequences, ones that prevent them from being as verbally driven as they may initially seem. *Margot at the Wedding* also employs this technique, with the film beginning and ending with Margot and her son sitting silently on public transport. By departing from expectations for how generic dialogue typically functions, silent scenes or characters can be seen to constitute something of a verbal pleasure.

Another form of verbal silencing, and one that is tied to our earlier consideration of verbally defined subcultures, relates to class and race. Although Hartley's, Jarmusch's and Linklater's characters often struggle financially, dialogue contributes to the impression that many of Anderson's, Baumbach's and Stillman's characters belong to a similar well-educated 'middle class'. In fact, the therapy-inflected speech already discussed also reflects an increased reliance on therapy among the social grouping to which many of the cinematic verbalists' characters belong. In terms of racial inclusivity, Jarmusch stands out among the group. With only a few exceptions,[20] major characters in Anderson's, Baumbach's, Linklater's and Stillman's work are overwhelmingly white. Anderson in particular has been criticised for the 'unbearable whiteness' of films such as *The Darjeeling Limited* (2007), which as Jonah Weiner (2007) surmises, tend to include 'nonwhite, virtually mute characters' as a way to 'import a whimsical, ambient multiculturalism into the films'. Although people of colour are marginalised in much of the independent cinema under discussion, it is worth restating that, through their frequent incorporation of multilingual scenes (as detailed in Chapter 3), these writer-directors do engage linguistically with a variety of cultures, albeit mostly European ones. If not racially inclusive, this at least pushes back against the monopoly that the English language holds over Hollywood cinema. Jarmusch can be seen to take a less tokenist approach to race, with prominent characters of African origin in *Ghost Dog, The Limits of Control, Coffee and Cigarettes* and *Paterson*.

In *Paterson*, although the titular character (played by Adam Driver) is white, nearly every other character in the film is a person of colour, including his girlfriend, Laura, played by Golshifteh Farahani, an Iranian-born, French-based actress. The racial makeup of the characters reflects the actual demographics of Paterson, New Jersey, a city where, as of 2012, only approximately 37 per cent of the population identified as white ('CLR Search' 2012). Roughly 31 per cent of the population identified as Black (ibid.), and the city has also been reported as having the second-largest Muslim population in the United States (Dovere 2013). Most of Paterson's friends are African American and he has other meaningful interactions with a Japanese tourist (also a poet) and a Black man (played by rapper 'Method Man') whose freestyle riffing he overhears, stops to listen to and praises. As with Jarmusch's work more broadly, the cultures and languages of people of colour are subtly rendered rather than presented as racial tokens. Laura's ethnicity or accent are never mentioned, but she does discuss a dream about ancient Persia as well as playing and singing along to relatively famous Persian songs, including the Mohsen Karbassi and Anooshirvan Rohani title song from *Soltane Ghalbha* (Ali Fardin 1968). Laura is presented as a genuinely transnational figure, a citizen of the world: she discusses Italian poetry and orders a guitar online from a man named Esteban whom she saw playing music on YouTube. But, even if the name Esteban suggests that the guitar may be intended for Spanish music, Laura intends to use it to accompany herself singing country music 'like Tammy Wynette or Patsy Cline'. Although Paterson is a man of few words, he supports even her flightiest dreams, recipes and interior designs with words of encouragement.

Like in Jarmusch's earlier films *Coffee and Cigarettes* and *Ghost Dog*, African American slang (and one of its musical variations, in the form of rap) is a recurring verbal motif in *Paterson*. Jarmusch has spoken in an interview about his fondness for hip-hop music, including its openness with regard to drawing inspiration from other places (Suárez 2007: 163), a response that is equally seen in the titular character. Even before Paterson has an exchange with the rapper whose private freestyling session he overhears, Paterson takes pleasure in the linguistic creativity of a group of young men channelling African American slang and speech patterns. They stop him on the street to warn him that his pedigree pooch is at risk of being 'dog-jacked'. The speaker, played by New Jersey native Luis Da Silva Jr, is identified as 'Blood in Convertible' in the credits.

> BLOOD: Hey yo, that's an English Bulldog, right?
> PATERSON: Uh … yeah.
> BLOOD (to men in his car): Yo I told you man, them dogs are poppin' right now.
> Yah that dog mad expensive, right?
> PATERSON: Yeah, well … expensive to feed.
> BLOOD (initially addressing the men in his car): Yeah, this guy yo …
> No, I feel ya though, but man, dog like that get jacked.
> Ya know what I mean? Like dog-jacked my G.

Even if this white character could be critiqued for racial and cultural appropriation, including that relating to his style of language and clothing, his dialogue is in keeping with scholar Maciej Widawki's (2015: ix) discussion of the strong influence of African American slang on American slang more generally. As Widawki explains in his book on the subject, African America slang is 'linguistically innovative and culturally revealing' (ibid.), traits that Jarmusch – and Paterson by extension – also seem to appreciate. In this scene, Paterson takes more heed of the term 'dog-jacking' (which he later repeats with mock concern to the dog) than the prospect of it actually happening. The dog inspires further verbal creativity later in the film, when the rapper (Method Man) refers to the pug as Pugsley. He initially spots the dog while Paterson (whom he later refers to as Pimpin') is out of view:

> METHOD MAN (to dog): Hey Pugsley, what are you lookin' at? Ah, I'm guessin' this is your human ball and chain, right Pimpin'?
> PATERSON: Sorry, I didn't mean to eavesdrop, but I think it's something really interesting that you are working on.

While Paterson seems to have a wry appreciation for the term 'dog-jacking', he displays a genuine interest and respect for the rapper's process. Notably, Paterson stops to listen to his casual riffing by choice – while previously it was the white man channelling Black slang who insisted Paterson stop to listen. Method Man's spontaneous riffing is presented as a source of inspiration and motivation for Paterson, particularly given the broader narrative in which he struggles at times with the process of writing his own poetry.

Paterson's exploration of race and vernacular serves to complement Jarmusch's earlier rendering of characters of colour. In *Ghost Dog*, the subject of racism is explored through direct and indirect verbal references to skin colour. Towards the end of the film, men wearing blackface refer to Ghost Dog (Forest Whitaker) as a 'black fucker'. Jarmusch mitigates the scene's offensive visual and verbal references to race when, at another point in the film, Ghost Dog and other characters with African ethnicity discuss the colour of their skin in positive, lyrical terms. In what seems like a clear allegory, Raymond (Isaac de Bankolé) notes that 'chocolate' ice cream is superior to 'vanilla', despite what most people think. Racism towards a black French taxi driver, also played by de Bankolé, is treated with similar nuance in *Night on Earth*. A sense of pathos is created when, after forcing aggressive, racist passengers out of his car, he sadly repeats *'bonne journée, bonne journée'* ('have a good day') under his breath. From the audioviewer's perspective, the intonation of his speech is used to create a gap between what he says and what he means, with the resigned indignation suggesting that such racist comments are an occupational hazard. There can be a similar knowingness to Anderson's inclusion of racist remarks, as when Royal Tenenbaum refers to Danny Glover's character of Henry Sherman as 'Coltrane': as Weiner (2007) acknowledges, 'Anderson frequently points out his white characters' racial insensitivities.' But, unlike with Jarmusch, Anderson's characters of Asian or African origin are generally talked down to, rather than being allowed to voice their own opinions.

The Role of Speech in Characterisation

As this chapter has aimed to make clear, there are various ways in which audiences' understanding of character is filtered through dialogue, with that which is constructed to reveal nuances of personality a key reason why independent film characters can be considered more complex. In Newman's (2011: 90–1) writing on indie cinema, he argues that interesting characters are more thought-provoking, lifelike or surprising. Attempts to identify and measure such traits are inherently subjective, but dialogue can be crucial to advancing the impression that these qualities are in play. In these filmmakers' work, speech also plays an important role in the development of 'thought-provoking' and 'surprising' characters, as well as helping them to create the kind of 'novelistic' characters theorised by Dyer, but in this case for film. 'Surprising' characters are ones that depart from type, with characters who are 'lifelike' displaying a higher degree of autonomy and discrete identity. The cinematic verbalists' work reveals the importance of using individuated dialogue to distance characters from clichéd character types. This applies to both individuals (for instance, characters who are notably direct or notably understated) and groups of characters (Linklater's and Stillman's philosophising youths).

In considering dialogue as action, Kozloff (2000: 41; emphasis in the original) uses the notion of 'verbal events' from speech-act theory and explains that 'all conversation can be thought of as events, as *actions*. When one talks, one is *doing something* – promising, informing, questioning, threatening, apologizing'. Analysis of the cinematic verbalists' dialogue as action demonstrates that such speech can focus on relatively inconsequential interpersonal contact, as opposed to expositional dialogue that focuses on moving the plot forward. When involved in verbal sparring, their characters tend to alternate unpredictably between being highly articulate and struggling to find the right words. In these films, articulation captures the idealised use of, and knowledge of, language as expressed through extensive vocabularies and characters' insistence on verbal accuracy. Inarticulacy, on the other hand, incorporates considerable hesitancies and 'phatic expression',[21] when words convey that characters are trying to communicate, but with insubstantial words.

Unsurprisingly, given Kozloff's focus on genre conventions in mainstream cinema, American independent film dialogue only partly conforms with her discussion of typical verbal 'events', including the disclosure of secrets, a declaration of love that 'solves' the romance plot and verdicts in courtroom scenes (41–2). Although the cinematic verbalists include the occasional disclosed secret, these tend not to resolve the narrative in the way that Kozloff discusses in relation to mystery films. Declarations of love are also rare, although philosophical discussion of the concept does take place. Indeed, in Chapter 3, we considered how the cinematic verbalists often have characters negotiate their feelings via source music, which again avoids the need for overt declarations. In this cinema, certain speech acts do involve the kind of informing, questioning and apologising that Kozloff identifies, but such speech acts tend to have less dramatic functions. Instead they serve to align or distance one character from another on the basis of speech. Similarly, bonds between characters are developed and revealed when they compromise linguistically (accepting words, or definitions of them, that were previously rejected). Verbal dynamics between characters are often structured so that (in a variation on cathartic plot finality) their words come full circle instead. The transferral of words and phrases from one character to another can therefore help give more unity to episodic narratives and more meaning to characters' apparently arbitrary exchanges. Although these and other findings are made in relation to the independent cinema under focus, concepts such as verbal games and verbal catharsis could be extended more generally to selected other film dialogue.

It would be difficult to consider how dialogue can contribute to certain characters being thought-provoking or surprising without the kind of reception-focused approach used here. Personalised dialogue that simultaneously reveals nuances of characters but hides factual information contributes to the sense that, although we are observing characters closely, they remain largely unknown like individuals in everyday life. Such dialogue adds to the impression that a character has a discrete identity. Adrian Martin (2008) warns scholars against projecting too much psychological depth onto character analysis by speculating 'on what fictional characters are "really" thinking, feeling or remembering at any given moment of their screen story'. Yet I would argue that, if projecting psychological depth onto characters is common and largely automatic, then theories of characterisation that attempt to understand this process, including the contribution of dialogue to this process, are more valuable than declarations that we should disregard projections of psychological depth on the basis that characters are not real. Furthermore, given the critical bias against dialogue and the various ways in which dialogue contributes to character construction in the cinematic verbalists' work, it seems reasonable to conclude that the interdependence of dialogue and characterisation is one reason why theories of character in cinema has been slow to develop. So although this chapter establishes a variety of ways through which characterisation can be established verbally, more work remains to be done on this complex area of film studies.

NOTES

1. Jaeckle (2013b: 8) observes how in *Psycho* the mother's 'verbally abusive' personality is established through insults. These are distinguished from Norman's hesitant and apologetic verbal style that 'characterise[s] him as boyish and placating'.
2. Tzioumakis is quoting Cassavetes as part of his discussion of Cassavetes' influence

on American independent cinema: when promoting a film on a late-night radio show, Cassavetes requested that listeners send him money so he could make a better film – a 'movie about people'. This early example of crowdfunding would lead to *Shadows* (Cassavetes 1959). This incident was first discussed by Ray Carney (1994: 29).

3. Characters' distinctive verbal styles are also discussed in *Analysing the Screenplay*. Both Ganz and Nelmes use dialogue from *Sideways* (Payne 2004) to demonstrate how characterization is developed through the central character's changing use of language (Ganz 2011: 133; Nelmes 2011: 229–31). In *The Phantom of the Cinema: Character in Modern Film* (1998: 10), Lloyd Michaels contends that characters can 'perhaps most obviously [be] defined by what they say and what others say about them'. Despite this, Michaels includes almost no actual discussion of characterization through dialogue, such as how dialogue can provide crucial clues about a character's arc over the course of a film, or how verbal exchanges can be used to create and sustain dramatic interest

4. Tarantino uses a similar naming strategy in *Reservoir Dogs* (1992) with Mr Orange, Mr Pink and so forth. *Last Year at Marienbad* (*L'année dernière à Marienbad*) (Resnais 1961) is an earlier example of the withholding of proper names, with characters instead referred to as A, X and M.

5. When Jaeckle (2013a: 158) discusses Anderson's use of rhyming effects, he extends this to characters' names, such as Ronny and Donny Blume in *Rushmore* and Ari and Uzi Tenenbaum in *The Royal Tenenbaums*.

6. These names also reflect Hartley's admiration for Howard Hawks who – as McElhaney (2006: 284) notes – uses direct, descriptive names (like Dallas, Dude or Feathers) to sum up a character.

7. As I discuss further in 'The Actor-Writer as Author in the *Before Sunrise* Trilogy' (O'Meara forthcoming), audioviewers familiar with the actors' role in writing the second film also have further reason to consider the characters as extensions of the actors, and so can read them as more 'real'.

8. Digressive dialogue can be considered the verbal component of what King (2005: 68) identifies as independent cinema's 'persistent tendency' to incorporate 'the dull bits' of life.

9. This definition of 'idiom' is from the online edition of the Merriam Webster dictionary, available at: http://www.merriam-webster.com/dictionary/idiom (last accessed 8 October 2016).

10. Newman (2011: 31) clarifies that such films are not generally vehicles for particular ideas about social reality, nor do they have a rhetorical agenda of encouraging social change. This lack of political motivation distinguishes the cinematic verbalists' representation of particular social realities from those of the *Nouvelle Vague* filmmakers.

11. For example, *Everybody Wants Some!!* opens with an inconsequential exchange that includes various mentions of 'fucking' and 'shit' as well as 'God' and 'Jesus'.

12. See Beach (2002: 196–204) for a more detailed analysis of the use of labels in *Metropolitan*. Perkins (2012: 35–6) also details some of the other labels propagated throughout Stillman's work, including 'titled (or untitled) aristocrats', 'Westsiders' and 'public transport snobs'.

13. As Perkins (2012: 82) notes, representation of children and teenagers in smart cinema frequently characterize them as 'precocious and articulate'. But, as suggested by my discussion of parroting, the dialogue of the young characters tends to suggest that their articulacy has been learned – as opposed to them being preternaturally gifted with language.

14. For instance, Perkins (2012) notes the veiled cinephilic references in the dialogue of

The Royal Tenenbaums. Richie delivers a line ('I'm going to kill myself tomorrow') from *Le Feu Follet* (Malle 1963), with Royal's 'I know you, asshole', taken from Peter Weir's *Witness* (1985) (100).

15. Elsewhere, I have considered competition and verbal games as part of a chapter on Anderson and Baumbach's collaborations and shared preoccupations (O'Meara 2014a).

16. Indeed, Perkins (2012: 11) applies Füredi's description of 'a diminished, emotionally deficit self' to the character of Roger and his casual references to therapy.

17. Beach also notes Woody Allen's tendency to mock therapy when characters repeat empty mantras. Commenting on the character of Mary (Diane Keaton) in *Manhattan* (1979), Beach (2002: 171) notes how she is 'part of a well-educated and affluent but intellectually and morally hollow culture', as exemplified by her psychobabble pronouncement that 'I'm beautiful, I'm bright, and I deserve better'.

18. Kozloff (2000: 74) refers to this technique as 'dialogue of the deaf'.

19. I use the term 'silence' to refer to an absence of words since, as Mary Ann Doane (1980: 39) points out, sound is never absent when room tone remains.

20. In Stillman's work, the casting of the Nigerian American performer, Megalyn Echikunwoke, in *Damsels in Distress* is a notable exception. Echikunwoke plays Rose, a member of the film's articulate clique.

21. For Bronislaw Malinowski (1923: 314–16), who coined the term 'phatic', such communication fulfils a social function rather than being the result of intellectual reflection. He describes it 'as a mode of action' since it serves to establish bonds between individuals.

5. EMBODYING DIALOGUE: RICH VOICES, EXPRESSIVE MOUTHS AND GESTICULATION

Performance analysis is naturally complicated by ambiguity regarding who (actor, director, screenwriter, editor) determines various elements of the final product. Nonetheless, attempts to single out who is responsible for various performed components are important to dialogue studies since, as Jack Shadoian (1981: 91) notes in his early consideration of the topic, '[b]oth the effect and function of dialogue is dependent on its delivery'.[1] This chapter considers the relationship between the cinematic verbalists' dialogue and its embodiment, including a certain emphasis on the expressiveness of the mouth, and their casting of actors such as Chris Eigeman and Greta Gerwig who have distinctive verbal and/or vocal styles. Although these writer-directors' favoured performance style cannot be reduced to a single set of characteristics, they share certain tendencies in relation to casting choices and the rehearsal process. Consultation with screenplays and interviews reveals how a great deal of their influence on the delivery occurs in written script directions and during rehearsals. At the same time, by working closely with actors in pre-production these independent filmmakers relinquish elements of control when they incorporate the performers' words or ideas into the formal script. Creating the impression of character interiority and performer improvisation appear to be significant aims of their dialogue's embodiment. This leads to speech that changes direction, and to actors performing dialogue as though thinking 'out loud' as when they 'talk' with their hands.

In addition to Chris Eigeman and Greta Gerwig recurring in the films of Stillman and Baumbach, there are various other overlaps in the performers featured in the cinematic verbalists' work. Bill Murray, Tilda Swinton and Cate Blanchett appear in Jarmusch's and Anderson's films (the first two recurrently) while Parker Posey appears in many of Hartley's and Linklater's films, and one of Baumbach's. Ben Stiller is featured by Anderson and Baumbach, while Julie Delpy is in four of Linklater's films and was cast by Jarmusch in *Broken Flowers*. More recently, Adam Driver's performances in two of Baumbach's films and Jarmusch's *Paterson* has confirmed his presence as a talented performer who is in demand by both independent filmmakers and Hollywood. For *Paterson*, Jarmusch also cast Jared Gilman and Kara Hayward as a pair of articulate teenagers, ones who previously played an articulate child couple in Anderson's *Moonrise Kingdom*. Each writer-director also has a set of actors with whom they work consistently and who are largely specific to them. For Hartley, his repertoire of performers includes Martin Donovan, Elina Löwensohn, Adrienne Shelly and Thomas Jay Ryan. Anderson reuses Anjelica Huston, Jason Schwartzman, Owen Wilson and Luke Wilson. Jarmusch's recurring actors include Isaach De Bankolé, John Lurie and Tom Waits. Although made eighteen years apart, Stillman cast Chloë Sevigny and Kate Beckinsale in both *The Last Days of Disco* and *Love & Friendship*.[2]

These filmmakers often write roles with one actor in mind, or cast non-professionals or non-US performers who bring different connotations to a part. Significantly, as part of their independent style of authorship, they generally insist on control over the casting process. Linklater claims, 'I've never had to cast anyone I didn't want' (Koresky and Reichert 2004) and, early in his career, Jarmusch explains that he could not work for a studio if it means being told which actors to use (Jacobson 1985: 54). For Hartley, his personal use of language is one advantage to working with certain performers repeatedly. He explains how this allows him to use 'the same terminology on the set to describe appropriate actions and gestures' (Fuller 1992: xxx). Hartley thus applies the efficiency and specificity of language of his scripted speech to the filming itself.

A cult following has been attributed to several of these writer-directors, or to their individual films, and in keeping with Ernest Mathijs's (2012) description of cult cinema acting as being referential 'acting about acting', existing literature on performance in their work tends to highlight the reflexive treatment of characters' own performances. Steven Rawle (2011) convincingly argues that Hartley foregrounds socio-psychological performance by drawing comparisons between Erving Goffman's work on the everyday performances of individuals – particularly *The Presentation of Self in Everyday Life* (1959) – and the performances of Hartley's characters.[3] For Goffman, a sociologist, individuals use external signs (like speech, as well as costume or gesture) to project a chosen identity. Goffman considers how speech can indirectly reveal things that were unintended and some of his findings have already been extended to Indiewood film dialogue by Coughlin (2008) in relation to the Coen brothers, and Peberdy (2012) in relation to Anderson. I too use elements of Goffman's work to explain the dynamic between dialogue and performance in the cinematic verbalists' work. In particular, the final section of the chapter relates their incorporation of lies to Goffman's (1959: 143; 217) claim that individuals' everyday performances include incompatible elements that typically go unnoticed. Since the execution of lies in the cinematic verbalists' films rest on a distinct combination of spoken language, performance and images, it can be seen to take advantage of lies as a particularly 'cinematic' use of speech, as well as one that actively engages the audioviewer.

Impressions of Improvisation and Interiority

One of the most notable features of the cinematic verbalists' treatment of dialogue and performance is the impression they create of a character thinking 'out loud'. Writing in *Stars*, Dyer (1998 [1979]: 118) stresses how, unlike in literature, characters on screen have few means for conveying interiority. He goes so far as to say: 'The biggest problem facing film in trying to construct character along more or less novelistic lines is how to render a character's "inner life".' Owing to the way that their dialogue is written and performed, our writer-directors navigate this difficulty particularly well in order to strongly suggest characters' internal processes.

Linklater incorporates elements of improvised dialogue into a re-written script to overcome the loss of spontaneity that typically results from using a script. Indeed, Johnson notes this link between Linklater's writing style and the work of Éric Rohmer:

> Rohmer was so attentive to his actors' own language that he famously claimed not to understand lines he had appropriated for the script of *La Collectionneuse* (1967) ... like Rohmer, Linklater listens to the language his actors use when not in character. (Johnson 2012: 29–30)

Creating a sense of improvisation was also an aim of the *Nouvelle Vague* more generally, with Linklater (and also Jarmusch and Baumbach) seeming to subscribe to Truffaut's (2009: 325) assertion that 'spontaneity is all the more powerful when it is the result of long and careful work'. Berliner (2010: 193–7) also highlights 'an air of improvisation' in John Cassavetes' dialogue from the 1970s, as well as identifying certain impressions of improvisation in the work of Woody Allen (who includes rambling speeches, but with definitive resolution) and Martin Scorsese, whose script for *Mean Streets* (1973) includes actor improvisations (193–4). In each case, incorporating actors' own language generally requires a long rehearsal process, and Linklater schedules performers for three weeks before shooting begins (Weston 2003: 287). He also incorporates actors' own language through more formal collaborations. For the *Before Sunrise* trilogy, he wrote or re-wrote the script with the main actors (Ethan Hawke and Julie Delpy), with several scenes in the initial screenplay for *Before Sunrise* deliberately left 'bare' for the actors to 'fill in'.[4] But once Linklater decides to incorporate elements of an actor's own speech then the dialogue is formalised in an updated script, which is memorised verbatim.

Jarmusch is equally keen to include actors in the writing process. For *Broken Flowers*, each of the main female characters were shown a draft of the letter that serves as a catalyst for the story and asked to write an in-character version of it. Jarmusch then rewrote the letter using what he describes as 'pieces of their own language' (Focus Features n.d.: 7). His actors are also encouraged to improvise during rehearsals, with Jarmusch rewriting parts of the script so that the actors 'feel [more] comfortable about the language' (Sante 1989: 94). Like with Linklater, the actors are then required to deliver lines verbatim from the updated script (von Bagh and Kaurismäki 1987: 71). Thus, both writer-directors ensure that their decisions regarding dialogue are not lost during the shooting. Jarmusch's complicated process for directing Japanese actors in *Mystery Train* further reveals both his collaboratory spirit and his firm control over the speech. Using an interpreter, the performers improvised in rehearsals, but their Japanese additions were translated back into English by a second interpreter so that Jarmusch could write his own subtitles using 'my choice of English' (Sante 1989: 94).

Although Hartley and Baumbach do not seem to encourage elements of the script to be improvised in rehearsals, they do stress the importance of the rehearsal period and incorporate their performers' contributions in other ways. For Hartley's first five features, the performers were hired for a month of rehearsals before shooting began (Avila 2007: 81), and Hartley describes completely rewriting scenes to incorporate their personalities. Anderson and Baumbach have also included actors in the writing process: Owen Wilson has a co-writer credit on Anderson's first three films; Jennifer Jason Leigh has a story (but not screenplay) credit for *Greenberg*, while Greta Gerwig has a co-writer credit for *Frances Ha* and *Mistress America*.[5] In these ways, when the cinematic verbalists write or rewrite their screenplays to incorporate some of the actors' contributions, verbal mannerisms or personality traits, the actor reclaims some of the autonomy typically lost due to cinema's recording technology.[6] It also seems reasonable to expect that actors who contribute ideas or dialogue to a script will have a deeper connection to the material. Although impossible to establish, this in turn may influence the execution of the dialogue.

Leaving such speculation aside, what is clear is that by incorporating actors' scripted hesitancies into the final film, characters' dialogue is imbued with a sense of spontaneous thought. As discussed in Chapter 4, the sense that characters are not entirely constructs is conveyed when their dialogue is argumentative in a pedantic or inconclusive way. Dialogue of this kind also requires actors to convincingly perform the dialogue so that interiority is suggested. Again, the *Nouvelle Vague* is a strong influence. Michael J. Anderson (2009) points out that Rohmer does not film dialogue per se, but conversations that are more than the sum of the scripted lines. Anderson describes a scene from *Ma nuit chez Maud* (*My Night at Maud's*) (Rohmer 1969):

> [W]e see Jean-Louis [Trintignant] perk up with that last quoted line, raising his finger and waiting for Vidal to finish the sentence ... We see him wait to deliver the line, not as an actor who has almost spoken before his turn, but rather as the participant in a dialogue, thinking on his feet.

Here, Anderson captures how Rohmer's conversations are constructed as dramatic events; characters not only speak but are shown as they listen, formulate thoughts, struggle for the right words and impatiently interject (ibid.). The cinematic verbalists also construct lines that stop and start or change directions in order to give the impression that a character is mid-thought, as in Anderson's *Bottle Rocket* when Dignan responds to the disappointing behaviour of his team as follows: 'He's out. You're out too. And I don't think I'm in either.' When compared with an alternate line that conveys a similar message (such as, 'You're both out and I can't do this by myself'), three separate fragments with pauses in between give the impression that Dignan is deciding each part in turn, giving a sense of spontaneity to the second and third parts, which also becomes an absurd punch line. The pauses suggest an interiority that would not be conveyed by the single alternate line, as does Wilson's tone, which moves from angry exclamation (for the first two lines) to a quieter sense of deflation in the last.

The tendency for lines to be updated while they are spoken extends to some of the other indie films under discussion, as when Bernard tells his sons in *The Squid and the Whale* that the subway station is 'four blocks from the house. Four or five. No more than six blocks.' Frank also describes a poster he has 'at home', before quickly shaking his head and correcting himself, 'at Mom's'. Given that he and Bernard argued over the correct terms for each location ('our house' versus 'your mother's house'), Frank's self-correction indicates his attempt to forestall Bernard correcting him. Yet such changes in the direction of the dialogue still require the actor to signal the change – as though they have just thought of something – through a simultaneous shift in expression or movement: Frank blinks quickly and shakes his head. Such dialogue contrasts with the tendency in mainstream cinema for characters who speak in unwavering statements, particularly when relaying plot information. By offering a contrast from such overly polished messages, this cinema can distance itself from the kind of dialogue that Jean Mitry (1997 [1963]) criticises in his early consideration of the topic. Mitry notes that since 'giving perfect form to the expression of a thought takes time, nothing is more contrived than putting well thought out ideas into the mouths of characters' (239–40).

Instead, the combined effect of such dialogue and its embodiment is more in keeping with cognitivist Murray Smith's (1995: 20–1) argument that 'as the imagined, fictive counterparts of human agents', characters must show most of the attributes expected of a real human. In addition to including 'the ability to use and understand a natural language', Smith notes 'perceptual activity' and 'self-awareness' among these attributes. Interiority can be so important to the execution of this dialogue that it can even be stressed in their screenplay directions, as with Hartley's for *Flirt* (1995) and *The Unbelievable Truth*, when lines are prefaced with '*thinks, then ...*', '*pauses, then*', '*realizing*' or '*considers*'.[7] The detail with which Hartley imagines his speech enacted is clear, although there is a danger that detailed directions for vocal tone and emphasis make it more difficult to achieve a sense of spontaneity. Baumbach took a rather different approach with *Frances Ha*, by only showing actors the script for their own scenes, with the hope that this would increase the sense of spontaneity (Brooks 2012). He explains how the strategy makes it easier for actors to perform 'the moment and what was in front of them', rather than imbuing scenes with their knowledge of the overall plot (ibid.).

GESTICULATION AND THE EXPRESSIVE MOUTH

Gesticulation is another important strategy for creating a sense of characters' speech as spontaneous, in addition to creating the impression that characters are 'real people' who are thinking 'out loud'. Chris Eigeman's performance style is a case in point. From 1990 to 1998, Eigeman plays six variations of the same fast-talking character in each of Stillman's and Baumbach's first three films. When their dialogue calls for passionate articulation, Eigeman not only emphasises words vocally (discussed later in the chapter), but he gesticulates in a variety of ways. During a brief rant in *The Last Days of Disco*, Des/Eigeman counts out the words of the acronym 'YUPPIE' on his fingers. Then, arguing that in order for a given group to exist people have to admit to being a part of it, he mimes a small box – the one he doesn't want to be placed in. While other characters sit calmly during conversations, Des/Eigeman grips anxiously at his drink. In addition to Eigeman using his hands to emphasise the spoken words (Figure 5.1), he also indicates interiority when his eyes dart from side to side as he speaks as though scanning his brain for an answer.

More generally, gesticulation allows spoken words to be shaped physically, and is particularly suited to mid or wide shots in which the cinematic verbalists' actors sit and talk, or walk and talk. Linklater even uses animation

Figure 5.1   Des/Chris Eigeman speaking with his hands in *The Last Days of Disco* (Stillman 1998). (Source: screenshot by author)

to exaggerate gesticulation, as in *Waking Life* when Shape-Shifting Man's (Eamonn Healy) hands shrink and grow while he uses them to speak.[8] The filmmakers also include reaction shots of hand gestures rather than of facial expressions. In *Rushmore*, when Miss Cross reveals that she is married a container of fish food falls from Max's hand into the tank below. Although Max masks his shock verbally and facially, the scene is cleverly choreographed so the audience can see his physical response to Miss Cross's words.

Hand gestures are also used to draw attention to gaps between what is said and what is meant, as in *Bottle Rocket* when Anthony asks Rocky (Donny Caicedo) to translate into Spanish what he wants to say to his romantic interest, Inez (Lumi Cavazos). Anthony pleads, 'Just give me two seconds,' but quickly follows this with, 'It'll take three minutes.' Two seconds, a common but misleading expression, is therefore revealed as such. Anthony holds up three fingers while saying this, as though forgetting that Rocky speaks English and (unlike Inez) does not need him to mime. Furthermore, when Rocky subsequently translates for Anthony he fails to replicate Anthony's use of air quotes (Figure 5.2), again signalled with fingers, which further alters the original meaning.

Writing on translation more broadly, Tessa Dwyer (2005: 303–4) sums up what is potentially Anderson's motivation for presenting scenes in this way: 'In attempting to translate, to make the foreign familiar, difference is inevitably reaffirmed and accentuated.' Hand gestures that accompany scenes of translation draw attention to this difference and strengthen the impression that speech cannot easily be converted or reduced to the verbal – even when all the characters speak the same language.

Figure 5.2   Amending speech with air quotes in *Bottle Rocket* (Anderson 1996). (Source: screenshot by author)

The independent cinema under discussion can also focus physical performance on speech by taking advantage of the expressive potential of the mouth. Bordwell (2005) notes that Hartley 'squeezes' characters into small spaces, sometimes with only their hands and faces visible. But, in some instances, the whole face doesn't even make it in to the frame. We see this in *Trust* when Maria talks to her mother who is only visible from the mouth down, with a cigarette hanging from her lips. The cigarette moves as she speaks and so draws our attention away from Maria who is otherwise the focus of the shot. The mouth is also an important focus for Adrienne Shelly's characters in both this film and *The Unbelievable Truth*. In the latter, Audry/Shelly is introduced when pushing her lips out in time with an imagined explosion. The camera later stays entirely on her when, lectured by her parents, she awkwardly holds her finger to the corner of her mouth (Figure 5.3). When she removes and replaces her finger several times it focuses our attention on the mouth, and suggests that the rigidity of the gesture is intended. In another highly choreographed sequence, Audry/Shelly falls off a step when applying lipstick.[9] She proceeds to have a long conversation unaware of the streak of red extending across her face. Since Audry/Shelly wears dark glasses and repeatedly bites her lip, further attention is kept on her mouth (Figure 5.4). Hartley's staging choices and Shelly's execution are consistent enough that reviewers refer to Shelly's 'swollen' or 'over-sized' lips (Rea 1990; Anderson 2007). The impression that Hartley is deliberately showing the mouth as visually as well as verbally expressive is strengthened by *Simple Men*'s promotional poster, which consists of two images: a hand holding a gun and an extreme close-up of a woman's mouth.

Figures 5.3 and 5.4   Audry/Adrienne Shelly focuses attention on her mouth in
The Unbelievable Truth (Hartley 1989). (Source: screenshots
by author)

Like Hartley, Anderson, Stillman and Jarmusch make frequent use of cigarettes as props that alter the rhythm with which lines are delivered, as well as
highlighting the mouth and connecting the hand to the mouth. As Peberdy
(2012: 49) notes of Margot in *The Royal Tenenbaums*, her cigarette functions
as an 'expressive object'[10] since her 'extended inhalations and exhalations'
amplifies the character's sense of boredom. Exhaling smoke also adds visual
and vocal interest to several scenes in Jarmusch's *Ghost Dog* and to a collection of static verbal moments across his work. In this way, the performance of

Jarmusch's dialogue aligns with Chion's discussion of pipes, cigars and ciga-rettes as 'the starring props' of verbocentric cinema (75). However, in keeping with the conclusion in Chapter 2 (that these writer-directors take features of verbocentrism and stylise them 'beyond' that of Hollywood) Jarmusch's use of cigarettes can be interpreted as intentionally excessive. For example, as the title of *Coffee and Cigarettes* indicates, the very premise of the short film col-lection is overtly verbocentric: each short focuses on conversations in which characters use coffee and cigarettes as props. At the same time, it is undoubt-edly more cinematic than a film such as Louis Malle's *My Dinner with André*, which consists almost entirely of a single conversation for close to two hours. Jarmusch's set-up adds dynamism to a similar situation.

Baumbach's work also incorporates a wide range of gestures that draw attention to the mouth. These include peeling skin off lips in *The Squid and the Whale* (Figure 5.5) and vicious ear biting and nervous nail-biting in *Margot at the Wedding*. In *Kicking and Screaming*, Jane (Olivia d'Abo) takes out her retainer during meaningful conversations, while Roger in *Greenberg* applies lip balm when uncomfortable. The use of cigarettes and overt gestures of the mouth is another detail of this work that can be traced back to Godard. Indeed, Baumbach explicitly references Godard's treatment of the mouth in *The Squid and the Whale* when Bernard explicitly quotes both a line of Jean-Paul Belmondo's dialogue and his quintessential gesture (parodying that of Humphrey Bogart) of repeatedly running his thumb over his lips.

Overall, by highlighting the expressive potential of the mouth, this cinema helps to maintain the focus on the spoken words and take advantage of

Figure 5.5   Gesturing tied to the mouth in *The Squid and the Whale* (Baumbach 2005). (Source: screenshot by author)

cinema's ability to use gesture, props and costume to highlight the mouths and hands of particular actors. The voice is equally, if not more, important to the execution of this dialogue.

Verbal Speed and Efficiency

As noted, the cinematic verbalists include a long rehearsal period prior to shooting. Given the small budgets with which they typically work, this allows them to shoot with relatively few takes.[11] Perhaps more importantly, a theatrical approach to preparation helps them to achieve the kind of fast-paced delivery and smooth transitions found in many of their films.[12] As acting coach Judith Weston (2003) explains:

> If you want the actors to go faster, you must [allow for] more substantive rehearsal ... [This] can create the safety, connection, and authority among the cast to allow them to pick up cues and pick up pace. (Weston 2003: 300)

Excluding Jarmusch's films, fast-paced dialogue is apparent in each of these filmmakers' work, and the intended speed of the delivery is evident in their screenplays, where dash marks are used to signal when one character is cut off by another. Certain reviews for the cinematic verbalists' films have acknowledged that their dialogue is delivered at an uncommon pace. Robert Downey Jr's speech in *A Scanner Darkly*, for instance, is described as 'hyperactive' (Vest 2009: 167), 'maniacal rapid-flow' (Eggert 2007), 'motor-mouthed' and involving 'verbal gymnastics' (Coyle 2006).[13] Indeed, 'pace' is identified by Wilkins (2013: 413) as a common, but not necessary, condition of 'hyperdialogue', and she cites Downey Jr's role in Linklater's film as an instance in which 'hyper dialogue' is contained to the speech of one character.

Perkins identifies *The Squid and the Whale*'s notable pace, but not the delivery of the dialogue's role in establishing it (61). Yet even Baumbach's directions (in the published screenplay) acknowledge the difficulty of delivering a point uninterrupted in a family in which everyone is quick to respond:

> Joan sits on the side of her bed ... She takes a deep breath.
> JOAN
> Hi.
> (trying to get it all out)
> I wanted to tell you about Ivan so you didn't hear it from anyone else.
> (Baumbach 2005: 65)[14]

Not only does Walt (Jesse Eisenberg) – the character Joan (Laura Linney) is addressing – speak quickly, but he cuts out pauses between his response and the previous speaker's last words. When his father recommends that he read Franz Kafka's *The Metamorphosis* (1915), Walt repeats 'metamorphosis' instantly, before any kind of beat. In Chapter 3, we consider how verbal repetition encourages audioviewers to infer meaning by comparing instances in which a word or phrase is used. We can also be actively engaged by the way in which repeated words are *performed*. In this particular scene, given that the book title and its author's name recur throughout, Walt/Eisenberg could have signalled the significance by repeating it slowly and deliberately. Instead, when the five syllables are run together quietly and robotically, the delivery suggests that Walt is committing the title to memory but without emphasising that we should expect the book to be mentioned again. More generally, keeping up with characters' exchanges, and their broader significance, requires close attention to be paid to the notably fast speech.

Our ability to follow notably fast speech is rooted in everyday perception. Gerrig and Prentice allude to this in their discussion of audience participation: in everyday exchanges, people often only get the chance to speak when they 'jump in' within milliseconds of the last utterance. Transition times of as little as 0.2 seconds have been recorded for someone to move from being addressee to speaker, a fragment that constitutes 'the quickest voluntary response humans can emit' (Gerrig and Prentice 1996: 394). In this way, notably fast-paced speech takes a feature of everyday conversation to an extreme that seems exaggerated, excessive even, in comparison to the pace of much mainstream dialogue.

These independent screenplays are also notable for the efficient pace through which actors' words are edited together with their actions. Consider the detailed directions in the following excerpt from *The Royal Tenenbaums* screenplay (co-written by Owen Wilson, who plays Eli and follows the directions as written):

> Eli standing near the circulation desk with a group of professors drinking cocktails.
> ELI
> Well, everyone knows Custer died at Little Bighorn. What this book presupposes is: (tentatively) what if he didn't?
> Eli shrugs and smiles.
> CUT TO:
> Eli placing a call from a payphone in the lobby. He unfolds a newspaper clipping and looks at it while he waits. He says suddenly into the receiver:
> ELI
> Let me ask you something. Why would a review make the point of saying someone's not a genius? I mean, do you think I'm especially not a genius? Isn't that –

> Someone gives Eli a book to sign. He scribbles his name on it and hands
> it back without looking. He says sadly:
> ELI:
> You didn't even have to think about it, did you? (Anderson and Wilson
> 2001: 21–2)

Each adverb used to describe Eli's speech is crucial to understanding the subsequent change in his emotion. He 'tentatively' shares his idea with the professors that he is trying to impress, but because he 'shrugs and smiles', the delivery seems to convey dramatic revelation rather than genuine insecurity. We are not shown the professors' reactions (or even anything to suggest that his work will be reviewed), yet the scene cuts immediately to a disappointed Eli, so frustrated by the reception of his work that he speaks 'suddenly' once his call is answered. The fast pace is maintained by cutting him off mid-rant and leaving out the interlocutor's response, which is unheard but inferred by (1) the next line, (2) him 'not looking' at his fan and (3) him 'sadly' responding. In this way, each line of speech is loaded with meaning – not naturally – but through the way they are combined to accumulate a distinct impression. In Chapter 2, we explore how American independent cinema often avoids redundant overlaps between dialogue and visuals, ignoring what Thompson (1999: 17) terms 'the rule of three' – whereby visual and verbal cues reinforce each other three times to ensure that the audience gets the message. In a similar avoidance of redundancy, this scene relies on the *combined* impression (from Eli's gestures, words and the speed/tone of delivery) to reveal how his career prospects and confidence have quickly gone from good to bad to worse.

CHRIS EIGEMAN, GRETA GERWIG AND THE CASTING OF DISTINCTIVE VOICES

Although there is a degree of physicality to the pace at which a performer can deliver speech, other elements of the embodied voice are also important – even if they can be more difficult to identify and put into words. Yet it is precisely *because* it is ephemeral that the voice is a particularly 'cinematic' performance tool. As Peberdy (2007) effectively explains:

> Unlike the film still, photographic image, script or screenplay, the voice
> cannot be 'captured'. An image can be paused, enhanced or magnified; a
> passage from a play or screenplay can be read, re-read, and reinterpreted.
> 'Capturing' a voice, however, proves much more problematic.

Since the turn of the century there has been increased focus on the voice as (1) a performer's expressive tool and (2) a technologically mediated element only partly under the actor's or actress's control (Sergi 1999; Robertson Wojcik

2006; Smith 2008). In *Vocal Tracks*, Jacob Smith (2008) makes a convincing argument for reconsidering twentieth-century acting in respect of the introduction of the closely held microphone. As he rightly notes, the microphone's 'ability to capture subtleties of vocal timbre and inflection faithfully opened up the possibility of new forms of performance marked by a quiet intensity' (8). Cognitive theorists like Persson (2003: 160) and Plantinga (2009) similarly consider the voice in cinema and distinguish 'verbal form' from 'verbal content'. Persson (2003: 160) explains how '[p]rosodic features, such as pitch (level, range, and variability), loudness, and tempo of voice are informative indicators of emotions and mental states'.[15]

When deciding who to cast, vocal qualities and verbal skills appear important to American independent cinema and this is one way in which performance in the cinematic verbalists' work aligns with that of cult cinema. As Sarah Thomas (2013: 48) notes in *Cult Film Stardom*, character actors often have an 'excessively distinctive "sound"'. Take Chris Eigeman, for example. In addition to his use of gesticulation, Eigeman brings a distinctive vocal embodiment to Baumbach's and Stillman's work. Stillman's dialogue requires Eigeman to enunciate thirteen-line monologues and tongue-twisters (like 'stepmother of untrammelled malevolence') at rapid speed. His scripted speech also benefits from Eigeman's ability to alternate between passionate articulation and an incredulous tone of sarcasm, as when Eigeman insults a character by repeating their words back in a scathing tone. Baumbach also makes a feature of Eigeman's voice through his writing and direction. In *Highball* (1997), his largely forgettable third feature film, Baumbach centres a joke on Eigeman's ability to project: wearing a costume he can't see through, Eigeman's character is too busy talking to realise he bored the person beside him into leaving. Eigeman's voice remains so loud through the costume that he is the only one in the party scene unaware that he is talking to himself. Baumbach and Stillman can also subvert sound-mixing conventions by maintaining music volume and requiring actors to speak over it. Eigeman's voice is resonant enough, and his words are enunciated clearly enough, that he can deliver extensive amounts of dialogue over loud music.

For *The Last Days of Disco*, producers at Castle Rock (a subsidiary of Warner Bros) wanted a high-profile actor to play Des, but Stillman insisted that the role had been written for Eigeman and only he would do (Everett 2012). Stillman's physical and vocal embodiment suggests that Stillman was right to insist that few actors had the precise skills necessary to embody the role. Alternatively, one could say that few roles require Eigeman's precise skills for embodying dialogue. As a result, Eigeman's career slowed notably when, at the end of the 1990s, Stillman and Baumbach took breaks from filmmaking. With Eigeman's distinct verbal talents not in demand by other filmmakers, his subsequent work has largely been in television where, more so than cinema, writers have been drastically increasing dialogue speed. As Emily Nelson notes in a 2002 article on the pace of TV dialogue, Aaron Sorkin's writing on *The West Wing* (HBO 1999–2006) and Amy Sherman-Palladino's for *Gilmore Girls* (Warner Bros 2000–7) took fast-talking to another level. It is telling that Eigeman was subsequently cast in a recurring guest role in the latter. At 20–25 seconds a page, *Gilmore Girls'* dialogue's is delivered more than twice as fast as the standard pace for television (Nelson), and Eigeman was apt to play a romantic and verbal match for Lorelei (Lauren Graham), the show's hyper-articulate central character.

Since his casting in *The Squid and the Whale*, Jesse Eisenberg's verbal skills have similarly shaped his career trajectory; leading him to appear in such notably 'wordy' films as *The Social Network* (Fincher 2010) and *Midnight in Paris* (Allen 2011). In fact, according to Fincher, Eisenberg's casting in the former was explicitly due to his speed of delivery, when he was the only actor able to replicate the speed that screenwriter Aaron Sorkin intended for *The Social Network*'s dialogue (Harris 2010). Both Eigeman's and Eisenberg's voices are in keeping with Martin Shingler's (2010: 112) description of a 'rich voice' as possessing some of the following qualities: 'full-toned, fully rounded, resonant, deep, energized, amplified and projected ... articulate, pure and clear'.

Shingler uses the term 'rich voice' partly because he discusses such vocal performances in relation to the *The Rich are Always with Us* (Green 1932). However, the 'rich' element also extends to Shingler's argument that, during the period of the Great Depression, Hollywood occasionally used 'rich voices' as a substitute for an expensive mise en scène:

> Visual opulence ... is more sensitive to the economics of film production than sound; therefore it is no wonder that in a time of financial constraint, extravagant *mise-en-scène* made way for rich voices, [and] screenplays swelling with streams of words. (Shingler 2010: 113–14)

Again, it becomes clear that dialogue is an effective means for creative differentiation for films with relatively small budgets. Like the fast-paced delivery of screwball comedies from the Great Depression period of the 1930s to 1940s, the casting of actors with strong verbal skills is another connection between American independent cinema and certain verbally stylistic Hollywood productions from decades earlier.

Shingler focuses on actors' voices largely independent of the dialogue that they deliver,[16] yet the style of writing can determine which aspects of a 'rich voice' are most important. A voice may be well-suited to the speech of one film and poorly suited to that of another. This point can be illustrated by considering Greta Gerwig's roles in Stillman's *Damsels in Distress* and Baumbach's

Greenberg, Frances Ha and *Mistress America*. Gerwig's vocal performances are in notable contrast to Stillman's collaborations with Eigeman, for whom Stillman's dialogue seems to come naturally. Instead, Gerwig found the verbal style of *Damsels in Distress*, with what she describes as its 'commas and caveats', to be a challenge:

> I would run out of steam for the character ... I would start off strong and feel like I was kind of distinguishing the points she was making, and finding it, but it was so tiring that by the end [the dialogue] was all running together. (Rea 2012)

Gerwig's description of trying to deliver Stillman's long and convoluted lines recalls James Naremore's (1988: 26) discussion of a 'performative sentence'. Naremore explains how a notably long line (whether in text, theatre or film) has to be kept 'in play', with the reader or speaker, 'stringing out parallel constructions like a singer holding his breath, until that final moment when the period brings us to rest' (ibid.). Gerwig's difficulty with Stillman's speech is unsurprising since it is at odds with most of her previous roles in 'Mumblecore' films.[17] Although dialogue-centred, films given the 'Mumblecore' label tend to include the kind of meandering speech more common of Linklater and Jarmusch than of Stillman. Therefore, despite Gerwig's voice being 'rich' in terms of expressivity (it is consistently energised with effective contrasts of tone), she generally delivers lines in a stop–start manner. Thus, when delivering Stillman's dialogue, she likely ran out of breath when running 'out of steam'.

Although Gerwig manages to overcome these difficulties to do Stillman's performative sentences justice, her more natural vocal delivery is more suited to characters that she plays in Baumbach's *Greenberg*, *Frances Ha* and *Mistress America*. Although aged from twenty-seven to thirty-two when playing these roles, Gerwig's voice is notably 'girlish' in quality (slightly breathy and nasal, with a relatively high pitch for someone of her age) and this is well-suited to her roles as creative, complex and somewhat flaky women who are lost on the road from adolescence to adulthood. Writing on the vocal traits of teenaged girls, Diane Pecknold (2016: 78) describes how 'the rasps, breaks, breathiness, straining' can 'sonically project an infinite state of restless becoming whose endpoint is never determined'. As Pecknold discusses, although the technical flaws associated with girls' voices are often criticised, the material 'grain' of their voices can also be read as authentic (78–82). In other words, while changes in vocal anatomy can lead to a certain amount of vocal incoherence, the breathiness and breaks can sound like genuine expressiveness. Such a description applies well to Gerwig who, although older, continues to imbue her youthful characters with a verbal-vocal delivery that sounds suitability liminal and earnest. Indeed, one of Baumbach's musical choices seems to complement and support such an interpretation: when Florence is being driven to an abortion clinic in *Greenberg*, the car stereo blares 'Hey little girl, what's the matter with you?' from The Sonics' song 'Shot Down'. Florence/Gerwig asks for the music to be turned down, straining her voice to be heard over it. Gerwig's character is not ready to be a mother, with the lyrics and her girlish vocal performance serving to heighten this impression.

In Gerwig's most recent collaboration with Baumbach, as co-author and co-star of *Mistress America*, her performance as Brooke Cardinas depends on a range of distinctive vocal traits. The audience is first introduced to Brooke aurally via an intense voicemail message, one that sounds self-possessed to the point of being forceful, and that leads the nervous Tracy (who has never met Brooke) to hang up altogether. Despite Brooke's voice being filtered through a phone speaker, Gerwig effectively captures the character's overzealous tone – one that is repeated and exaggerated further when Brooke physically enters the frame. Brooke suggests that she and Tracy meet in Times Square, a notably congested space in which she nonetheless finds way to make a grand entrance: after shouting at Tracy from the top of the imposing TKTS steps, Brooke/Gerwig addresses her, 'Welcome to the great white way!' – a line described in the screenplay directions as to be delivered in an 'awkwardly grand' way (Baumbach and Gerwig n.d.: 15). In a subsequent scene in which Brooke teaches a soul cycle class at the gym, Gerwig continues to vocally signal the enjoyment Brooke takes from making a scene and filling sonic space: while using a microphone to motivate her tutees she chooses to address Tracy loudly through the microphone when she enters the room (Figure 5.6). For this role,

Figure 5.6   Brooke/Greta Gerwig uses a microphone to enhance her vocal sound in *Mistress America* (Baumbach 2015). (Source: screenshot by author)

which generally requires Gerwig to signal Brooke's free-wheeling exuberance and/or irritation, the actress seems to build on her vocal performance as Violet in *Damsels in Distress*. Because in *Mistress America* it is Tracy who struggles at times to articulate herself, or to be verbally and vocally forceful. At the same time, although the two women learn from each other they also begin to critique each other, with the ambiguity of their respective roles (is Brooke really wiser because she is older?) supported by differences in their voices. Even though Brooke/Gerwig is twelve years older than Tracy, Lola Kirke who plays Tracy speaks in a lower pitch, with her almost gravelly tone making her, paradoxically, sound like she could be older than Brooke.

The script itself includes an explicit reference to vocal tone, one that supports this interpretation that Gerwig (and perhaps Baumbach) carefully designed a vocal style for Brooke. Late in the film, Brooke exclaims to her nemesis Mamie-Claire that 'you are so annoying when you get calm voice!' It is telling that his remark seems to come from nowhere, with the phrase 'calm voice' never explained and used as though a common expression. The implication of Brooke's remark, however, is that she herself chooses to speak passionately. Indeed, Brooke/Gerwig is prone to emphasising key words to the point of shouting. Brooke's frustration in this small moment suggests something that seems crucial to the relationship between dialogue, character dynamics and performance in the cinematic verbalists' work more generally: tone is crucial, and refusing to match someone's tone (as Mamie-Claire refuses to do with Brooke) can become a form of retort.

As some of the Gerwig examples begin to demonstrate, the vocal skills required to effectively deliver the cinematic verbalists' dialogue can thus involve more than the ability to project loudly, or to rattle off lines coherently or confidently. Jarmusch's dialogue is often delivered at a slow lethargic pace by characters more concerned with smoking than with making their point. Rawle (2011: 173) explains how, with Hartley's *Amateur* (1994), the short statements, questions and retorts of the dialogue *as written* would seem 'rapid and punchy', and look like those of *His Girl Friday* (Hawks 1940), but that Thomas (Martin Donovan) and Isabelle (Isabelle Huppert) perform the dialogue at a slow and methodical pace. Alluding to the relationship previously discussed between interiority and performance, Rawle notes that such a delivery gives us time to reflect on the 'unusually internal contrastive nature of the [film's] characters' (ibid.). Like with Jarmusch's dialogue, the less Hartley's actors 'do' with the material, and the longer they spend doing it, the more time that we have to reflect on what they actually mean by their words.

Jarmusch (2010: 16) tends to use actors whose voices are 'distinctive and easily-identifiable', two criteria that Shingler identifies for a voice to be well-suited to cinema. Consider John Lurie's and Tom Waits's use of expressive vocal sounds in *Stranger Than Paradise*, *Down by Law* and *Coffee and*

Cigarettes. Waits has been described as having a 'gravelly, "whisky" voice' (Solis 2007: 41), while Ben Stiller – who appears in several of Anderson's and Baumbach's films – is another example of an actor with a distinctive rather than a conventionally pleasing voice. In fact, his emphatic delivery in *Greenberg* is described as 'knifelike' by Denby (2010). By allowing actors to include unpleasant or coarse sounds in their vocal performances, Jarmusch and Baumbach incorporate the kind of idiosyncratic sound that Shingler praises. As discussed in relation to sound design in Chapter 3, at times these filmmakers intentionally sacrifice dialogue audibility. While these unclear vocal components can be signalled by the director with screenplay directions for lines to be mumbled or delivered under their breath, they also allow their actors the freedom to incorporate vocally expressive moments. For instance, when Nicole Kidman picked up on Baumbach's use of vocal sound effects in *Margot at the Wedding*, she added a heavy sigh of her own. Baumbach subsequently praised her initiative in interview when he explains how her sigh was used as a sound bridge across two scenes (Feld 2007).

For Jarmusch the voice is such a priority that he does not allow his films to be dubbed. As his agent Bart Walker explains, despite causing difficulty with financiers of his films in Europe and Japan, Jarmusch insists that '[t]he integrity of his film changes when the actor's voice is changed' (Walker cited in Hirschberg 2005). Jarmusch's refusal to dub also recalls our consideration of polyglot films in Chapter 3, particularly the way that European imports to the United States were relegated to the art cinema unless dubbed into English. Assuming that subtitles are perceived by filmmakers and distributors to be off-putting to potential audiences, Jarmusch effectively recreates this relationship when he insists that his films are not dubbed for non-English-speaking countries. Jarmusch further aligns his films with the exclusivity of art cinema but, perhaps more importantly, his aversion to dubbing reveals his understanding of the emotional message conveyed by the dialogue's tone. As Plantinga (2009: 122–3) explains, emotion can often be accurately judged by 'picking up cues from variables such as changes in loudness, pitch, and temporal sequences of sound (utterance length, speech rate, and silences)'. Crucially, vocal delivery can allow for dialogue that avoids stating characters' emotions, similar to the way these filmmakers structure dialogue to convey a sense of interiority.

Jarmusch's attention to the voice, and his subtle treatment of race, also extends to accents. For *Broken Flowers*, he was keen for Winston (Jeffrey Wright) to capture the 'slight touch of South Asian' that distinguishes an Ethiopian accent ('Focus Features' n.d.: 8). Jarmusch wrote the role specifically for Wright, who in turn called the Ethiopian Embassy during shooting in order to ask questions that would help him perfect Winston's pronunciation. Again, the delivery of the dialogue depends on the actor and director aligning in terms of what they consider important; Wright pays his vocal performance the kind of close attention that Jarmusch desires. Furthermore, Jarmusch uses his technical knowledge of music and recording to develop a verbal directorial style that suits the musicians he often casts as actors (such as Waits and Screamin' Jay Hawkins). Since Hawkins was unfamiliar with film terminology, during the production of *Mystery Train* Jarmusch spoke to him as though they were in a recording studio: 'I'd say, "don't overlap her line, because you're going to bleed through, like one guitar part over another"' (Sante 1989: 96). Like Jarmusch's use of in-character letters written by the actors, or Hartley's development of a 'shorthand' language for directing actors on set, their creativity with language can thus be said to occur *during* the production process as well as in the finished films.

Having outlined the significance of the voice, verbal skills and written and performed impressions of interiority to this independent cinema, let us now consider lying as a kind of dialogue particularly reliant on these performative elements.

Lying as a Tangled Web of Words and Performance

In a brief discussion of lies on film, Chion (2009: 362) argues that cinema fails to take advantage of the dramatic potential of characters 'inventing imaginary facts or altering [the] truth'. Also addressing lies in cinema, Nelmes (2011: 229) notes how the audience tends to be made 'aware of the deception'. Here the concern is with precisely *how* the audience is made aware of such deceptions in these films, and if this suggests that the writer-directors *are* taking advantage of lying characters' cinematic potential. According to Joseph Anderson (1998: 87), lies require audioviewers to engage in 'cross-modal comparison and correction'. Although he focuses on how conflicts between musical and visual cues force the audioviewer to re-evaluate their previous interpretations (87), the same can be said of (1) conflicting words or (2) conflicting combinations of words and images. Lies can therefore take advantage of cinema's combination of words, images and performance by having one or more element(s) undermine the remaining element(s).

First, a lie or deception can be identified entirely based on the scripted dialogue when a character makes inconsistent points. Depending on who a character is speaking to in each case, the audience can be the only ones aware of the full range of their words, and we may have to decipher tone and/or expressions to determine which utterances are more likely to be true. This is somewhat the case with 'hyper-dialogue', which Wilkins (2013: 412) describes as creating 'a distance between what is stated and what is felt'. As an example, she provides two scenes from Anderson's *The Darjeeling Limited* in which Francis explains his physical injuries. First, in a detailed account, Francis tells his brothers about the motorbike that led to his visible injuries. When his mother subsequently asks about the same injuries, Francis gives a dramatically shorter account: 'I smashed into a hill, on purpose, on my motorcycle'. Wilkins notes how the two words 'on purpose' reveal Francis's underlying anxiety, which was omitted from his first, verbose answer (418). As she identifies, the conflicting accounts compel the audience 'to recall and reconsider the initial explanation offered to the brothers and the audience' (ibid.). Wilkins alludes here to the power of repetition with variation to cognitively engage audio-viewers, a feature identified in earlier chapters to be a more general feature of dialogue in American independent cinema.

Arguably more 'cinematic' than lies detected based on dialogue content are lies detected on the basis of *how* the words are delivered. In *Don't Believe His Lies: The Unreliable Narrator in Contemporary American Cinema* (2008), Volker Ferenz argues that audience members are likely to detect lies from facial expressions and body language. He downplays verbal and vocal delivery, going so far as to suggest that 'in the cinema we pick up most of the story information from the image-track, and tend to play down the information provided by the sound-track' (93). And yet, in the cinematic verbalists' work, pauses and shifts of pace and tone are often key to signalling that a character is speaking without conviction, or is lying outright. This is the case in *The Royal Tenenbaums*, with the screenplay directing Gene Hackman (as Royal) to make several telling pauses when asked about his divorce by his daughter:

> MARGOT
> Was it our fault?
> ROYAL
> (long pause)
> No. Obviously, we had to make certain sacrifices as a result of having children, but no.
>
> (Anderson and Wilson 2002: 5)

The pause here signals interiority, with Royal/Hackman taking a moment to decide whether to say what he wants or something more sensitive to the child asking. Aside from the delayed response, his true feelings are hinted at with the qualification he makes between the two 'no's.

The use of vocal tone to signal truthful qualifying remarks is also a feature of Blanchett's dual performances in *Coffee and Cigarettes*. Inspired by Blanchett's acting range, Jarmusch invited her to play herself and a fictional cousin (Shelly) in one of the eleven shorts. Shelly's resentment of Cate's fame and lifestyle is indicated by the script, but Blanchett develops this impression by isolating words associated with celebrity and delivering them in a mocking tone. At the end, when the character of Cate leaves to do press interviews, Shelly enthusiastically reciprocates ('Send my love to everyone your end'). But, after a six-second pause (that allows Cate to move further away), Shelly sits back down and adds: 'If they even remember me.' The enthusiasm in both her face and voice are gone to reveal a sense of hurt. Cate shouts back in voice-off ('Hey, maybe next time I'll get to meet Lou!'), and Shelly smiles again as she answers ('Yeah!'), but then mutters under her breath ('It's Lee'). Although here Shelly's 'true' feelings are accompanied by a closer-shot, it is her private speech that is particularly revealing. Shelly's qualifying remarks – made under her breath – convey that while the character of Cate is the professional actor, Shelly was also acting.[18]

These scenes demonstrate how the tone and content of a character's speech can together indicate a character's negotiation between their public and private self. Aural signalling of this kind complements Dyer's focus on the use of the 'long held close-up' to signal a character's 'true' feelings, by capturing an expression that no other character *sees* (123). Similarly, Naremore discusses a scene in *True Heart Susie* (Griffith 1919) in which Lillian Gish uses a raised fan to hide her 'true' feelings from the other characters, while allowing the audience to see them. In *Coffee and Cigarettes*, it is instead the tone of the 'private' speech that encourages us to reconsider the truthfulness of what Shelly previously said, much as the close-up or the shielding fan does in the scenes Dyer and Naremore discuss.

When a character is revealing a truth they would rather not, their speech may also come out at such volume or intensity that it seems they have partially lost control over it. In *Greenberg*, rushed dialogue accompanies Roger's speech that is more outspoken in content, as though he is revealing waves of ordinarily suppressed thoughts. This is in keeping with Dyer's (1998 [1979]: 121) description of characters seeming more 'true' when they 'pour forth their thoughts and feelings in an untrammelled flow'. Alternatively, if a character's words lack the normal level of detail then this too can indicate that they are hiding something. As these examples suggest, a notable change – of any kind – in a character's verbal style can indicate that they are either trying to hide the truth, or that they are revealing the truth unintentionally. It follows that, in order for audience members to perceive such a change, the character's dominant verbal style must already be well-established.

A lie can also be signalled to the audioviewer through camera work and editing. In the independent cinema under discussion, lies signalled in this way still tend to require some contextualising dialogue. This is the case in a scene from the *The Squid and the Whale* in which Frank sees on the floor the food that Bernard has cooked. When Bernard serves the food in the next room Frank feigns ignorance and asks: 'Why'd you yell goddamn it?' Although Bernard answers quickly and casually, 'I burned myself,' we have been *shown* that he actually yelled because the food fell. Frank does not reveal the truth, however, in keeping with Baumbach's general unwillingness to 'spell out' things for the audience when they can be reasonably inferred.

Each form of lie discussed here is signalled to the audience through a combination of performance, scripted speech and images. These lies, or unintended revelations of the truth, are inconsequential from the perspective of plot. Indeed, these filmmakers typically script inconsistencies for characters that signal self-deception or a discomfort with openness, rather than scripting the kind of dramatic lies more likely to impact the narrative. Characters' negotiations with the truth instead reveal the struggles Royal, Shelly, Roger, and Bernard face when deciding what to say openly and what to keep to themselves. In this way, the cinematic verbalists continue to foreground a sense of interiority and self-awareness in their characters. Like the actors playing them, the characters are therefore revealed to be performing. As a result, they are further aligned with the performance style of cult cinema which, as Mathijs summarises, is often referential 'acting about acting' (136-7).

These uses of lies to actively engage the audience can be unpacked further with reference to Goffman's concept of performance 'witnesses' in everyday life. For Goffman (1959: 210), disciplined performers remember the part they are playing and do not 'commit unmeant gestures'. He notes that most everyday performances include 'incompatible' elements, but that witnesses rarely collect and organise the inconsistencies 'into a usable form' (143). But, unlike in reality, the cinematic verbalists seem to carefully design the visual and verbal signs so that they can be detected – positioning the audioviewer as a Goffman-style 'witness' who decodes inconsistencies in speech or behaviour. Typically, if we suspect that a character is lying then we need to recall both what we have seen (actions and facial expressions) and heard (dialogue and tone) in order to pick up on and reconcile inconsistencies. Even if a lie has few narrative consequences, it can create a de-dramatised sense of suspense with the viewer waiting to see if it is uncovered. And, if we are better informed than any one character, then there can be a certain pleasure in tracking the lie and characters as it evolves over the course of a scene or the film. In fact, given the ability of both camera and microphone to magnify the kind of subtle details that can indicate that a lie is in play, cinema is probably the medium best-equipped to represent this kind of deceitful behaviour.

There is also some evidence that the cinematic verbalists are intentionally foregrounding lies, since a number of their characters explicitly discuss lying. Characters in Stillman's *Metropolitan* even debate whether lies are necessary for smooth relationships. Of course, mainstream and classical cinema also incorporates lying and can reveal speech to be a lie through the way that the words are delivered, or through the accompanying images. Distinguishing the cinematic verbalists' use of lies, however, is the frequency and the subtlety with which they are used.[19]

Shaping Dialogue through Performance

Taking this chapter's various insights into performance together, the cinematic verbalists can be said to use a number of novel strategies to ensure that their dialogue is effectively embodied. Although an auteurist approach to performance risks taking away credit from both editor and actor, analysing performance style in these films alongside their screenplays and interviews, reveals notable overlaps in the ways that this dialogue is executed. While the six filmmakers can be wary of undue interference from industry players, they embrace close working relationships with actors, particularly those who bring other creative skills (such as screenwriting or music) to the process. Even though filmmaking is generally conceived of as a collaborative art, it is rare for performers to be so involved in the development of their characters' dialogue. Since their contributions from the rehearsal process are formalised prior to shooting, the cinematic verbalists ensure that their dialogue is still executed as desired. Interviews with the cinematic verbalists suggest that their creativity with language occurs *during* the production process, in addition to in the finished films. Consideration of their screenplay directions also reveals how actors' style of delivery is firmly guided by the writing, and thus demonstrates the value of consulting their screenplays when attempting to distinguish the actor's, director's or writer's contributions to a given performance.

In order to imbue characters with a sense of spontaneity and interiority, specific performance skills are beneficial to the delivery of the kinds of independent dialogue discussed here. Given the significance of nuanced vocal performances to the impact of this dialogue, it is understandable that these filmmakers are particular about casting particular actors' voices, and, in Jarmusch's case, to then refuse to let them be dubbed. Performers in the cinematic verbalists' work tend to display verbal dexterity, or emote vocal expressiveness that is only hinted at in the content of the speech itself. Furthermore, in keeping with previous scholarship on the role of the voice in character acting and cult stardom, these actors' voices are 'rich' in terms of expressivity, but they are not necessarily pleasing in a conventional sense.

Since cinema can alter the representation of time in certain ways that text cannot, it is intuitive that some of the cinematic verbalists' most memorable techniques for dialogue embodiment are precisely a result of its pace; speech is either accelerated or intermittently slowed down with revealing pauses. Since there is no way to control the speed with which dialogue is read (although punctuation, or lack of, can approximate this effect) neither could be fully realised in literary formats. In these ways, the effect created by the cinematic verbalists' dialogue is execution-dependent and specific to the medium.

Performances that do the cinematic verbalists' dialogue justice require more than just vocal embodiment, however. Gestures in this work can be somewhat localised to the hands and the mouth. By encouraging actors to physically shape the words as spoken, the cinematic verbalists' dialogue further indicates a sense of spontaneity or interiority, or reveals disparities between the words as scripted and the intended message. Overall, such dialogue offers certain challenges and rewards for performers and audiences, as when actors are required to convey that their character is lying or performing a contrived identity by alternating between different types of vocal delivery or physical expression.

NOTES

1. Dyer (1998 [1979]: 151) similarly indicates the need to first appreciate the source material: 'Performance is what the performer does in addition to the actions/functions she or he performs in the plot and the lines she or he is given to say.'
2. Unlike Sevigny, who is strongly associated with American independent cinema, Stillman is one of very few filmmakers to cast Beckinsale in roles out of Hollywood – ones in which she can embrace the more intellectual roles that one may associate with Beckinsale's attendance at the University of Oxford.
3. Rawle (2011: 306; 312) argues that Hartley's main contribution to art cinema is an experimental approach to acting that emphasises 'the illusionistic nature of performance in mainstream cinema'.
4. Elsewhere, I discuss Delpy and Hawke's collaboration with Linklater, as well as their individual creative projects, in 'The Actor-Writer as Author in the *Before Sunrise* Trilogy' (O'Meara forthcoming).
5. Leigh, who was married to Baumbach at the time, gave feedback on drafts of *Greenberg* and *Margot at the Wedding,* as well as acting in both. When Ben Stiller was concerned that *Greenberg* was written for somebody younger than him, he discussed the character with Baumbach who 'came back with a very different draft' that incorporated some of Stiller's ideas (Stiller cited in Deevy 2010).
6. For instance, Sharon Marie Carnicke (1999: 76) describes the potential of montage to 'redefin[e] the relationship between director and actor from one of collaboration to one of authority and control'.
7. The screenplay directions are found in Hartley's published screenplays to *The Unbelievable Truth* (78; 79; 82) and *Flirt* (7).
8. Starr A. Marcello (2006: 69) analyses Linklater's *Waking Life* in her discussion of the interplay between film acting and sound design. Marcello argues that, given the film's unconventional rotoscoped animation, Linklater should be given further attention 'as the creator of the performances'.
9. Rawle (2011: 109–49) details the choreographed nature of performance in Hartley's films, both in a chapter on dance and in a discussion of violence.
10. The term 'expressive object' was coined by Naremore (1988: 83–8). Peberdy (2011) also draws attention to other moments of performance centred on the mouth in Anderson's work. Such moments include the use of a toothpick that reveals vulnerability in *Hotel Chevalier* (51), Peter (Adrian Brody) licking and chewing on his lips in *The Darjeeling Limited* (ibid), and a cigarette hanging limply from Herman's mouth in *Rushmore* (66).
11. Another explanation for the cinematic verbalists' extensive rehearsal periods is that Linklater, Jarmusch, Baumbach and Anderson all make use of non-professional actors.

12. F. Thomas (2013: 128) identifies a similar connection between rehearsal and smooth transitions in his study of Orson Welles's verbal style. However, in the case of Welles, the transitions often involved overlapping speech.
13. It should be noted that such a fast-paced delivery is also characteristic of Robert Downey Jr's performance style, and is not particular to his role in *A Scanner Darkly*.
14. The intention for characters to cut one another off is also evident in Anderson's and Linklater's screenplay directions. For example, *Before Sunrise*'s includes descriptions like 'he jumps on her words' and 'interrupting' (Linklater and Krizan 2005: 95–6).
15. Sonnenschein (2001: 138–9) makes a similar point in his discussion of the voice as an instrument that carries two meanings, one that is verbal, and the other that is intonational and reflects the speaker's feelings.
16. Shingler's (2006b) discussion of Bette Davis's voice does, however, carefully relate her delivery to *All About Eve*'s most famous line: 'Fancy your seatbelts, it's going to be a bumpy night.'
17. Lyons (2013: 164) describes Mumblecore as 'cult micro-budget films' that are 'character-based, predominantly (often acutely) naturalistic films detailing the conversational minutiae and relationship dynamics of drifting twenty-somethings'. Gerwig appears in such Mumblecore films as *LOL* (Swanberg 2006), *Hannah Takes the Stairs* (Swanberg 2007) and *Nights and Weekends* (Gerwig and Swanberg 2008).
18. I have considered Blanchett's broader performance style, including some further discussion of that in *Coffee and Cigarettes* in 'Cate Blanchett's Deconstruction of Performance through Performance' (O'Meara 2014b).
19. Again, the cinematic verbalists appear to be influenced by the *Nouvelle Vague* filmmakers who also use lies to creative effect. Michael J. Anderson notes that lying characters are a 'central motif' of Éric Rohmer's work, while in *Jules and Jim* (*Jules et Jim*) (Truffaut 1962) issues of trust and deception are key to the relationship between the central characters. Chion (2009) also cites Rohmer's incorporation of lies, as does Tamara Tracz (2003) who notes that mystery in Rohmer's films, 'manifests itself in the lies people tell', and that these are both 'to each other and [to] themselves'.

6. GENDERED VERBAL DYNAMICS: SENSITIVE MEN AND EXPLICIT WOMEN

Dialogue in contemporary independent cinema often complicates certain generic expectations of what forms of speech are 'male' and 'female', resisting the tendency to script male and female dialogue in decidedly different ways. Although, in terms of gender balance, the filmmakers under discussion tend to be associated with telling men's stories (and so foregrounding male voices) the reality is not quite that extreme. Hartley has produced several female-centred narratives (including *Trust*, *An Unbelievable Truth* and *Fay Grim*), with Stillman's last three films (*The Last Days of Disco*, *Damsels in Distress* and *Love & Friendship*) and Baumbach's last three films (*Margot at the Wedding*, *Frances Ha* and *Mistress America*) all focused on female characters. While Linklater may have chosen to chronicle *Boyhood* rather than girlhood, his *Before Sunrise* trilogy offers extensive and equal time to each half of its central couple. And, even if relegating women to minor roles is an offence (one that Anderson and Jarmusch are most guilty of), then it is one that can be lessened when minor female characters are given disproportionate verbal authority.

Discussion of gender and dialogue in film studies tends to focus on genre in Hollywood cinema and, in relation to the voice-over, to take a psychoanalytic approach – as in Kaja Silverman's *The Acoustic Mirror* (1988). In terms of male characters, the view that cinema predominantly represents men of action, not words, is captured by Richard Dyer's (1982) and Steve Neale's (1983) discussion of the masculine ideal as one of 'masculinity-as-activity' (Dyer 1982: 66–7). Neale (1983: 12) identifies the centrality of battles between individual or groups of men to the 'male' genres of the war film, the gangster film and the

Western. Writing explicitly on dialogue in the action film, the other quintessentially male genre, Yvonne Tasker (1993: 87) sums up how 'speech and silence' are central to establishing its representation of masculinity. Tasker discusses Sylvester Stallone and Clint Eastwood as two sides of the same near-silent coin, with Eastwood considered to artfully withhold words, while Stallone's muttering instead suggests 'an artless inability to speak' (86–7). In contrast to these physically brave and taciturn men, the tortured male protagonist of *film noir* often reveals existential concerns through a voice-over that confides in the audioviewer. Despite their pensive moments, the men of *film noir* (like the men of action) are situated in a dark and violent world, and they rarely disclose their feelings to other characters.

Generic discussions of gendered dialogue tend to characterise male and female speech by contrast, as though the two must exist in opposition to each other. In Scott Simmon's (2003: 112) discussion of the Hollywood Western, he positions the verbal style of female characters (who propose 'pacifist solutions') against that of male characters who listen awkwardly to the women's suggestions before tersely dismissing them and asserting that they, as men, must *act*. In Tasker's (2002: 57) analysis of *The Quick and the Dead* (Raimi 1995), she highlights the novelty of a female protagonist (Sharon Stone) who is 'strong and silent'. Tasker explains how the female character's one-liner put-downs are also more associated with the 'tough-guy' type (57). It is no coincidence, then, that melodrama (historically considered the genre of 'women's films') instead privileges 'the open discussion of emotions' (Kozloff 2000: 238).[1] As Peter Brooks (1985: 4) equally notes, a fundamental characteristic of the genre is the 'desire to express all', with characters voicing 'their deepest feelings'. Less concerned with openly discussing their emotions are Maria DiBattista's *Fast-Talking Dames* (2001) of the 1930s and 1940s, who were verbally empowered in unique ways. DiBattista is right to praise the cycle of articulate heroines in this period; they 'won' sparring matches with male characters and astonished with the speed of their delivery (14). Other discussions of women's dialogue in this progressive period take a more critical view, with Kozloff (2000: 183) identifying a tendency for female 'blathering', which uses 'vague vocabulary and referents, and [jumps] from one topic to the next in a process of mindless, freewheeling association'.

This chapter's analysis of American independent cinema's nuanced scripts will reveal the ways that verbal style can be made specific to the individual character, rather than being determined a priori by that character's gender. In order to demonstrate this, it is first necessary to analyse aspects of male and female speech separately, by considering points of contact between the cinematic verbalists' work and other iterations of the verbally (in)expressive man and the verbally (dis)empowered woman. Case studies include *Henry Fool*, *Greenberg* and *Paterson* in relation to men's speech, and *Love & Friendship* and *Mistress*

America when considering women's speech. As in earlier chapters, characters' speech is considered here from a socio-psychological perspective. Findings on gendered speech from socio-linguistics can help to contextualise scripted gender dynamics. Such an approach is less precarious than it may initially seem, since there are considerable overlaps in the ways that film scholars and social linguists discuss their human subjects. Throughout *Men Talk – Stories in the Making of Masculinities* (2003), linguist Jennifer Coates refers to individuals as 'protagonists' who 'perform' masculinity through their creation of verbal 'narratives'. Nancy Lee's (2010) analysis of male speech in the HBO series *Entourage* (2004–11) has much in common with Coates's analysis of everyday speech. Lee analyses how *Entourage*'s dialogue reveals speech to be 'the act – the *performance* – of internalised social ideals of gender' (183; emphasis in the original).[2] Her analysis unpacks how verbal dynamics between characters help to place them at various points on a hierarchy of masculinity, and, in the process, demonstrates the suitability of taking a socio-linguistic approach to the gendering of scripted language.

In Coates's analysis of everyday discourse, she identifies certain themes and forms of communication as typical of men's speech and others as typical of women's speech. She qualifies this by noting that, when binary distinctions such as 'masculine' speech and 'feminine' speech are made, it obfuscates the considerable overlaps between the ways in which men and women talk. By taking a dualistic approach, existing literature on gender and dialogue can create this same kind of false dichotomy. Instead, this chapter is concerned with the overlaps between female dialogue in the cinematic verbalists' films and elements of speech that are typically considered 'male', and vice versa. Thus, while Lee argues that dialogue in *Entourage* functions to express 'the internalised ideals of gender' (195), in the independent cinema under discussion, language is also used to question or reject these ideals. The overall effect from this is the creation of characters who have nuanced verbal styles, distinctive to him or her, and that are removed from generic gender types.

THE VERBAL EXTREMES OF 'BIPOLAR MASCULINITY'

Kozloff (2000: 13) cites a societal association between talkativeness and femininity as a key reason why dialogue has been undervalued in film studies, but the cinematic verbalists' male characters are often more talkative. Certain characters in Hartley's and particularly Jarmusch's work use words sparingly, but the men in Anderson's, Baumbach's, Linklater's and Stillman's work generally detail thoughts and feelings in long meandering conversations – ones that can echo Woody Allen's brand of neurotic ranting. The recurring character of Antoine (Jean-Pierre Léaud) in François Truffaut's films is another important antecedent to this kind of expressive male character. Antoine is described as a 'solitary declaimer' by Bart Testa (1990: 96–7) and, like many of Hartley's,

Baumbach's, Linklater's and Anderson's male characters, he gives speeches with little narrative consequence.

More broadly, these characters can be seen as part of a distinct trend, emerging in the 1990s, for verbally expressive male characters. The form and delivery of such speech has already considered by Peberdy (2007, 2011, 2013b) and Debbie Ging (2012) in respect of selected contemporary cinema. In *Masculinity and Film Performance: Male Angst in Contemporary American Cinema* (2011), Peberdy details how various films of the 1990s and 2000s began to portray less conventional images of men, as well as revealing how selected male vocal performances are used to reflect angst. One of her conclusions, based on analysis of male characters including Don in Jarmusch's *Broken Flowers*, is that angst is presented as 'the breakdown of stereotypically "male" social roles', with the acknowledgement that men can be both 'hard' and 'soft', helping to establish how normative masculinity is constructed (169). Peberdy considers the performative relationship between masculine opposites, to argue that masculinity is increasingly portrayed as inherently 'bipolar' (in contrast to studies that argue that masculinity shifts from forms considered 'hard' to ones considered 'soft' depending on the historical period). She uses the term 'wimp' to capture male characters portrayed as ineffectual, pathetic and emasculated (97), with her argument that the wimp's impact is strengthened by his opposite (the 'wild man') particularly relevant to my interpretation of male dialogue in the cinematic verbalists' work. Because although the six writer-directors more often script male speech that highlights 'soft' masculinity, the impact of the dialogue is partly down to a recurring tension between 'hard' and 'soft' language. This is neatly exemplified in Hartley's *Henry Fool*.

In the film, Hartley incorporates both extremes of male speech to capture the bipolar dynamic that Peberdy identifies. Rather than the 'wimp' and the 'wild man' being embodied by a single performer, Simon and Henry take on the respective roles.[3] An early scene encapsulates the ways in which their exaggerated verbal styles represent the two extremes. Shortly after meeting Henry, Simon is taken in by one of his far-fetched, boastful and violent stories. Henry's speech includes various stereotypical traits of male narratives, as outlined by Coates. It is full of claims to greatness ('I've been bad, repeatedly') and danger (his story is set in a 'dangerous location' with 'water so foul the natives wouldn't even piss in it'). Henry also speaks with pride and aggression about his capacity for violence, both in the present ('let's go break their arms') and in the past, as in the following excerpt:

> This crowd of drunken motherfuckers hired by the local drug cartel shows up at my hotel room and threatens to tear me limb from limb. And I say, listen, hombres, OK, you've got me outnumbered here four to one and you're gunna kill me here tonight and not a soul in this dimly lit

world is gunna notice I'm gone. But one of you ... one of you ... one of you is gunna have his eye torn out.

Simon listens to Henry, impressed and uncritical. His single question ('and then what happened?') also allows Henry to end his story on an enigmatic high note ('Well, here I am, still, after all'). Simon's passivity is initially characterised by his refusal to speak or defend himself. When he does talk he gives one-word answers or gives up mid-sentence.[4] Rather than being the kind of strong silent type associated with the Western, war or action film, these are all traits that Amy Lawrence (1991) identifies in relation to disempowered female speech in *Echo and Narcissus: Women's Voices in Classical Hollywood Cinema*. Like Simon's passive silence, Henry's speech is presented in exaggerated form and, together, they indicate Hartley's awareness and desire to parody the two male extremes of 'the wimp' and the 'wild man'. This bipolarity alludes to the fact that neither verbal extreme is accurate, with a more 'realistic' style of male speech combining elements of both.

Verbal aggression, bragging and open discussion of sexual conquests are discussed by Coates throughout her study as stereotypically, if not realistically, male. Such traits could be said to align with 'hard' masculinity, with the cinematic verbalists more often using dialogue to highlight 'soft' masculinity. This is reflected in the topics on which they wax lyrical. J. J. Murphy (2007: 89) describes how Hartley's male characters are 'tortured by existential doubts' about such topics as love, trust, ambition, success, philosophy and theology, with his references to existential doubts raising an important point of comparison between the cinematic verbalists' men and the conflicted males of *film noir*. Although the efficiency of Hartley's speech recalls the 'terse' nature of hard-boiled dialogue (cf. Krutnik 2006 [1991]: 40), aphoristic *noir*-style dialogue is employed by male and female characters.

The dialogue delivery by female performers can also channel elements of the typical *noir* male. Peberdy (2013a: 327) describes Mark McPherson (Dana Andrews) in *Laura* (Preminger 1944) as a 'quintessential "tough guy"' who speaks in monotone, with a cigarette resting in his mouth that barely moves as he speaks. Yet females in Hartley's films can also speak in an inexpressive tone, and with cigarettes in their mouths limiting facial expressivity. The content of Hartley's *noir*-style dialogue can also differ from the generic norm. Henrik Gustafsson (2013: 59) notes that *noir* dialogue often uses metaphors to comment on the 'savage and predatory' nature of social relations, but the social relations commented on in the cinematic verbalists' work is generally of less consequence. The metaphors they script tend to draw on less dark and violent imagery. Indeed, Stillman's characters often use flowery euphemisms rather than 'dirtying' their mouths with words that have negative connotations. For example, as Beach (2002: 197) notes of *Metropolitan*, when Tom's father moves in with another woman Tom is 'disinherited', and when Tom's friends find out that he lives in a poor part of New York they describe how his 'resources are limited'.

In Chapter 5, Chris Eigeman's vocal and verbal skills were highlighted as central to his embodiment of Baumbach's and Stillman's dialogue. Another noteworthy aspect of Eigeman's characters is the way that they self-disclose 'soft', incompetent masculinity through speech. In *Barcelona*, Fred tells his romantic interest how he's just realised that he has been shaving 'the wrong way' and would probably have continued to do so for 'all of [his] life'. Within Fred's monologue of more than a dozen sentences, he also expresses concern that *if* he had a son he could have taught him to shave incorrectly. This hypothetical expression of paternal instinct is atypical of male film dialogue and, if shaving is taken symbolically as a basic act of manhood, then Fred's lengthy admittance is more in keeping with the socio-linguistic norm for women to self-disclose negative personal information (Coates 2003: 118). The character Eigeman plays in *The Last Days of Disco* is further distanced from normative masculinity when, repeatedly, Des pretends to have 'just realised' he is gay in order to break up with women. Despite Des feigning homosexuality to achieve commitment-free sex, Stillman uses speech to construct a space in which, verbally at least, alternative forms of masculinity are desired and accepted.

Much has been written on homosexuality in relation to masculinity. R. W. Connell (2005: 78) argues that since 'gayness' constitutes a rejection of hegemonic masculinity then homosexual men are relegated to the bottom of the hierarchy of maleness. Lee draws on Connell in her analysis of *Entourage*, in order to argue that male characters who make homophobic taunts not only suggest their distaste for homosexuality, but use such comments to distance themselves from the incompetent masculinity of gay men (190-191). Also drawing on Judith Butler's (1997: 32) concept of the 'sovereign power' of speech, Lee (2010: 193) argues that for the characters in *Entourage* 'saying [it] is as good as being it: speech acts produce masculinity'. In *The Last Days of Disco*, Des's repeated claim to be gay has a similar performative effect, only he uses speech to refute rather than produce hegemonic masculinity. In contrast to the males of *Entourage*, Des reacts defensively ('I could be gay!') when Alice scoffs that he doesn't even deserve to lick the boots of her 'real gay friends'. Both Alice's and Des's speech signals male homosexuality as something desirable to both heterosexual men and women, in contrast to *Entourage*'s dialogue that has characters verbally mark out gayness as inferior.

The analysis thus far has focused on the content of male speech, but the voice itself has significant cultural impact in the creation of male angst (89). In Peberdy's study of the vocal performances of William H. Macy, she reveals how male verbal authority is undermined through vocal dynamics in *Oleanna* (Mamet 1994) when John's/Macy's voice changes from a 'matter-of-fact tone' to a shrill and whining one (87). A similar undermining of verbal authority can be identified in respect of selected male characters in the cinema under focus. Staying with Des/Eigeman in *The Last Days of Disco*, although his speech generally occupies the mid-register of his voice, in moments of frustration (as when he exclaims 'we're not yuppies') his pitch intermittently jumps to create the same kind of shrill, whining effect as Macy. Similarly, Rawle (2013: 131–3) argues that, throughout Hartley's work, Martin Donovan invokes anger through changes in vocal pitch and 'absurdist' dialogue outbursts. He gives an example from *Surviving Desire* (Hartley 1991) in which Jude's/Donovan's 'restrained vocal tone changes and he shouts with clipped phrasing' (131).

Male angst in the cinematic verbalists' work is thus captured through the content and delivery of speech, with both components channelling stereotypes of female film dialogue: shrillness, flowery language, reflecting on feelings and reacting with hypersensitivity to others' comments. With the exception of Jarmusch's films, monologues of self-revelation (like Fred's in *Barcelona*) are also a fixture of male dialogue in the other cinematic verbalists' films. In Baumbach's *Greenberg*, angst is signalled both vocally and verbally, as in the following outburst in which Roger/Stiller answers his own question about whether the teenagers in his company are really that different to him:

> You're mean. The thing about you kids is you're all kind of insensitive. I'm glad I grew up when I did cause your parents were too perfect at parenting. All that Baby Mozart and Dan Zanes songs. You're so sincere and interested in things. There's a confidence in you guys that's horrifying. You're all A.D.D. and carpal tunnel, you wouldn't know agoraphobia if it bit you in the ass. And it makes you mean. You say things to someone like me who is older and smarter with this blithe air. I'm freaked out by you kids. I hope I die before I end up meeting one of you in a job interview.

Despite Stiller's aggressive delivery, Roger's attack on the younger generation reveals ways in which he is incompetently masculine. For one thing, he is aware of his own sensitivity, in contrast to his description of the kids as 'mean' and 'insensitive'. Roger also signals his low self-worth both by describing their confidence as 'horrifying' and suggesting that they will quickly surpass him in terms of employment. Roger's casual diagnosis of psychological conditions like attention deficit disorder (which he attributes to the teens) and agoraphobia (which he attributes to himself) is also in keeping with contemporary independent cinema's use of dialogue to reflect the parlance of contemporary therapy culture. Both the content and one-sided nature of Roger's speech demonstrate how Baumbach writes dialogue that is a 'talking cure' for his characters, with the emotional revelations of his male characters often melodramatic (and so stereotypically 'female') in nature.

Roger's outbursts and various others by male characters in Anderson's, Baumbach's and Stillman's films also align with Wilkins's (2013: 407) description of hyper-dialogue as serving 'to displace, an existential anxiety that cannot be directly accessed and is thus masked, or suppressed beneath a blanketed verbosity'. Overall, the frequency of male outbursts in these films indicates both a lack of control and difficulty accepting this lack of control. Tasker previously discussed the vulnerability indicated by such speech in relation to minor characters in action films. She identifies 'hysterical rambling' as a characteristic of 'weak and unthreatening' males who need protection (1993: 87). While such male characters tend to be side-lined to minor roles in the action genre, the cinematic verbalists unapologetically allow these characters to take centre stage. Indeed, it is telling that Tasker uses the word 'hysterical' (a term etymologically tied to women) to describe the verbal style of male characters who, like those of the cinematic verbalists, align with dialogue that is generically associated with females.

Earlier Iterations of the Verbally Expressive Male

The examples thus far have been drawn from the 1990s until present, but the trend for vulnerable male speech is not entirely a contemporary one; childish tantrums and neurotic rants by characters like Roger in *Greenberg*, Fred in *Barcelona* and a variety of Anderson's characters can be considered an update on the kind of anxiety-ridden characters in the films of John Cassavetes and Woody Allen. Indeed, in Wilkins' discussion of hyper-dialogue, she cites Allen as a 'direct precursor' to such speech, in exception to the New Hollywood kind of naturalism (422). Various male stars of the 1950s also delivered vulnerable styles of speech. According to Sidney Skolsky ([1957] cited in Cohan 1997: 201), actors like James Dean and Montgomery Clift came with neuroses and were 'diminished version[s] of the rugged, physical masculinity' personified by the likes of Jimmy Stewart and John Wayne (ibid.). Skolsky concludes that Clift and Dean (as well as Marlon Brando and Paul Newman) act adolescent, regardless of their actual age, with neuroses substituting for the physical masculinity of actors like Clark Gable and John Wayne (ibid.). As part of Steven Cohan's broader argument that post-war masculinity challenged the symbolic positioning of 'boys' as the opposite of 'men' (203), he argues that certain young male actors in the fifties 'played up the performative elements of their youth' in terms of clothing and, more importantly given our focus here, speech (202).

A similar fetishisation of youth has been noted of some of Anderson's male characters (Olsen 1999; Kunze 2014: 3; 91–109), and the same immaturity can be seen in many of Baumbach's, Jarmusch's and Linklater's male characters. While the cinematic verbalists' men often exhibit the kind of 'deeply rooted (and unresolved) emotionality' that Cohan (1997: 202) identifies, the characters of

Anderson, Baumbach, Hartley and Stillman are generally far removed from the 'mumbling diction emphasizing inarticulate (and uneducated) speech' that Cohan describes as typical of the 1950s. Instead, the pedantic and articulate speech of the cinematic verbalists' characters typically *reveals* their educational background. Cohan's description of mumbling and inarticulate speech does, however, capture some elements of male characterisation in Jarmusch's and Linklater's films. Significantly, Silverman (1988: 61–2) argues that classical cinema ties *women's* voices to bodily spectacle by presenting them as 'thick with body' when they cry or breathe heavily. Yet, in earlier chapters, discussion of the voices of John Lurie and Tom Waits identifies their coarse vocal performances in Jarmusch's work. Their 'emanation speech', in particular, is tied to the body in a way that Silverman attributes to the female voice. This means that, although Jarmusch's male characters tend not to align with female film dialogue in terms of content, the expressive 'spectacle' of their voices can be considered more stereotypically female than male.[5]

A more current comparison can also be made between the cinematic verbalists' male characters and the trend that Ging (2012: 111) identifies for 'idiosyncratically garrulous' Irish male characters in films like *Intermission* (Crowley 2003), *Garage* (Abrahamson 2007) and *In Bruges* (McDonagh 2008). Like Peberdy and Wilkins, Ging focuses on psychological angst, which she contends is indicated by dialogue that alternates between fast-talking and silence. She convincingly argues that, through the difficulties the men have communicating, audiences are allowed access to 'the complex emotional worlds' that the characters are unable to properly express (128). To situate these verbose Irish males, she looks at broader trends in male representation. Indeed, Ging briefly identifies American smart cinema as another grouping of male-oriented films underpinned by clever dialogue (112). Her comparison is focused on male protagonists in Irish cinema and the 'smart, angsty voice-over and dialogue' of contemporary British gangster films like *Trainspotting* (Boyle 1996) and *Snatch* (Ritchie 2000). There are notable differences between the cinematic verbalists' male characters and the juxtapositions that Ging summarises in relation to selected action heroes, with these differences highlighting how the cinematic verbalists' men are less conventional in terms of gender dynamics. First, Ging notes that the gangster heroes are physically *and* verbally adept:

> Although most of the characters still engage in physical action and acts of bravado, including armed conflict and robbery, bare-knuckle and kung-fu fighting, stealing cars and joyriding, the films frequently employ highly articulate and intelligent voice-over and dialogue, in which characters self-consciously ponder their fate, their identities and other existential issues. In many ways the paradoxes thrown up by this juxtaposition of

body and mind/voice, of brute physicality and articulate self-reflexivity, encapsulate the key paradoxes of contemporary masculinity politics. (Ging 2012: 112)

While the cinematic verbalists' male characters self-consciously and articulately ponder their identities, their films include virtually no physical action and bravado. Unlike the angsty action heroes on whom Ging focuses, the cinematic verbalists do not use acts of physical prowess to compensate for sensitive speech, with *discussion* about violence (as in *Henry Fool*) as close as they come. This unwillingness of the cinematic verbalists' male characters to physically fight is captured in a scene in Baumbach's *Mr. Jealousy*, when two writers attempt to fight with their fists (instead of their usual verbal bickering) but they quickly and politely give up.

Ging identifies incongruity in *Trainspotting*, *Fight Club* and *Die Hard* (McTiernan 1988) between characters' speech and their other traits, yet articulacy in American independent cinema generally fits with broader elements of character construction and narrative. Ging (2012) explains how Renton's (Ewan McGregor) witty and articulate voice-over in *Trainspotting* jars with the 'linguistic atrophy' of heroin addicts. She also identifies inconsistency in *Fight Club* between Tyler's (Brad Pitt) aversion to therapy as a 'talking cure' and the narrator's (Edward Norton) smart, existentialist voice-over (112). By contrast, most of the cinematic verbalists' males are unashamedly verbal. One-sided monologues by male characters are in keeping with their explicit references to attending therapy, while their articulacy is grounded with references to their background, education and occupation. Hence, no attempt is made to balance out the characters' preferences to define themselves through their words.

Ging successfully highlights a certain trend for expressive male dialogue around the turn of the millennium, by tracing links between articulate action heroes and Irish male characters whose speech signals internal angst. Here, bringing these together with other incarnations of the verbally expressive male characters has helped to reveal this to be a substantial 'type' – one that takes on a particularly exaggerated form in male-centred contemporary cinema, particularly indie cinema when words are the unapologetic focus. Perhaps it is because this type has fluid parameters, spanning various genres, countries and time periods, that it has been largely disregarded in order to focus on the man of action, who has little use for words, or at least words that reveal his deepest hopes and fears.

The Problem of the Speaking Woman

Our understanding of women's speech in the cinematic verbalists' work can similarly benefit from comparisons with existing literature and trends in female dialogue. According to feminist film theorists like Silverman (1988, 1990) and Lawrence (1991, 1994), women in cinema are frequently attributed unreliable speech, punished for talking or silenced altogether. In *The Acoustic Mirror*, Silverman demonstrates how, from a psychoanalytic perspective, the female voice is held to as many normative representations and functions as is the female body. In addition to the female voice being tied to her body more than the male voice is tied to his body, Silverman (1988: 46) argues that the female voice is often made to speak 'on command'. In *Possessed* (Bernhardt 1947: 59), for example, an unconscious woman (Joan Crawford) is injected with a truth serum that forces her to speak against her will. Silverman (1990: 309) later adds that, owing to 'her prattle, her bitchiness, [and] her sweet murmurings', the woman of film lacks linguistic authority. For Lawrence (1991: 145), 'the problem of the speaking woman' manifests in a range of classical thrillers, including *Blackmail* (Hitchcock 1929), *The Spiral Staircase* (Siodmak 1945) and *Notorious* (Hitchcock 1946). As she explains, in these films 'the woman's voice does not set her free', with female characters who are mute, who struggle to articulate themselves, or who have their words dismissed or used against them (109–46).

Silverman and Lawrence ground their discussion in a very specific historical and generic context, but a more recent approach to female dialogue is so broad as to be near-useless. Despite originating with a comic artist rather than in film studies, the 'Bechdel Test' is frequently employed to address a perceived silencing of women in cinema. Alison Bechdel's (1986) comic strip suggests that to pass the test a film must (1) include at least two women, (2) who have at least one conversation, (3) about something other than a man or men.[6] Understandably, given its comic-strip origins, the test is too simplistic to serve as a serious model for the analysis of gender representation. Nonetheless, due to its propagation in the popular media *and* the relative lack of nuanced criticism on the subject of female film speech,[7] the Bechdel Test has received an unwarranted amount of attention, with discussions around it tending to highlight how a significant portion of films fail.[8] Given the dominance of male characters in the cinematic verbalists' films, they too can fail. But it is not enough to ask how many female characters talk, and whether they talk about men, without also considering the broader complexities of their speech; including the language used, its delivery and the dialogue's eventual reception.

With a focus on these complexities in relation to American independent cinema, the analysis to follow begins to call into question the blanketed negativity that DiBattista directs towards female film speech post-1950. For DiBattista (2001), the release of *All About Eve* (Mankiewicz 1950) marked the beginning of the end for smart-talking female characters. Roles played by the likes of Marilyn Monroe, with her 'unsteady relation to language', instead established the 'dumb blonde' character type (335):

Smart girls, wise girls, bad girls, even silly girls who defined themselves by and through their words became increasingly rare apparitions, and indeed their muting has lasted into the twenty-first century. (DiBattista 2001: 332)

There are clear exceptions to this 'muting' of female characters in the cinematic verbalists' work. Through speech that is considered 'unladylike', their characters have a verbal freedom that is at odds with more conservative estimations of female film dialogue. Instead, the content and/or delivery of their female characters' speech seems to align with verbal and vocal traits that Kathleen Rowe (1995) includes in her influential conception of 'the unruly woman'.

The Explicit Speech of Verbally Unruly Women

In Coates's (2003: 4) socio-linguistic work on gender, she demonstrates how masculinity can be 'constructed in talk' with 'approved' ways for males to speak. The same can be said for femininity and these social conventions can, in turn, influence the development of 'approved' ways for female *characters* to speak on-screen. There are considerable overlaps between Rowe's conception of cinema's 'unruly woman' and Coates's description of female speech that challenges conventions of 'feminine "niceness"' (134), and it is partly through profane language and an unrepentant discussion of sexuality that the cinematic verbalists' female characters break away from norms for how women tend to speak in more mainstream cinema. In Jarmusch's *Night on Earth*, Corky's (Winona Ryder) constant cursing and wide-mouthed gum chewing highlights the unexpected nature of a female taxi-driver character, while Eva (Eszter Balint) in *Stranger Than Paradise* is quick to tell Willie (John Lurie) to 'bugger off' when he tries to tell her what to do. Explicit language is also a reoccurrence among Hartley's female characters, as in *Henry Fool* when Mary addresses the title character with 'you bastard', or when Amy tells Simon to 'kiss my ass'.

The function of cursing in cinema is typically analysed in terms of the performance of masculinity. Discussing the theatre and film dialogue of David Mamet, Peberdy (2007, 2011: 3) argues that his male characters often use 'coarse language' or an 'eruption of expletives' to assert power. Similarly, Ging (2012: 111) argues that the use of expletives by male characters in *In Bruges* and *The Guard* helps position them 'outside of respectability and political correctness'. Given that swearing is typically discussed in relation to males, and considered as unfeminine (both in cinema and society generally) (Coates 2003: 148), expletives position these female characters outside of respectability and, in the process, allow them to assert power through language. This is not to say that their male characters do not also curse, but rather that profane language is not attributed predominantly to them.

More radical still is the female characters' open discussion of their sexuality. Rowe (1995: 37) sees an intrinsic link between female sexuality, female garrulousness and female fatness: 'the mouth that both consumes (food) and produces (speech) to excess, is a more generalized version of that other, more ambivalently conceived female orifice, the vagina'. As a result, she considers it no coincidence that unruly women are considered to speak too much or eat too much, with a similar condemnation for those who are too sexually active. By combining two of these elements, extensive discussion of sex by females is doubly unruly.

Writing on *Jennifer's Body* (Kusama 2009) – penned by Indiewood darling Diablo Cody – Martin Fradley (2013: 214) identifies in the female characters' slang for sexual terms and body parts 'the unbounded pleasure-seeking of postfeminist culture'. A similar tendency for sexual pleasure-seeking can be identified earlier in relation to female characters in the films we are focused on. In *Henry Fool*, Fay's (Parker Posey) speech also includes the kind of references to sexuality and female biology considered to break the norms of female decorum. Fay casually says, 'God, I wanna get fucked', and later tells her brother that she's not alright since his 'poem brought my period on a week and half early'. In *The Squid and the Whale*, Bernard's student Lili is introduced when she reads out a piece of her creative writing: 'I absorb sex indiscriminately, numb and impartial. I suck men of their interiors, a fuck that unites John, Dan, Scott, Whomever ...' Bernard and his son stare at Lili as though mesmerised by her words and, acknowledging the 'risky' nature of her writing, he commends the 'racy' content. In Baumbach's next film, *Margot at the Wedding*, the title character and her sister compare sexual histories. Margot even suggests that they each list their exploits to determine who has had more. Combining competitive bragging with a discussion of sexuality, the character defies Coates's (2003: 135) description of women's stories as rarely involving competition or foregrounding achievement. In each case, female characters are unapologetic about the sexual desires. Indeed, Lili's sexualised speech is implied to be a turn-on for both father and son in *The Squid and the Whale*.

Responses such as these, by male characters, are in notable contrast to the kind of 'slut shaming' expressed in various contemporary genre films. In *Jack Reacher* (McQuarrie 2012) and *Guardians of the Galaxy* (Gunn 2014), for instance, male characters refer to female characters as 'sluts' and/or 'whores'. In fact, the plot of the romantic comedy *What's Your Number?* (Mylod 2011) is driven by the 'fact' – uttered by a female character in this case – that '96% of women who have been with twenty or more lovers can't find a husband'. In each case, speech is used to punish women for their sexual activity, or to deter them from pursuing (further) casual sex. Incidentally, two of these films pass the Bechdel Test, thus providing a good example of how flawed it is as a measure of progressive gender representation. But, rather than further lamenting the inadequacies of the test, it is perhaps more productive to further illustrate the cinematic verbalists' tendency to script more progressive forms of women's speech by looking at their recurring collaborations with particular actresses, including Parker Posey, Julie Delpy and Anjelica Huston.

Given her status as 'Queen of the Indies' (Negra 2005), it is rather fitting that Posey appears in eleven of the cinematic verbalists' films. In this work, it is often the content and delivery of dialogue that distances her characters from dominant Hollywood types. In addition to Fay's previously mentioned cursing in *Henry Fool*, Posey's character counters insults about her appearance and challenges a number of male characters with assertive lines (such as 'don't you dare talk that way to me' and 'keep your hands off my brother').[9] The tone of Posey's voice is particularly notable. Discussing the speech of the 'unruly' woman, Rowe (1995: 62) gives the voice of comedienne Roseanne Barr as an example of a performer whose voice is 'excessive' (and therefore 'unruly') in its tone and volume. Posey's ability to project her voice is similarly 'excessive', but the cinematic verbalists' films tend to highlight rather than downplay these qualities. This is evident early in Posey's career in her portrayal of Darla, the bullying cheerleader in Linklater's *Dazed and Confused*. Darla/Posey shouts abuse at other characters and often changes volume or pitch mid-word or phrase in order to intimidate them. Her ability to dominate via projection is particularly evident in a scene in which Posey's voice drowns out those of two other characters, as well as being the only voice that can be heard over the car radio. Drawing on Chion's (1999: 78) distinction between male shouting (delimiting a territory) and female screaming (limitless), Peberdy (2007) argues that the male shout is 'a marker of power' that implies a degree of control, while the scream implies powerlessness or a loss of control. As these examples suggest, Posey's voice is clearly associated with the power of the male rather than female exclamation. Darla's/Posey's control over her voice (and, as a result, her control over others), is further signalled when she accurately mimics the tone of one of the other girls in the car.

There are certain overlaps between the speech of Posey's characters and the recurring character of Céline (Julie Delpy) in Linklater's *Before Sunrise* trilogy.[10] In another instance of the *Nouvelle Vague* serving as an influence on the cinematic verbalists' work, Stone (2013: 120) notes that the character of Angela (Anna Karina) in *Une femme est une femme* (*A Woman is a Woman*) (Godard 1961) is 'a fitting forerunner of Céline' in that both are wilful and neurotic. Such terms are also used in descriptions of Posey (Kord and Krimmer 2005: 129; Rybin 2014) and, like various females in the cinematic verbalists' work, Céline's wilfulness is advanced through blunt speech. Stone describes the following questions that Céline asks Jesse in *Before Sunrise* as 'probing': 'Is this why you tried to get me off the train? Competitiveness? To make sure the guy behind you didn't pick me up?' (122) Discussing Céline and Jesse as standing for stereotypical representations of, respectively, American and European approaches to narrative, Stone also argues that their dialogue in the film:

> blurs, even subverts any distinction between the problem-solving intellect of American 'movies' and the dilemma-probing intuition of European 'films' by showing repeatedly how Jesse's capacity and need for reflection ('I feel like this is some dream world we're walking through') is answered by Céline's penchant for intellectual cynicism: 'Then it's some male fantasy: meet a French girl on the train, fuck her and never see her again.' (Stone 2013: 122)

In addition to the American character aligning with the European 'dilemma-probing' intuition, subversion takes place in relation to gender. Jesse's constant references to his feelings are more typical of female film dialogue, with Céline's profanity and 'intellectual cynicism' more typical of male dialogue. Aside from calling Jesse out on what she perceives to be a territorial (rather than genuine) interest in her, Céline's speech reveals how she is unafraid of being perceived as incompetently feminine. Two decades later, in *Before Midnight*, Céline candidly questions the idea of maternal instinct as a panacea:

> I don't think I've recovered since giving birth. When they were born, I had no idea what to do. People expect women to have instinct that kicks in, like a female baboon. But I had no idea how to do anything.

Céline's openness is in contrast to Lawrence's (1991: 5) suggestion that female characters are not permitted to tell the truth about their experience in the roles they are placed in by patriarchy. Recalling Céline's guarded and cynical response to Jesse in *Before Sunrise*, she also reveals her fear to him (now the father of her children) that every man 'want[s] to turn me into a submissive housewife'. In *Before Midnight*, generic representations of female speech are also inflated and suggested as absurd when Céline tries to prove a point by impersonating a more vacuous female 'type', one who fawns over a man by speaking softly and with hesitancy as though in awe of him. Like with Henry's exaggerated and violent boasting in *Henry Fool*, the performative nature of gendered speech is highlighted and parodied when Céline 'tries on' the kind of 'dumb blonde' type that DiBattista criticises for replacing the kind of fast-talking dames in her study.

Like with Céline in the *Before Sunrise* trilogy, the speech of Hartley's female characters allows them to question the ways that they are treated and discussed by men. Berrettini attends to elements of gendered speech in his discussion of a monologue by Maria (Adrienne Shelly) in *Trust*, in which she realises how she was never respected by the father of her unborn child. Maria's speech ends with the following:

> I go over it in my head, and now I know what it was he was seeing. It's really simple. He's seeing my legs. He's seeing my breasts. My ass. My mouth. He's seeing my cunt. How could I have been so stupid? That's really all there is to see, isn't it?

Berrettini (2011: 20–1) draws on Hartley's and Shelly's description of the scene as Maria's rock-bottom moment, as well being 'a moment of "performance crisis"' for Shelly who didn't want to say the word 'cunt'.[11] Hartley agreed with Shelly that a woman would be unlikely to refer to her anatomy using the derogatory term, but thought that Shelly's personal discomfort would contribute to the character's distress. Regardless of whether Hartley's rationale here was respectful of Shelly, Maria's self-description provides a powerful commentary on gender norms since she literally describes herself through the eyes of a man (much like Céline does in *Before Sunrise*, when describing herself as the token French girl of male sexual fantasies). Within film studies, discussion of the fragmentation of the female body (using camera techniques and editing) is common, but Hartley/Maria instead use speech to explicitly discuss her body from the perspective of an objectifying male. Since 'he' remains unnamed, and so potentially stands for 'man' more generally, the dialogue allegorically highlights women's disappointment at being reduced to their physicality. Also worth noting is the way in which Maria's father (John MacKay) loses his life as a result of 'slut shaming' his daughter. On hearing that she is pregnant in the opening sequence, he refers to her as a 'tramp' and 'slut'. Maria reacts by slapping him, which in turn gives him a heart attack. Although the overblown drama of the scene is not typical of the cinematic verbalists' films, the price that the father pays for his misogynistic remarks illustrates Hartley's attention to language's gender dynamics.

In his study of Hartley's work, Rawle (2011) considers the ways in which both male and female characters reveal the performed nature of gender roles. He acknowledges that Hartley's female characters more often provide 'a stable centre of the narrative, whereas the masculine performance descends into chaos and futility' (271), but I disagree with the conclusions he draws from selected excerpts of female dialogue in *Flirt* (1995). He asserts that women in the third, Japanese segment of the film 'exist as speculative objects', with their appearance more important than the 'aphoristic, platitudinous' words that they speak (207). Rawle dismisses the speech, quoted below, as unimportant, and yet the contrasting female speech recalls the way that Hartley was shown to capture the 'bipolar' nature of masculinity through contrasting speech:

KAZUKO: Fuck him! He's manipulating you! What the hell does he think he is! A gift from God! Tell him to get lost! His leaving Japan is the best thing that ever happened to you! The fuck!

SHOKO: Don't let him go! He'll get away! You were wrong to want more time! A girl has got to make a choice! You won't be young forever! Western men are more open-minded! They like Asian women!

Like the extreme contrast between Henry's and Simon's speech in *Henry Fool*, the impact of Kazuko's (Eri Yu) and Shoko's (Yuri Aso) speech is largely a result of what their opposing views suggest; Shoko expresses the traditional pressures aimed at women to find and commit to a man while young, and Kazuko represents a more independent and defiant perspective. The overall effect is (to extend Peberdy's term to the other gender) a sense of 'bipolar' femininity that draws on, but complicates, familiar female types.[12] A more balanced and 'realistic' type emerges when the two extremes are brought together. Again, the design and eventual impact of Hartley's dialogue depends on audiences' ability to infer things from the way that he manipulates the norms of mainstream dialogue.

When it comes to examining women's dialogue in Wes Anderson's work, Felando's (2012) article on Anjelica Huston's roles in *The Royal Tenenbaums*, *The Life Aquatic* and *The Darjeeling Limited* is a useful point of departure. Felando argues that, as uncharacteristically independent, accomplished and resilient women, Huston's characters represent female middle-age in progressive ways. For the most part, Felando's argument is grounded in the communication style of Huston's characters who are 'forthright', 'both stern and sensitive' and 'do not gush or seek approval' (68; 73; 68). Patricia in *The Darjeeling Limited* addresses her children with an 'off-putting' greeting, for instance, but also offers 'prescient advice' (78; 74). Unlike the foregrounding of feelings in melodrama, Patricia refuses to enter into highly emotional exchanges. Furthermore, while the strong, silent type is typically associated with male characters, Felando suggests that Eleanor's trademark move in *The Life Aquatic* is her ability to silently walk away from her husband's provocations (74). With back-and-forth bickering so often characterising the dynamics between male and female romantic interests, Eleanor's confident refusal to engage is powerful; figuratively, she gets the last word. Her relationship with language is thus in marked contrast to the range of female characters that Silverman (1988: 59) identifies as forced to speak against their will in the 1940s.

Huston's characters are not the only wise women in Anderson's films, nor is age a prerequisite for offering men good advice or calling them out on lies. In *Bottle Rocket*, a dynamic of this nature is created between Grace (Shea Fowler), an elementary school student, and her brother, Anthony, who is roughly twice her age. Grace pulls no punches when he seeks her out for comfort: 'You haven't worked a day in your life. How could you be exhausted?' Female speech again serves to highlight the immaturity of a typical Anderson man-child, with the girl's preternatural ability to detect bull-shit in amusing contrast to Anthony's naïveté throughout.

Women's Verbal Victories in *Love & Friendship*

Like the women discussed thus far, the character of Lady Susan (Kate Beckinsale) in Stillman's *Love & Friendship* explicitly critiques the patriarchal system in which she must live. Based on Jane Austen's epistolary novel, written in about 1805, Stillman maintains much of the syntax of the time and the vocabulary of the novel. Of more interest to the gendered verbal dynamics, however, are the ways in which Susan's clever strategies and playful spirit are revealed through interactions with other characters. These include confidantes, such as Alicia – played by Chloë Sevigny, and so reuniting the Beckinsale and Sevigny pairing from *The Last Days of Disco* – and the other players in the social games. The latter group generally lack Susan's sharpness and articulacy.

Stillman's engagement with, and updating of, Austen is crucial to the presentation of gender in the film. Scholars of Austen initially dismissed suggestions that the author was a proto-feminist, since her female characters are almost invariably married by the story's end (cf. Butler 1975; Ascarelli 2004). But this perspective has been countered. As Claudia Johnson (1990: xxiv) explains, rather than vindicating the status quo Austen found ways to 'expose and explore those aspects of traditional institutions – marriage, primogeniture, patriarchy – which patently do not serve her heroines well'. Stillman's scripting of *Love & Friendship* makes such exposures clear, particularly in relation to Lady Susan's well-thought-out views on marriage and motherhood.

Like Céline in the *Before Sunrise* trilogy, or Anjelica Huston's characters in Anderson's films, Lady Susan openly and amusingly complains about her own child and provides an ambivalent commentary on the experience of parenthood:

> Having children is our fondest wish, but in doing so, we breed our acutest critics. It's a preposterous situation, but entirely of our own making ... Of course, when the little ones are very small, there's a kind of sweetness which partially compensates for the dreadfulness which comes after.

While such a description is not taken from Austen's novel, Stillman does channel the Lady Susan from the source text who criticises her own daughter as 'the greatest simpleton on earth' (Austen 2005 [1805]: 2).

Susan's conflicted perspective on marriage – that it is rarely desirable but that it can provide relief from certain problems – is even more apparent from the character's film dialogue. In particular, she explains to Reginald DeCourcy (Xavier Samuel) why she is willing to have her daughter marry 'such a blockhead' as Sir James: 'You can afford to add another layer to your pride. If you realized the full extent of ridiculous manhood a young girl without fortune must endure, you'd be more generous to Sir James.' Here and elsewhere, Stillman reveals Susan's pragmatic insightfulness: the only way to avoid the advances of 'ridiculous manhood' is by agreeing to be aligned with just one man. This comment builds on one of Susan's previous musings, wherein she wonders aloud if the trait of 'great wisdom' is 'even desirable in a husband'. Taken together, such comments build a strong impression that Susan's recommended strategy, for herself, her daughter and women more generally is to marry a man who is dim enough not to notice or mind that the woman is not especially dedicated to him. This scenario provides both financial security and relative independence. It is also worth noting that Stillman writes the recently widowed character, and Beckinsale plays her, without any signs of mourning. Although Susan wears black, and so again satisfies aspects of what is expected of her, she appears aloof and shows no signs of emotional distress.

By contrast, and with only the exception of Reginald, the men in *Love & Friendship* are presented as some combination of bumbling, dim or outright dumb. Sir James in particularly becomes the kind of exaggerated male simpleton that Stillman also includes in *Damsels in Distress*. While the college students in *Damsels* had trouble naming colours, Sir James is foiled by both the portmanteau name, 'Churchill', of the Vernon's estate (he is bemused that it features neither a church nor a hill) and by the humble garden pea. He praises the vegetable at length: 'How jolly. Tiny green balls. Mm. Yes. Good tasting, quite sweet. What are they called?' Although Sir James's rendering borders on farcical, the relatively sensible Charles Vernon is equally revealed as foolish when he attempts to find substance in James's rambling: 'I'm enjoying Sir James's visit. His conversation's lively – brings a new angle to things.'

As the film nears its conclusion, Stillman's implicit commentary – on the foolishness of even the most supposedly powerful and well-bred men of this time (the early nineteenth century) – is made all the more apparent when, in keeping with Sir James's general ignorance, he makes overtly sexist remarks:

> For a husband to wander is not the same as vice versa. If a husband strays, he's merely responding to his biology. That is how men are made. But for a woman to act in a similar way is ridiculous. Unimaginable. Just the idea is funny.

By placing these remarks, which assert that men are biologically predetermined to cheat and that women should just accept this, with the film's most idiotic character, they are rendered all the more absurd. It seems clear that if Sir James believes something then the audience understands that it cannot be true. And, given that each one of James's ignorant comments is outnumbered by multiple sharp remarks by Lady Susan, Stillman ultimately presents their marriage as one that makes sense from her perspective: a rationale articulate woman, existing in irrational times, must learn to take pleasure in the small victory of a clever put-down.

Taking the cinematic verbalists' female characters as a group, then, their verbal assertiveness marks them out from expressions of deference common in classical Hollywood cinema, such as those that Susan Smith (2007) identifies of Kay (Elizabeth Taylor) in *Father of the Bride* (Minnelli 1950), when she describes her fiancé as 'absolutely, terribly wonderful' (169). With the cinematic verbalists' female characters often serving as voices of reason, they are also in contrast to the tendency Diane Carson identifies for *male* characters in screwball comedies to 'conquer' verbally adept females by revealing the 'nonsensical nature of [their] loquacious ramblings' (1994: 214). Because, aside from the aforementioned example of Darla/Posey verbally deriding her peers in *Dazed and Confused*, expressions of female assertiveness in the cinematic verbalists' work are generally aimed at *male* characters who are behaving badly or immaturely. This is in contrast to the kind of 'bitchy' female-to-female remarks more typical of romantic comedies and teen films; often, films based around cliques of young women–such as *Heathers* (Lehmann 1988) *Clueless* (Heckerling 1995), and *Mean Girls* (Waters 2004)–represent female friendships as superficial and catty. Exchanges between girls in these films are frequently characterised by put-downs, particularly on the basis of appearance. Such lines tend to be played for comedy, but the vitriolic image that they present of girls and women is problematic, making it worth noting the relative absence of such dialogue in the cinematic verbalists' work.

Thus far, the analysis of male and female speech in American independent cinema highlights the relationship between speech and power or control. While Posey's performances reveal her to have an uncommon control of her vocal delivery, Anderson scripts dialogue for Huston that is measured and controlled. By contrast, frequent male outbursts in the cinematic verbalists' films indicate their difficulty controlling the tone and content of their speech. This indicates that, even when these writer-directors foreground male characters, they tend to allocate female characters a disproportionate amount of linguistic authority. Discussion of the verbal power dynamics present in their work also requires a consideration of the use of voice-over, and the cinematic verbalists generally maintain a less divisive approach to gendered speech when this technique is in use.

VOICE-OVER AND GENDERED AUTHORITY

Historically, there has been a tendency for gender to be foregrounded in discussions of voice-over narration. In *The Acoustic Mirror*, Silverman focuses on the rarity of the disembodied female voice-over during the 1940s and early 1950s. Siding with Silverman, Shohini Chaudhuri (2006: 52) explains that female characters are allowed to serve as first-person narrators, but generally only if they can be overseen and overheard when consigned to 'a safe place' within the diegesis. In contrast, when the male voice is situated in a framing space 'outside' the diegesis he is aligned with the transcendental vision, hearing and speech (ibid.). So established is the male voice in disembodied voice-overs that it serves as the basis for *In a World* (Bell 2013), an independent film written, directed and starring Lake Bell, one that charts the overt sexism of the niche voice-over artist profession. Significantly for our consideration of gender and voice-over, Chaudhuri argues that even male characters whose voices are synchronised with their bodies possess the 'utmost authority' of the disembodied narrator's 'voice of the Law' (ibid.). By contrast, the cinematic verbalists tend to use extra-diegetic narration to question the authority of male characters, as well as complicating the norm that Chaudhuri suggests for women's letters to be overheard by audiences in the form of the narration of private letters.

Hartley's *The Book of Life* employs a male voice-over by Jesus (Martin Donovan) in a knowing, ironic way. Although Jesus is granted the right to narrate from off-screen (unlike the character of Satan (Thomas Jay Ryan) who instead directly addresses the audience from microphones in the diegesis),[13] his existential voice-over parodies the ubiquity of Hartley's angst-ridden male characters:

> What twisted fairy tale had I allowed myself to be tangled up into? What misplaced gratitude had I believed to be awe? Why had I let those souls believe there was anything other than sacrifice? Why were they comforted with dreams of vengeance? Why hadn't I interfered more? Agitated? Questioned? Panicked by both the legitimacy and hopelessness of their cries I rose to the occasion, and lied.

Jesus's torrent of unanswered questions takes the indecisive, sensitive male type to the extreme. There are also two references to people dying for 'the word of God' in the full-length version of the monologue. Thus, in addition to revealing Jesus's indecision and resort to lying, Hartley makes light of references to omniscient frame narrators as 'the voice of God'.[14] Because although Jesus is granted such a voice, he uses it to reveal very *human* insecurities and a 'soft' masculinity.

Silverman (1988: 57–8) explains how one strategy for keeping the female voice 'overheard', and therefore less authoritative, is to constrain it to a letter. Yet, as already noted when considering the relationships between dialogue and images in Chapter 2, Anderson and Baumbach include voice-overs of male characters narrating letters, as when Roger's stream of pedantic letters in *Greenberg* mocks voice-over connotations and shows how Roger victimises himself. There are strong contrasts between the impression that Roger tries to project through the letters (of a mature, well-educated adult) and the accompanying images that convey him as childlike (as when he is shown struggling to swim, or looking at his eye through a magnifying glass). The ironic use of voice-over in this and several of Anderson's films undermines the linguistic authority that often accompany a voice-over. Hartley's, Baumbach's and Anderson's male voice-overs thus depart from the kind of discursive mastery, knowledge and power that Silverman (1988: 87–100) describes as phallic traits attributed to the cinematic enunciator.

One could argue that, since Silverman and Chaudhuri base their findings on classical Hollywood cinema, we are not comparing like with like. But there are equally differences between Roger's voice-over and Kozloff's (2012) analysis of contemporary male voice-overs in *High Fidelity* (Frears 2000) and several films featuring Hugh Grant, including *Notting Hill* (Mitchell 1999) and *About a Boy* (Nick Weitz; Paul Weitz 2002). First, Rob (John Cusack) in *High Fidelity*, William in *Notting Hill* and Will in *About a Boy* all acknowledge the presence of an audience and speak directly to them. In contrast to their apparent choice to address us, the audience overhears Roger reading his letters, further aligning him with overheard female characters. Second, the use of the voice-over to grant Rob authority in *High Fidelity* is reflected in the way that, as Kozloff (2012: 8) notes, we initially 'only see the women [he refers to] through his narration and warped perspective'. This creates the impression that Rob is controlling the image track, unlike Roger whose words are instead undermined by the images that accompany them. The final contrast of note is between William's opening voice-over in *Notting Hill* – which, as Kozloff notes, primes the audience for the narrative focus on his loneliness and heartbreak (9) – and the way that Roger's agency is reduced before he is even present in the diegesis; the audience is introduced to him through a negative description by his sister-in-law.

Unsurprisingly, then, Kozloff's conclusions about the male voice-over in the contemporary rom-com do not hold in relation to Roger. She summarises that contemporary male voice-overs generally offer audiences 'intimate connection with attractive male stars in order to woo (heterosexual) women viewers and offer (heterosexual) male viewers attractive role models' (10). For one thing, Ben Stiller's distinctive face and small build depart from conventional notions of what constitutes an 'attractive male star'. Also, although Roger does start off 'emotionally stunted', as Kozloff identifies of contemporary male voice-overs more generally, he only makes marginal progress towards 'greater sensitivity, emotional commitment, and marriageability' (ibid.). Instead, in several ways, Roger has more in common with various male leads in Woody Allen films like *Annie Hall* (1977) or *Manhattan* (1979). Roger is not granted the authority that comes from Allen's use of direct address, though, nor the authority that comes with the knowledge that Allen has scripted and directed the films in question.

Jarmusch takes a notably different approach to voice-over in *Paterson*, but using one that also takes the form of an interior monologue as the laconic titular character writes poetry. This use of narration seems bound up in Jarmusch's interest in poetry, discussed in further detail in Chapter 7, but it also expands upon the writer-director's tendency to write men of few words. My earlier discussion of speech and masculinity concludes that male characters in the cinematic verbalists' work are typically verbose. In this regard, Jarmusch's films are exceptional. In *Ghost Dog*, we hear the title character reading in voice-over, but he does not speak diegetically until thirty-five minutes in. Instead, Ghost Dog communicates with his boss through carrier pigeons. The birds deliver hand-written message back and forth and, at one point, Ghost Dog eats what he has just read. This action captures his distrust of words, which he both literally and figuratively swallows. As Suárez (2007: 68) explains, Jarmusch's males are generally uncomfortable communicating, with their silence paired with 'a fastidious attention to style'. To a certain degree, then, they let their clothes speak for them. More specifically, Murphy (2007: 35) identifies the poignancy of a scene between Willie and Eddie in *Stranger Than Paradise* when an extended awkward silence conveys that there are things that cannot be verbally communicated by these characters. Yet the length of this silence also encourages the viewer to consider what Willie and Eddie want to say but cannot.

Paterson uses voice-over narration to convey a similar discomfort with words, with an unconventional approach to both subject matter and delivery (by Adam Driver) revealing Paterson's thought process, his writing process and his preference for expressing himself through written rather than spoken words. Throughout the film we are privy to the rewarding but tedious nature of Paterson writing poetry, with the same lines (or variations on them) repeated back, either within the same scene or a later one, thus signalling his rereading or editing of his own writing. As he writes, the words are superimposed on-screen in a font that approximates human handwriting. Initially such an approach suggests a certain redundancy – do we really need to read the words as we hear them? – but the technique gives way to a number of experimental and even profound moments. Although similar to *Greenberg*, wherein we also see the writing process and hear the words spoken aloud by the author, the

Figure 6.1   On-screen text combines with voice-over to enhance the impression of thought in *Paterson* (Jarmusch 2016). (Source: screenshot by author)

tone and content differs – with Paterson's writing and thoughts treated with a kind of patient reverence, unlike Roger's that are often ironically deflated through the corresponding images or the nihilism of the letters themselves.

At points, Paterson's/Driver's speech slows as he writes/narrates, creating a kind of liveness to the words, as well as highlighting the direct correspondence between the words as written and those as heard. The varied pacing of the delivery highlights the fragmented, time-consuming nature of writing: words do not necessarily stream out of an author, who may pause to re-read things or decide what word should come next. The idea that Jarmusch crafts a voice-over that is as focused on Paterson's thought process as on his final expression (in the form of either speech or poetry) is further supported by the narration of the word 'hmm', and the corresponding appearance of the word on-screen (Figure 6.1).

In choosing not only to include this moment of consideration, or hesitation, on the soundtrack, but also to foreground it through on-screen text, Jarmusch continues to draw attention to the fragmentary nature of expression. Highlighting the word 'hmm' further contributes to the impression that Paterson embodies the cliché that still waters run deep. He says little, but thinks a lot. Paterson hesitates when he writes, just as he hesitates before he speaks. Although his way of being could have been rendered as dysfunctional (a man incapable of expressing his feelings), there are a number of moments in which Paterson's thoughtful nature is eloquently verbalised to another character. He casually mentions to partner Laura that he is writing her a poem and, after she asks him about it, he explains, 'I guess if it's for you it's a love poem.'

With a different character, or in a different kind of film, such a line could come across as trite, but Paterson/Driver delivers it with a matter-of-factness. He may not make grand declarations of love, but he makes genuine allusions to it nonetheless. In a later scene, when asked if Laura minds that he does not have a cell phone or a laptop, Paterson notes that this is not an issue for them since 'she understands me really well'.

The appearance of Paterson's writing as on-screen text can in fact be tied to Laura's respect for his poetry. Relatively early in the film, she implores him to photocopy the filled pages of his poetry notebook. She fears that this single record will somehow be lost, preventing others from one day reading Paterson's work. Indeed, the revelation that her dog has destroyed the book (and before he has made a copy) is the film's key dramatic moment. Although clearly upset, particularly since looking after the dog was already a source of frustration, Paterson insists, 'It's okay, they were just words, written on water.' This reference to water is part of a broader verbal motif in the film, and yet his statement is also at odds with his poetry as presented in the film. Because although Paterson's words were never photocopied, they have been copied onto the surface of the screen – indirectly expressing Laura's desire for others to read his words, and for them to be archived. In fact, just as developments in digital technologies allowed Jarmusch to add such text in post-production, Laura takes some comfort in salvaging the tiny scraps of writing for technology to fix: 'I saved all the pieces. Maybe somehow they could be puzzled back together, with a computer programme or something.' This idea, and Paterson's lack of response, is in keeping with their respective approaches to digital media: while he does not even have a cell phone, Laura buys her guitar online, where she also searches YouTube for cultural treasures and instructional videos.

In this way, aspects of *Paterson*'s voice-over align with that of *Greenberg*: both use the image track to somewhat undermine the wishes of the narrator. Although male voice-overs in the cinematic verbalists' work do not serve to empower them, female characters in their films are only granted voice-overs infrequently – *Mistress America* provides the only sustained example. While Suzy is heard narrating letters in *Moonrise Kingdom* she must share the voice-over with Sam. Given that Lawrence's (1991: 111) configuration of 'the woman's voice' includes 'her possession of [an] authorial point of view', then female voices are somewhat contained in these films. When female voice-overs are used, however, they can be granted an uncommon amount of authority. As Berrettini notes of Hartley's *Amateur*, certain images are suggested as Isabelle's 'imaginative illustrations' of a text she writes and is heard narrating (38). In addition to briefly controlling what the audience sees (unlike Roger whose words are undermined via images), the power of Isabelle's narration is underlined when her comments ('This man will die. He will. Eventually') are revealed to be a premonition when Thomas dies in the closing scene. As discussed in Chapter 2, Violet's speech in *Damsels in Distress* is also reflected in the film's intertitles, as well in texts that are embedded in the mise en scène. Although Violet does not speak to us through a voice-over, her words nonetheless have an impact on the image track, much like a voice-over that appears to control what we see. Male characters in *Damsels in Distress* are instead shown as comically slow-witted, to the point where they have to be taught the names of colours.

In Baumbach's *Mistress America*, co-written by Gerwig, a voice-over is attributed to the eighteen-year-old Tracy, whose words are gradually revealed to be the narration of a story she wrote, entitled 'Mistress America'. The story, about a character named Meadow, is strongly based on the film's other female lead, Brooke, who is Tracy's soon to be step-sister, and with whom she becomes fascinated. The narration is notable for a number of reasons, none more so than the orientation of its focus: one young woman is talking with insight about another, in a way that complicates both their individual characterisation and the relationship between the two. Tracy's perspective on Brooke, who is not identified as the subject for some time, is initially one of admiration, veering on obsession, for a woman so different to Tracy herself: 'She did everything and nothing and spent time like I always mean to – purposefully.' The tone of the 400 or so words of narration shifts considerably over the course of the film and, although its content is gradually clarified by the events within the main story-world, a crucial ambiguity remains: nearly three-quarters of the way through the film, Tracy narrates, in reference to Meadow's/Brooke's inability to see herself and her fate clearly, that 'because I was in love with her, I decided I couldn't see it either'.

This is the only direct reference to Brooke as an object of Tracy's affection and yet, in keeping with Baumbach and Gerwig's subtle style of writing, there are other lines of dialogue that support it. Discussing Meadow/Brooke in voice-over, Tracy describes how Brooke's 'beauty was that rare kind that made you want to look more like yourself not like her'. This line is initially framed as one of empowerment (that Brooke is helping Tracy to feel more comfortable in her skin), but it equally helps ground the idea that Tracy is physically attracted to Brooke. Furthermore, one of the first questions that Brooke asks Tracy is whether she is gay, given that she chosen to attend Barnard College (historically, only women could attend). Tracy answers with a perfunctory 'no', and yet, since she initially has a male romantic interest in the story, we could reasonably interpret her answer as either a lie by omission, from someone who identifies as 'queer' or 'bi' rather than 'gay', or as a hesitant denial by someone who is still unsure of their sexual orientation, and so is unwilling to casually disclose it to someone who she has just met.

Interestingly, despite Tracy's casual declaration about being 'in love' with

Meadow/Brooke, there are no references to Tracy's possible bisexuality in popular media reviews, with the film almost exclusively interpreted as a story of female friendship. However, actress Lola Kirke/Tracy has made a number of references to being cast in this period as a lesbian (Rickman 2014; Merry 2015). If, as Tracy's narration suggests, *Mistress America* is as much about unrequited romance as it is about female friendship, then there is again a reasonable justification for why the romantic elements are not more fully teased out – rather than interpreting this as a suppression of queer sexuality. Tracy's mother is engaged to Brooke's father, while Brooke shows no signs of being attracted to women – thus Tracy has two good reasons not to express her feelings outside of her 'Mistress America' story and, by extension, the narration. The very decision to include this declaration of love, without fully substantiating it, is another testament to Baumbach's willingness to use dialogue to raise complex questions about his characters, rather than to provide didactic explanations for an audience. And even if we disregard Tracy's brief declaration of love, the voice-over is still notable for providing a very rare example of narration delivered by a woman, about another woman – a direct affront to the issue that the Bechdel Test highlights in relation to two women often only talking about a man or men. In fact, Tracy's lyrical descriptions of Meadow/Brooke can recall, at times, the hardboiled detective of *film noir* as he laments his desires the *femme fatale* figure.

Tracy's narration also revises another stereotype of voice-over and gender – that of the tragic female author. As noted in Chapter 4 when discussing how Tracy's verbal style gradually evolves to mimic that of Brooke, Tracy also becomes more confident as a writer. In fact, when giving Tony a copy of 'Mistress America', the short story from which the voice-over is drawn, she tells him that she does not want his feedback on it. Tracy will later defend her story when Brooke realises she has written about her, a trope that recurs across Baumbach's work. As such, Tracy is a departure from female writer characters associated with mental illness, such as those based on real women in *An Angel at My Table* (Campion 1990), *Girl, Interrupted* (Mangold 1999), *The Hours* (Daldry 2002) and *Sylvia* (Jeffs 2003). In such films, narration is used to allow audiences to 'overhear' the female protagonists' creative work, typically with the female reading her work or letters via the trope of an internal monologue. The focus of the voice-over, however, is generally on the psychological struggles of the woman author, whose writing is suggested to emerge from their inner turmoil. In *The Hours* Virginia Woolf (Nicole Kidman) narrates her suicide note while the audience is shown scenes of Woolf's husband reading the note, interspersed with shots of her drowning. The note is filled with self-revelation:

> Dearest, I feel certain I am going mad again. I feel we can't go through another of these terrible times again and I shan't recover this time. I begin

to hear voices and can't concentrate. So I'm doing what seems to be the best thing to do …

Sylvia also opens with a revelatory voice-over by the title character (Gwyneth Paltrow), who has also committed suicide, and who explains her vision for life through the metaphor of a tree.[15] While Woolf's letter is addressed to her husband, in *Mrs. Parker and the Vicious Circle* (Rudolph 1994) we instead see Dorothy Parker (Jennifer Jason Leigh) deliver heartfelt poetry about a man directly to the camera ('The sun's gone dim, the moon's turned black, for I loved him and he didn't love back'). In each film, voice-over or direct address encourages the viewer to sympathise with the women's psychological struggles, which are suggested to be crucial to their writing: without the suicidal tendencies, there would be no narration. Tracy's narration, by contrast, has no pathological connotations. While the characters in *The Hours*, *Sylvia* and *Mrs Parker and the Vicious Circle* are based on actual authors who committed suicide or attempted to, *Mistress America* gives voice to a young woman who is relatively well-adjusted and confident in her writing, even without receiving any external validation for her work. Tracy, and particularly her voice-over, thus serves to normalise and validate the everyday woman writer: she need not have died for her art, or even to have had her work recognised as exceptional, in order for her to provide a kind of 'voice of God' commentary on the film world.

FREEDOM FROM GENDERED SPEECH

Overall, the cinematic verbalists' male and female characters tend to resist internalised ideals of gendered speech, both in relation to cinema and society more generally. Their dialogue offers more nuanced representations of what type of speech is 'appropriate' for males or females, revealing a refusal to divide characters' verbal styles on the basis of gendered stereotypes. At times, this is done with a sly knowingness, as in the following exchange between Francis and her romantic interest Lev (Adam Driver) in Baumbach's *Frances Ha*:

> LEV: Just because you bought dinner doesn't mean I'm going to sleep with you.
> FRANCES: I'm not trying to sleep with you.
> LEV: No – I was pretending to be a liberated woman.

In addition to such moments of gendered role reversal, the language of male characters in these films is used to advance a complex representation of vulnerable masculinity, in keeping with Coates's discussion of 'alternative' forms of male speech. Their work further establishes the verbally expressive male as an enduring (but often overlooked) character type.

Although the cinematic verbalists' male (and female) dialogue tends to be articulate, their male characters are more likely to lose verbal control or lack verbal authority. This subverts Silverman's (1988: 61) argument that female characters are made to seem more vulnerable when they vocalise 'linguistic incapacity', of one form or another. Male characters are allowed to remain silent, to voice their deepest feelings or to verbally align themselves with homosexuality and alternate forms of masculinity. The dialogue content and delivery (and extreme changes in each) can be seen to reflect men's responses to perceived and real changes in their roles in contemporary society.

This avoidance (or knowing appropriation) of binary distinctions between male and female dialogue is one of the commendable aspects of their characterisation via speech. The cinematic verbalists' female characters reveal how 'unruly' female speech can be inseparable from representations of female rebelliousness, as Rowe previously suggests. Describing the screwball comedy heroine, Kozloff (2000: 185) describes how her verbal unruliness may be advanced 'not because she babbles, but because she dares to speak so frankly ... Moments when you'd think that the heroine would be polite, evasive, coy, or blathering, she speaks with complete candor.' Kozloff's description of the candid heroine applies well to the communication styles of various female characters throughout the cinematic verbalists' work. Their dialogue gives female characters the freedom to curse and discuss their sexuality and difficulties with motherhood, as well as being allowed to question the ways that they are treated and addressed by men. More generally, this analysis of gender and verbal dynamics has begun to question the applicability of findings on female film dialogue by Silverman, Lawrence and DiBattista to contemporary US cinema, particularly independent films produced outside of the studio system.

NOTES

1. For a detailed discussion of dialogue in melodrama, see Kozloff's chapter 'Misunderstandings: Dialogue in Melodramas' in *Overhearing Film Dialogue* (2000: 235–67).
2. Lee uses Judith Butler's (1997: 196) theorisation of speech's performative and subjective power in *Excitable Speech: A Politics of the Performative* to conclude that power in *Entourage* is constructed through characters' dialogue.
3. Rawle (2011: 219–20) correctly identifies that Simon and Henry are 'polar opposites', but discusses this on the basis of physical appearance, gesture and movement rather than speech.
4. Although Rawle (2011: 214) does not contrast Henry and Simon in terms of speech, he does describe Simon's verbal style in more detail. He notes that Simon's speech 'is marked by a restraint of language', including short sentences 'that are punctuated by mid-sentence pauses to grasp for the correct words or simply trailing off'.

5. Other actors whose vocal performances are similarly 'thick with body' include Humphrey Bogart and James Earl Jones (cf. Peberdy 2013b), and Woody Allen. As Berliner (2010: 193) explains, Allen's 'linguistic stumbling has become a signature'. Indeed, Ben Craw and Oliver Noble (2013) have combined all of Allen's on-screen stammers into an audiovisual essay that is forty-four minutes in length.

6. The 'test' was originally included in Bechdel's *Dykes to Watch Out For* comic-strip series. The strip, entitled 'The Rule', can be accessed easily online, including on the website for the separate Bechdel Test Fest film festival, at http://bechdeltestfest. com/about/ (last accessed 15 January 2017).

7. There are a number of notable exceptions, including several studies published in the period 2014 to 2016, but these generally focus on voice rather than speech: Britta Sjogren's (2006) *Into the Vortex: Female Voice and Paradox in Film*, Liz Greene's (2009) 'Speaking, Singing, Screaming: Controlling the Female Voice in American Cinema', Pooja Rangan's (2015) 'In Defense of Voicelessness: The Matter of the Voice and the Films of Leslie Thornton' and Barbara McBane's (2016) 'Walking, Talking, Singing, Exploding ... and Silence: Chantal Akerman's Soundtracks'. Although focused on female singing, as presented on-screen, Jennifer Fleeger's (2014) study of *Mismatched Women: The Siren's Song through the Machine* incorporates compelling analysis of the treatment of the female voice in films such as *Frozen* (Buck; Lee 2013).

8. For example, the website http://bechdeltest.com gives the percentage of film releases that pass the test each year, with approximately 6,500 listed in terms of which parts of the test they pass (as of 25 July 2016). I discuss the limitations of the Bechdel Test, and the need for greater research into women's dialogue, in more detail in 'What "The Bechdel Test" Doesn't Tell Us: Examining Women's Verbal and Vocal (Dis)Empowerment in Cinema' (O'Meara 2016a).

9. I discuss Posey's collaborations with Hartley in greater detail elsewhere, as part of Steven Rybin's *The Cinema of Hal Hartley: Flirting with Formalism*, in a chapter entitled 'Parker Posey as Hal Harley's "Captive Actress"' (O'Meara 2016b).

10. Delpy also has a small but crucial role in Jarmusch's *Broken Flowers* as the woman who walks out on Don in the opening sequence. Many of the verbal characteristics discussed in relation to Delpy in this chapter could also be applied to *2 Days in Paris* (2007) and its sequel *2 Days in New York* (2012), both of which were written by, directed by and star Delpy.

11. It should be noted that although Bernard praises the explicit content of Lili's writing in *The Squid and the Whale* he, like Maria in *Trust*, does so using the same derogatory term: 'She's a very risky writer, Lili. Very racy. I mean, exhibiting her cunt in that fashion is very racy.' However, when Bernard uses the term 'cunt' in *The Squid and the Whale* he does so with a view to impressing his son by casually using sexual slang, rather than to be intentionally derogatory towards the woman whose sexual writing he praises.

12. Rawle also quotes a third female character, not cited here, since her dialogue is of less relevance to the 'bipolar' argument.

13. Rawle (2011: 35–7) also identifies the reflexivity and irony of voice-over in *The Book of Life*. As Rawle explains, the voice-over does not follow its usual function 'as a suture, tying up any holes in the plot and promoting a reading of the text that explains everything to the viewer'.

14. Lawrence (1994: 175) explains the use of the phrase 'voice of God' to describe narration that is omniscient, with 'a disembodied male voice reciting "facts" while speaking the dominant language without noticeable accent or use of the vernacular'.

15. Sylvia narrates the following in the opening voice-over: 'Sometimes I dream the

tree, and the tree is my life. One branch is the man I shall marry, and the leaves my children. Another branch is my future as a writer, and each leaf is a poem. Another branch is a good academic career. But as I sit there trying to choose, the leaves begin to turn brown and blow away, until the tree is absolutely bare.'

7. ADAPTING DIALOGUE AND AUTHORIAL DOUBLE-VOICING

Dialogue's association with the literary arts is a key reason why it has been historically undervalued within film studies. It is perhaps no surprise, then, that *Literature/Film Quarterly* was the journal willing to highlight film dialogue more generally in the 1980s, when it published Jack Shadoian's (1981) 'Writing for the Screen ... Some thoughts on Dialogue', and John Fawell's 'The Musicality of the Filmscript' (1989) – as explored in Chapter 3 when considering dialogue's relationship to the soundtrack. Given the general lack of attention paid to dialogue at this time, these articles were significant. But although adaptation scholars have demonstrated particular interest in voice-overs, as part of a broader interest in the transcodification of narration techniques across media,[1] the discipline has tended to downplay the significance of dialogue more broadly. As Linda Hutcheon explains in her influential book, *A Theory of Adaptation* (2013 [2006]: 40–1), when theorists discuss shifts from text to performance media 'the emphasis is usually on the visual, on the move from imagination to actual ocular perception'. By focusing on the verbal elements of the cinematic verbalists' adaptations, as well as other literary influences on this independent cinema, this final chapter begins to address the imbalance that Hutcheon identifies.

One of the overriding arguments in this book is that, if well-performed and carefully integrated, dialogue can be cinematic. Because although the cinematic verbalists have strong literary influences, they channel these into their dialogue in complex and medium-specific ways. Each of the six filmmakers studied literature at university, or initially pursued a literary career or literary side projects.

Their love of words was apparent from their selective adaptation of literary works, in addition to their more general crafting of dialogue. Linklater's *A Scanner Darkly* (based on the Philip K. Dick (1977) sci-fi novel of the same name) and Anderson's *Fantastic Mr. Fox* (co-written by Baumbach) based on the Roald Dahl (1988 [1970]) children's book are both relatively direct adaptations, but both films' verbal styles are notably inflected with independent cinema's broader approach to scripting. Stillman's work provides more complex examples of intertextuality – including his novelisation of *The Last Days of Disco* and the influence of the work of Jane Austen on *Metropolitan* and, more recently, *Love & Friendship* – and we will pay particular attention to his films.

Since dialogue is central to the development of narrative and character in both film and literature, it seems intuitive that speech would be a crucial creative device for filmmakers, such as these, with a strong interest in both. But precisely how do the cinematic verbalists' literary interests influence the dialogue in their original and adapted works? This question is the chapter's guiding focus, and it appears that even though cinematic verbalism can depend on filmmakers directing *and* writing their own work, dialogue can also be used to create verbal consistency between these writer-directors' adaptations and their original screenplays.

As part of our aim of reframing adaptation from a verbal perspective, the final section of the chapter theorises the cinematic verbalists' reflexive approach to authorship by extending Bakhtin's concept of 'double voicing' from literature to film. For Bakhtin, double-voicing:

> serves two speakers at the same time and expresses simultaneously two different intentions: the direct intention of the character who is speaking, and the refracted intention of the author. In such discourse, there are two voices, two meanings and two expressions ... it is as if they actually hold a conversation with each other. (Bakhtin cited in Holquist 1981: 324)

As is clear from Bakhtin's summary, such dialogue is inherently complex for the reader. Similarly, it will be argued that film dialogue can also employ double-voicing, which engages audiences who are encouraged to identify the screenwriter or writer-director's refracted intention, beneath the character's more direct message. In fact, in an article on Stillman, Perkins (2008: 23) briefly argues that through double-voicing Stillman is 'ever present on the surface of the text'. Here Bakhtin's concept is extended to the group of independent filmmakers, with a focus on Anderson and Stillman, by analysing the kinds of conversation they can have with an audience through the 'mouthpiece' of a character. I suggest that their double-voiced discourse can be considered as annotations, so to speak – inscribed by the writer-directors 'on the side of' the film.

'Unabashedly Bookish' Material

While the filmmakers under focus express a high degree of cinephilia, literary texts and influences are also foregrounded; and this constitutes another way in which verbal style, of various forms, is key to understanding their work. Mark Olsen (1999: 17) notes that Wes Anderson is 'as likely to make a literary reference as a cinematic one'. Scholars and critics of Anderson's (and the other cinematic verbalists') work similarly draw out literary comparisons. With its family of child geniuses and 'fetishizing of childhood artefacts' (MacDowell 2012: 10), *The Royal Tenenbaums* is regularly compared to the work of J. D. Salinger (cf. Kertzer 2011: 6). Framed visually as a book, the film is divided into chapters using title cards.[2] Indeed, it was journalists and literary – rather than film – scholars who initially wrote about Stillman's work in Henrie's (2001) edited collection *Doomed Bourgeois in Love* on Stillman's first three films. One of these contributors, Lauren Weiner (2001: 19), asserts that Stillman's films 'strongly attract the analyst of culture because the material is so unabashedly bookish'. Stillman encourages such literary comparisons in interviews when referencing authors like Leo Tolstoy, Jane Austen, J. D. Salinger and F. Scott Fitzgerald (cited in Hogan 2000).

Similarly, although Jarmusch is reluctant to offer much commentary on his own films, he claims to 'admire poets more than any other artists' since their work isn't fully translatable (cited in Von Bagh and Kaurismäki 1987: 78).[3] Indeed, such a comment will be echoed nearly three decades later in an exchange in *Paterson*, wherein a Japanese poet explains to the title character that 'poetry in translation is like taking a shower with raincoat on'. *Dead Man*, with its central character of Bill Blake – who is considered by other characters to be the poet William Blake reincarnated – was perhaps Jarmusch's most overt homage to poetry until *Paterson*. His admiration for the medium goes beyond mere citation, however, to impact the thematic and verbal motifs in his work. In addition to the lyrical elements of Jarmusch's dialogue identified in Chapter 3, he regularly makes a feature of rhyme. The central characters in *Down by Law* bond over rhyme in their prison cell, chanting, 'I scream, you scream, we all scream for ice cream' – with various intonations – for approximately two minutes. More recently, alliteration is used to create a lilting title for *Only Lovers Left Alive*. Literal books are also central to Jarmusch's narrative structures, with *Ghost Dog* foregrounding text most prominently.

Books also have narrative and conceptual importance in the other cinematic verbalists' work. In Hartley's *Fay Grim*, Henry's book takes on an almost mythical status since the plot centres on whether the version of the book in the first film (*Henry Fool*) was a fake. Indeed, in another instance of Hartley's dialogue serving to confuse rather than clarify, the character of Simon refers to the various competing versions of Henry's self-proclaimed masterpiece as 'a collection of fakes of a book that has never itself been written'. In *The Girl from Monday*, a book helps to provide commentary on censorship in the media when a rogue copy of Henry David Thoreau's *Walden* (1854), banned in the dystopian Big Brother society, circulates to dramatic effect. In the film, Hartley also includes an experimental voice-over to reflect a character scanning a pile of books on a variety of subjects and from a variety of cultures. In the scene, we hear overlapping, whispering voices in a variety of languages. Elsewhere, Hartley incorporates literary quotations directly into the dialogue. In *Flirt*, a definition of flirting – 'chaste amorous relations generally devoid of deep feelings' – is taken directly from Toril Mio's (1994) book on Simone de Beauvoir (Hartley 1996: xvii).

Books also function as catalyst for romance, and thus serve as alternatives to the 'declarations of love', which Kozloff (2000: 42) identifies as a central 'speech act' in mainstream romances. Books serve as a romantic catalyst for Cèline and Jesse in *Before Sunrise*,[4] Walt and Sophie in *The Squid and the Whale*, and Audrey and Tom in *Metropolitan*. In *The Unbelievable Truth*, Audry and Josh bond over a book on George Washington (a shared interest), as well as Molière's *Misanthrope* (1958 [1666]).

Hartley has spoken about the influence of Molière on the rhythm and tone of the dialogue in his earlier films, since his 'words were the action' (Hartley and Kaleta 2008: 19). Using an example from *Tartuffe* (1882 [1664]), Rawle (2009) details this further when he explains the strong similarities between Hartley's and Molière's verbal repetition. Rawle also draws a comparison between Hartley's trapping of characters in 'repetitions of which they are unaware' to Samuel Beckett's *Waiting for Godot* (1953) (65). Hartley's distinctive verbal style therefore borrows heavily from experimental literary figures. Yet in Hutcheon's discussion of adaptation she observes that 'radical' texts by writers like James Joyce and Samuel Beckett are more difficult to adapt than 'linear realist novels' (ibid.). Hartley does not attempt to adapt their work directly but, by drawing on the dialogue style of Beckett and Molière, he incorporates their writing as an intertextual influence.

Comparisons can equally be made between Linklater's use of stream-of-consciousness dialogue and his other, more direct, allusions to writers like James Joyce and Fyodor Dostoevsky. David T. Johnson identifies various references to Joyce, including the reading aloud of *Ulysses* (1922) in *Slacker*, and *Before Sunrise* taking place on 16 June, which is 'Bloomsday' (6–7).[5] In addition to Linklater adapting two plays (Eric Bogosian's *subUrbia* (1994) and Stephen Belber's *Tape* (2000)), he has adapted a non-fiction book (*Fast Food Nation* (2006)) and, with *Bernie* (2011), an article from a Texan newspaper. Neither Hartley nor Linklater aims to directly adapt Beckett's or Joyce's texts, but both Hartley's repetitive and non-developmental dialogue, and Linklater's digressive, meandering speech seem to have their origins in the kind of 'radical'

Modernist texts that Hutcheon classes as particularly difficult to 'translate' to cinema. Unsurprisingly, given the centrality of dialogue to Linklater's original screenplays, it is also central when he adapts literary sources more directly, as in *A Scanner Darkly*.

Maintenance of Authorial Verbal Style in Adaptations

Despite the visual creativity of *A Scanner Darkly*'s rotoscoping, it is a verbally digressive scene that is most frequently discussed in analyses of the film. Barris (Robert Downey Jr.) enters with a bike that he has just bought and describes his finding it as 'Total, total, total, totally, total, total ... total providence'. Barris subsequently postulates about whether the bike was stolen, and if it is missing gears. This scene from Philip K. Dick's novel was excluded in Charlie Kaufman's earlier adaptation of Dick's book – a screenplay that never made it to production. Doreen Alexander Child (2010: 97) notes this when describing the gear scene as a highlight of Linklater's adaptation. Indeed, writing on the source material, Johnson expands that since Dick presents the dialogue as a transcript (separate from the rest of the text), it reveals Dick's fascination with his characters' language (98–9). Johnson also draws a comparison between Dick's transcript, which slows the pace of the novel, and Linklater's scene that slows the narrative, 'even if the pace of the conversation compensates with speed' (ibid.). Since digressive conversation is typical of Linklater's verbal style (although the 'total, total, total ...' line is not found in the book), it is understandable that he would incorporate – and exaggerate – the feature that Dick made of the characters' language. Kaufman's adapted screenplay, on the other hand, ignores the scene altogether. So although *A Scanner Darkly* has been received as a particularly 'faithful' adaptation, it equally maintains Linklater's own auteurial tropes, including verbal style, since he and Dick share a tendency for digressive or ambling conversations.

Fantastic Mr. Fox also bears the verbal marks of its adapters, alongside those of the original author. Anderson and Baumbach's screenplay incorporates Roald Dahl's short story as 'the middle chapter of a three-chapter plot' (Kertzer 2011: 5). Although adaptation studies have fortunately progressed far beyond notions of 'fidelity' when comparing film and literary versions, Adrienne Kertzer's analysis of *Fantastic Mr. Fox* deftly combines theories of adaptation with Anderson's manipulation of extra-filmic materials to *suggest* fidelity. Kertzer details how Anderson appears keen to stress the endorsement of the film by Dahl's wife (who praises the film in a DVD interview), but also makes sure that the film fits comfortably alongside the rest of his work.[6] There are strong parallels, for instance, between the opening of *Fantastic Mr. Fox* and that of *The Royal Tenenbaums* (8).

Significantly, the film's plot is not primarily concerned with Mr Fox (as in the book) but, as is typical of both Anderson and Baumbach, with family dynamics between Mr Fox, Mrs Fox (Meryl Streep), their son (Jason Schwartzman) and their nephew (Eric Anderson). Chapter 6 reveals how empowered female voices are a notable feature of Anderson and Baumbach's treatment of dialogue and gender, and this too is evident in their adaptation – as when Mrs Fox cuts through Mr Fox's showy statements to the reality of the situation:

> MRS FOX: They'll kill the children!
> MR FOX: Over my dead body, they will.
> MRS FOX: That's what I'm saying. You'd be dead, too, in that scenario.

The exchange is in sharp contrast to the same scene in Dahl's book, in which Mrs Fox instead gets upset:

> 'They'll kill my children!' cried Mrs Fox.
> 'Never!' said Mr Fox.
> 'But darling, they will!' sobbed Mrs Fox. 'You know they will!'
> (Dahl 1988 [1970]: 27)

Kertzer argues that Mrs Fox's vocal criticism challenges the complicity of women in Dahl's work. As Kertzer notes, Mrs Fox seldom speaks in the book 'and when she does, Dahl restricts her to some version of telling her children how fantastic their father is' (17). In other words, assertive dialogue is crucial to distinguishing Mrs Fox from her incarnation in the book, but also to aligning her with Anderson and Baumbach's other verbally assertive female characters, including Lili in *The Squid and the Whale* and those played by Anjelica Huston in Anderson's films.

Another verbal trope that aligns the adaptation with Anderson and Baumbach's other work is the substitution of cursing with the word 'cuss':

> BADGER: The cuss you are!
> MR FOX: The cuss am I?
> MR FOX: Don't cussing point at me!
> BADGER: Are you cussing with me?
> MR FOX: Do I look like I'm cussing with you?

Their films are littered with profanity and, rather than excluding this as is customary in children's films, here they make a humorous feature of it as forbidden. As with their verbal style more generally, we are called upon to fill in the blanks – literally in this case. Also, unlike in Dahl's book, the characters regularly cut one another off mid-sentence. Like with *A Scanner Darkly*, then, continuity of verbal style strongly contributes to the impression that *Fantastic*

Mr. Fox is as much an auteur film by Anderson (and Baumbach) as an adaptation of Dahl's classic.

STILLMAN'S MULTI-DIRECTIONAL ADAPTATIONS

Like Baumbach, whose film *Greenberg* was loosely influenced by the Jewish American tales of Saul Bellow, Stillman incorporates literary sources loosely to create an indirect style of adaptation. As Perkins (2012: 35) explains, Stillman is often described as a contemporary Jane Austen, with both of them uncovering aspects of human nature through the lens of a particular class and era. It is predominantly dialogue that allows Stillman's first four films, particularly *Metropolitan*, to channel Austen's work. *Love & Friendship*, as a period film based on Austen's novella *Lady Susan* (2005 [1805]), supplements verbal similarities with historical costumes and locations. Overlaps between Stillman's and Austen's verbal style are especially apparent on consultation of Bharat Tandon's *Jane Austen and the Morality of Conversation* (2003). Tandon discusses 'the vortex of eloquence' in Austen's work, explaining that her novels are 'short on action of any kind', instead gaining impact through Austen's 'creative ear for familiar and familial conversation' (1–3). Tandon's summation recalls Chapter 4's discussion of Stillman's creation of a diegetic vernacular for his characters, as does Tandon's description of Austen converting 'bitchy social conversation' into a more refined debate (99). Stillman's characters can equally express two sides of an argument without there being a clear outcome. They can also depart from the kind of harsh one-liners that would align with Tandon's description of the kind of 'bitchy social conversation' that Austen's characters do *not* engage in. Through the voicing of opinions, debate as action is thus central to both Stillman and Austen.

In 2000, Stillman chose another direction for his adapting process, publishing a novelisation of *The Last Days of Disco* entitled *The Last Days of Disco, With Cocktails at Petrossian Afterwards* (2000a). Examining Stillman's rationale for this uncommon move helps to reveal the ways that, more generally, he uses dialogue to creatively explore the boundaries between cinema and literature. The premise for Stillman's book is that it is written by the character, Jimmy Steinway, after the release of *The Last Days of Disco* – a film based on his group of friends. The novelisation is sparse in terms of direct dialogue: Jimmy instead tends to summarise his friends' words. However, the detailed monologues in Stillman's films are equally phrased with the same long 'performative sentences',[7] and with sections where characters' words are marked out explicitly with quotation marks (to indicate the speakers' self-awareness and ironic intent). Elements of the novelisation's vocabulary can also be considered as a bridge between the *The Last Days of Disco* and Stillman's next film, *Damsels in Distress*. In the latter, Violet is given some of Jimmy's words from the text, such as 'hackneyed' (Stillman 2000b). She also makes the same distinction as Jimmy does between moods that are 'funks' and those that are 'depressions'. In this way, characters' vocabulary spreads intertextually from book to film.

Stillman claims that, prior to the novelisation, a strong aversion to writing description prevented him from writing novels (Hogan 2000). Alternatively, this could be framed as Stillman having a strong preference for writing dialogue, as when he explains his struggle to 'give the dialogue a context' when describing scenes from the film in the book (ibid.). In the novelisation, Stillman negotiates this problem by making author-character Steinway's literary descriptions of events very similar to characters' monologues in his films. Like in many of the cinematic verbalists' films, Stillman's characters recount past events in their life to another character, and thus the audience. As a result, there can be little difference between the film character's dialogue and the literary narrator's: it is as though Stillman's film characters are verbalising inner monologues more typical of literary formats. This is not always the case – as with the speedy back-and-forth exchanges between characters discussed elsewhere – but storytelling dialogue allows Stillman's films to have cross-over appeal. When a character recounts things at length, they temporarily employ the descriptive mode of literature, returning to more cinematic verbal norms when that moment has passed.

Dialogue as Storytelling

In the cinematic verbalists' adaptation and incorporation of unconventional literary sources, they again overlap with their *Nouvelle Vague* antecedents. Indeed, Chris Wiegand's introduction to *French New Wave* follows the heading 'The Men Who Loved Films' with one reading 'The Men Who Loved Books'. Wiegand (2012: 21) explains that the *Nouvelle Vague* filmmakers departed radically from the kind of '"safe" adaptations of tame work' common in France at that time. The cinematic verbalists similarly adapt literary sources in a way that is more experimental and less 'safe' than is typical. As Bordwell (1979: 58) describes, implying once more the importance of dialogue to 'art' cinema in general, its characters frequently tell one another stories, or recount dreams, fantasies or autobiographical events. However, when the cinematic verbalists use storytelling dialogue it tends to take on a somewhat unconventional format.

Kozloff (2000: 55–6) briefly discusses dialogue that functions as 'storytelling', and she explains how storytelling in cinema is generally used for narrative causality, when 'a character will tell a story to explain some key gap in the plot'. Instead, storytelling dialogue in these independent films tends to take on the least common form that Kozloff identifies – dialogue that is 'tangential to the plot' (55). In addition to these moments of digressive storytelling,

Anderson uses storytelling in a reflexive way that draws attention to the artifice of more narratively causal forms. Indeed, when Francis recounts his injuries in *The Darjeeling Limited*, Wilkins (2013: 418) implies that Anderson plays with audience expectations that a standard form of storytelling is being used. Because, as she rightly suggests, the standard expectations for how storytelling functions in cinema are destroyed when Francis tells a much briefer version of the story, one that reveals the accident described initially as an attempted suicide.[8] Anderson's use of reflexive 'storytelling' is also discussed in Chapter 2 when we consider how, as an alternative to voice-over narration, his characters can discuss themselves in the third person. In *Fantastic Mr. Fox*, the impression that characters are narrating their lives as they happen is taken even further in a scene that cuts to a close-up of the title character as he says of his impending adventure: 'And so it begins ...'

Storytelling dialogue could be critiqued as a particularly 'literary' form of film speech, but socio-linguists have identified the same trend for explicit storytelling in everyday discourse. Returning to Coates (2003: 5), she explains how '[m]ost conversations are full of stories', with storytelling significant to the way that individuals 'present to each other what has been happening in [their] lives'. Yet despite the connection between verbal storytelling and literary *storybooks*, Hutcheon explains how the visual elements of film adaptations tend to be analysed at the expense of their spoken words. She too betrays this bias, arguing:

> Film is not supposed to be good at getting inside a character, for it can only show exteriors and never actually tell what is going on beneath the visible surface ... It is decidedly the case that elaborate interior monologues and analyses of inner states are difficult to represent visually in performance. (Hutcheon 2013 [2006]: 58–9)

But characters' inner states need not be represented *visually* since, for instance, Stillman's characters verbalise certain thoughts through extensive storytelling. Like Hartley, who realised that his initial filmmaking urge was to have characters discuss unseen events rather than for him to record them,[9] recounting stories is a crucial element of Anderson's, Hartley's and Stillman's writing style. In the process, they use dialogue to blur the line between prose narration and narrative development in their films.

Issues of audience response are crucial to theories of adaptation and Hutcheon's discussion of reception provides useful context for a more general analysis of the cinematic verbalists' use of dialogue to engage audiences. Hutcheon (2013 [2006]: 120–1) uses the descriptors 'knowing' and 'unknowing' to classify how adaptations are experienced by different viewers/readers. The significance that adaptation theory attributes to audience members' knowledge of a source text(s) can be linked to the role that contemporary auteur theory attributes to the audience. Staying with the literary comparisons: like the satisfaction collectors get when they locate a rare edition for their collection, the fan of an auteur enjoys spotting intertextual references, be they visual, verbal or thematic. Pleasure can equally be found in identifying para-textual consistency, in the form of 'double voicing', when a character's dialogue mirrors, or alludes to, the filmmaker's own words in extra-filmic material. With a focus on Anderson and Stillman, the discussion to follow argues that – rather than a book – the 'text' that oscillates in our minds when watching the cinematic verbalists' films can be an interview with the filmmaker or the scripts from an earlier film.

'DOUBLE VOICING' CHARACTERS AS AUTHORIAL 'MOUTHPIECES'

Throughout this book, the filmmakers' discussion of their work has been incorporated in a way that grants them a degree of authority over the meaning of their films. By drawing on Bakhtin's literary concept of 'double voicing', such commentary can be reframed: the writer-directors' own speech can also be considered as a complementary level of discourse to the words of their characters. Put differently, we could say that depending on what the filmmakers say in interviews and DVD commentaries, we may recognise characters' dialogue as reflecting the filmmaker's voice.

While Bakhtin developed the concept of double-voiced discourse in relation to literary texts, the same two speakers (the character, and the author speaking through the character's dialogue) can be identified in the cinematic verbalists' dialogue. 'Double voicing' offers writer-directors the potential to advance an auteurist reading of their work through dialogue that actively engages the audioviewer in multiple levels of meaning. Discussing Bakhtin's concept of double-voiced discourse, Gary Saul Morson (1989: 65) explains how the audience of double-voiced words are supposed to hear (1) the original utterance as the embodiment of its speaker's point of view and (2) 'the second speaker's evaluation of that utterance from a different point of view'. Morson describes double-voicing as a kind of palimpsest 'in which the uppermost inscription is a commentary on the one beneath it' (ibid.). The first speaker is the character, with the second speaker the writer who comments on his/her character *while* the character themselves comments. The same two speakers can often be identified in relation to our independent filmmakers and their characters. Clarifying Bakhtin's discussion of double-voiced discourse, Morson and Emerson (1990) divide it into three meta-linguistic categories: (1) unidirectional passive-double-voiced words; (2) varidirectional passive double-voiced words; (3) and active double-voiced words (147). Again, as in our study of engaging dialogue, the reader or audioviewer's role is tied to these concepts of activity or passivity.

Perkins incorporates a few references to double-voiced discourse in respect of Stillman (2008: 23; emphasis in the original), noting that his self-awareness results in a fresh approach to auteurism: 'he is ever present on the *surface* of the text, where his double-voicing specifies only that he, like his characters, is "not entirely joking"'. She rightly identifies how Stillman both agrees with what his characters say and intends for their words to be amusing. In this way, Stillman's use of double-voicing is generally in line with unidirectional passive double-voicing, in which the writer 'constructs his utterance so that the voice of the other [the character] will be heard to sound within his own' (Morson and Emerson 1990: 151). Unlike with parody – the main form of varidirectional double-voicing that involves the writer providing a harsh critical commentary on the direct speech – Stillman's unidirectional double-voicing instead creates a perceivable slippage between character and creator. His awareness of the indulgence of this dialogue is also extended to the character's self-awareness about the indulgence of their speech, thus blurring the line between him and them.

Elements of Stillman's self-mocking through dialogue depend strongly on audience awareness of Stillman's own biography, as when Violet in *Damsels in Distress* describes a male character as '[a] journalist, so you can imagine the mindboggling arrogance and conceit'. Our recognition of this as double-voicing depends on knowledge of Stillman's background in publishing. Its effect thus relies on references to extra-filmic materials like interviews or published profiles. So although Violet's derogatory comments about journalists in *Damsels in Distress* are independently humorous, they are potentially more amusing to those aware that Stillman was a journalist himself. Again, like with Sconce's discussion of irony as dividing audience members into those who get the joke and those who do not, double-voicing can be equally divisive when it requires background knowledge of the filmmaker to be fully appreciated. Such double-voicing is also evident in Stillman's novelisation: part of the reason he wrote the book from the perspective of Steinway was that 'my faults as a first-timer could be masked, or made amusing, by having this other first-time would-be novelist be responsible' (Stillman cited in Hogan 2000). Again, the slippage between Stillman and his narrator is strong. Interview comments by Stillman's performers also suggest that there are strong overlaps between him and his characters. Much as his characters use flowery euphemisms rather than 'dirtying' their mouths with uncouth language, Greta Gerwig notes that Stillman did not allow cursing on the set of *Damsels in Distress* (PageSix.com staff 2012).

Unidirectional double-voicing is also apparent in the work of the other cinematic verbalists, giving the impression that a given character in their film serves two roles: (1) a fictional construct in the narrative and (2) a dummy who addresses the audience on the filmmaker's behalf. Nayman (2009: 49) alludes to double-voicing in his *Cineaste* review of Jarmusch's *The Limits of Control*: 'In a talky film where the speakers are never just making conversation, [actress Yûki] Kudoh's everything-old-is-new-again prophecy sounds suspiciously like a statement of [Jarmusch's] artistic intent.' After describing another scene in which the character of 'The Nude Woman'(Paz de la Huerta) delivers the words 'no guns, no mobiles, no sex', Nayman concludes that these characters 'may be speaking for Jarmusch', and asks, 'Are they – and by extension, their creator – begging our indulgence?' (ibid.). As these comments suggest, it is tempting to criticise double-voicing as self-indulgent. Is it not enough that a given writer-director communicates to the audience through the narrative as a whole and their choice of images and soundtrack, without also labouring a message through speech? Yet, in order to recognise double-voicing, we generally need to be aware of the writer-director's extra-filmic commentary. As a result, it functions productively as another layer of intertextual pleasure for what Hutcheon would term (in relation to adaptations) a 'knowing' audience.

Other forms of double-voicing are even more complex, and so potentially more rewarding, for clued in audience members. In *Trust*, Maria's repeated pronunciation of naïve (as 'nave') allows Hartley to comment on her ironically. Because the word (and its pronunciation) provides a commentary on the character it can be seen as a verbal alternative to the way in which many filmmakers use non-diegetic music to comment on a character – something Hartley avoids altogether. The cinematic verbalists also incorporate the third category of double-voicing, the active form of what Bakhtin refers to as 'hidden polemic', and that has been explained further by Morson and Emerson:

> In hidden polemic, the author's discourse is partially directed at its referential object, like discourse of the first type. But at the same time, it seems to cringe in the presence of a listener's word, to take a 'sideward glance' at a possible hostile answer. It responds to this anticipated answer by striking 'a polemical blow … at the other's discourse on the same theme'. (Bakhtin (1984: 195) cited in Morson and Emerson 1990: 155)

Bakhtin (1984: 196) gives speech that is overly self-deprecating and 'repudiates itself in advance' as an example of hidden polemic. When the cinematic verbalists use character dialogue to respond to potential criticism that their films could receive, their reflexivity has the same self-deprecating effect.

In *Henry Fool*, Hartley seems to anticipate and address possible critiques of his own writing through characters' speech. The title character's self-aggrandising statements are arguably Hartley mocking his authorial ego, as when Henry describes his unpublished book as 'A philosophy. A poetics. A politics, if you will. A literature of protest. A novel of ideas. A pornographic magazine of truly comic-book proportions.' The variety of terms seems to mock the assumed authority of artists' statements of intent, particularly since Henry finishes by saying that 'it is, in the end, whatever the hell I want it to be'.[10] Hartley also uses unidirectional, passive double-voicing: when Henry announces that 'a prophet is seldom heeded in his own land', it is difficult not to consider Hartley's personal comments about having a stronger following overseas, and his temporary move to Berlin where he received a writing fellowship.[11]

Such uses of hidden polemic also seem influenced by the *Nouvelle Vague* filmmakers. Consider Louis Malle's in-joke in *Zazie Dans le Métro*, as identified by Wiegand (2012: 67): '"Screw the New Wave," cries Zazie to anyone that will listen. "Screw you," says Malle to the New Wave's increasing number of detractors.' Similarly, Godard's use of unidirectional double-voiced discourse is alluded to by Michel Marie who asserts that Godard transforms male characters 'into a sort of mouthpiece for the director' (106). Indeed, although in Chapter 5 I attribute the slowing of Chris Eigeman's career, post-1998, to both Stillman and Baumbach taking a break from filmmaking, double-voicing could also be partly responsible. Given how recognisable Eigeman has become as a 'mouthpiece' for Baumbach and particularly Stillman, other filmmakers may have been reluctant to cast him in other parts. With Linklater, his tendency to speak through his characters is particularly apparent in *Boyhood*. Despite the audience watching Mason (Ellar Coltrane) evolve into a young adult from the age of five, in the closing scenes he suddenly begins to philosophise in the same style as earlier Linklater characters. Since Mason is notably restrained with language up until this point, the sudden change in his verbal style is jarring and creates the impression that Linklater is now using him as a kind of 'mouthpiece' – a stand-in for the author himself.

Taken together, the cinematic verbalists' use of double-voicing constitutes another example of the tendency that Pat Brereton (2012: 2) notes for smart films to engage cineastes through 'an ironic and playful exposition of the filmmaker's work'. Cognitively, our ability to pick up on double-voicing can also be considered in terms of Bordwell's (1989a: 3–7) discussion of individuals' attunement to 'specialized domains' and to their ability to mobilise learned structures when certain cues are identified. Taking a filmmaker's verbal style as one such specialised domain, the words of the character can be the cue that is cross-referenced both with what other characters have said, and with what the writer-director has said, in order to perceive the filmmaker's doubled voice.[12]

SELF-SCRIPTED AUTHORSHIP

This interpretation of double-voicing is in marked contrast to Perkins's (2012: 27) summation that 'the practice of decipherment is entirely eluded' by the openness of 'celebrity' auteurs in interviews and commentaries. In the case of these independent writer-directors, their double-voicing is executed subtly and requires decipherment, regardless of their explicit revelations of intent in interviews. Considering how double-voicing relates to the marketing of Anderson and Hartley as auteurs will now allow for more critical reflection on the form and content of the cinematic verbalists' speech in interviews and other extra-textual material.

Hartley's verbal style in interviews can be uncannily reminiscent of his characters' dialogue. Using the kind of circular phrasing that recurs in his scripts, Hartley describes explicit sex scenes as 'embarrassing. It's redundant. Redundancy is embarrassing' (Fuller 1992: xxxv). Furthermore, like the Sheriff in *Simple Men* who states a list of qualities ('Safety, Guarantee, Promises, Expectation, Consideration, Sincerity, Intimacy, Attraction, Gentleness, Understanding'), Hartley uses a list format to describe what his films explore: 'Attraction, flirtation, disappointment, affection, resentment, contempt' (ibid.). Again, recognition of this as double-voicing depends on an audioviewer being invested enough in Hartley's work to read or watch extra-filmic commentary. Regardless, Hartley seems to incorporate such references into interviews – potentially to satisfy fans who may look out for clues that the filmmaker is similar to his own characters.

Anderson's extensive gesticulation in interviews is another way in which slippage is created between him and his characters. As discussed in Chapter 5, Anderson's characters (and those of the other cinematic verbalists) are prone to amending the content of their speech by simultaneously 'speaking' with their hands. Watching Anderson's filmed interviews, it would seem that his characters' embodiment of words is partly an extension of the way Anderson embodies his. This is not to suggest that Anderson purposefully gesticulates in interviews, but that he is aware of his tendency to do so and thus encourages performers to be equally expressive with their hands when speaking.

Anderson's *The Life Aquatic*, co-written by Baumbach, even includes an overtly reflexive commentary on the authorial image. Various scenes in the film play on the notion of celebrity auteurs, as when Zissou is asked to autograph an endless supply of cards. Devon Orgeron (2007: 54) goes so far as to say that the real story of the film is not the search for the beast that killed documentary filmmaker Steve Zissou's partner, but the search for the author himself. One scene in particular ties together several aspects tied to dialogue and verbal authorship. Sceptical of the hype around Zissou, Jane (Cate Blanchett) opens her interview by asking: 'Don't you think the public reception of your work has significantly altered in the last five years?' Zissou responds, 'I thought this was supposed to be a puff piece,' since he had been expecting to begin with 'some stock dialogue ... you know ... Favourite colour: blue.' With his response, Zissou stresses that publicity material is crucial to the creation and management of the auteurial image, much as scholars Timothy Corrigan (1990) and

Catherine Grant (2000) argue in relation to film authorship more generally. Zissou's dialogue allows Anderson (and Baumbach as co-writer) a unidirectional double voice, with their on-screen counterpart, Zissou, expressing clear views on the kind of questions he wants to be asked. Indeed, although the DVD edition of *Rushmore* includes an interview Anderson did on the Charlie Rose show, Anderson's subsequent films instead include what Orgeron (2007: 60; emphasis in the original) refers to as 'craftily produced *fake* television interviews' that are 'equally signed and authored'. Furthermore, Zissou's reference to 'stock dialogue' explicitly reveals both Anderson's and Baumbach's awareness of the kind of stock film speech against which they generally position their verbal style.

REFLEXIVE ADAPTATIONS, REFLEXIVE COMMENTARY

As this chapter has revealed, the cinematic verbalists' literary interests influence their dialogue, and work in general, and yet they also manage to design and integrate dialogue in ways that show awareness of, and take advantage of, the specifics of the medium. Dialogue in their adaptations complements the verbal style in their original screenplays. Continuity of verbal style between the filmmakers' adapted and original screenplays contributes to the impression that, although based on someone else's material, the film still fits within the filmmaker's body of more personal work. While I have considered literary aspects of all six writer-directors' work, Stillman's approach to literary materials warrants particular attention. By having characters recount stories of unseen events rather than show them, 'storytelling' dialogue is crucial to his verbal style. Notably, Stillman (cited in Levy 1999: 198) describes his films as 'novelistic' rather than literary, explaining that 'literary is a way of treating the material, while novelistic implies that the story is somehow bigger than the vessel you're putting it into'. By writing a novelisation of *The Last Days of Disco*, Stillman put this unconventional perspective into practice. The book proves to be an ideal medium for commenting on authorship and the relationship between dialogue in film and literature.

Since adaptation studies tend to focus on the transcodification from text to images then dialogue is frequently overlooked. The analysis provided here indicates why this is a worrying blind-spot for scholars of both film and adaptation. For example, while Hutcheon rightly observes that 'radical' texts by writers like Joyce and Beckett are difficult to adapt, Hartley's and Linklater's experimental dialogue (which is digressive, repetitive or stream-of-consciousness) is one element of Modernist literature from which Hartley and Linklater borrow. Ignoring verbal literary influences means that less direct forms of intertextual references can go undetected.

Furthermore, in keeping with these writer-directors' engagement with a range of literary outputs and processes, their double-voiced discourse can be considered as a form of marginalia, inscribed by the writer-directors 'on the side of' the film. Such knowing comments are likely to be noticed only by those audience members who are familiar with their body of work, with recognition of double-voicing often depending on an audioviewer having experienced the filmmaker's verbal style, or personal comments, in interviews or commentaries. By using interviews to maintain the impression that they share common ground with their characters, Anderson and Hartley make it difficult for commentators to discuss their work independent of the creators. More broadly, double-voicing reveals itself to be an important channel through which the cinematic verbalists, and potentially other filmmakers, can engage an audience. Like with other forms of pattern recognition identified in their work, this can be a source of pleasure for those suitably attended to pick up on overlaps between the words of the character and the filmmaker. Therefore, although the cinematic verbalists' dialogue can be withholding in terms of expositional and background information, it can still create the impression that the audioviewer can 'get to know' the filmmaker by paying close attention to the characters' words. Analysis of double-voicing thus reveals the value of developing connections between dialogue and auteur and reception studies. Double-voicing can be seen to appeal to 'fans' who seek out consistencies between a filmmaker's body of work and their media image. Both 'fans' and film scholars can selectively perceive auteurial verbal tropes (and find them rewarding), thus revealing the importance of considering dialogue alongside extra-textual utterances.

NOTES

1. Andrew Crisell (1986: 138) defines 'transcodification' as the process of replacing one code or set of codes by another.
2. Suárez (2007: 23) also identifies how books and a letter help 'generate the main sequence of events' in *Ghost Dog* and *Broken Flowers*, respectively.
3. Even when Jarmusch is asked if he would like to make a larger scale movie, he frames his answer by comparing himself to poets, not filmmakers: 'I consider myself a minor poet who writes fairly small poems' (cited in Sante 1989: 92).
4. Throughout his study of Linklater, Johnson (2012: 7) details Linklater's incorporation of literary references and literal books. Johnson discusses how in *Before Sunrise* 'books inform Jesse and Céline's romance', from their initial meeting when they discuss the books they are reading on the train, to their initial reunion at a reading of Jesse's book based on his time with Céline.
5. Murphy (2007: 245) also identifies how in *Slacker* the character of 'Dostoevsky Wannabe' recites a passage from Dostoevsky's *The Gambler* (1866).
6. For further analysis of this subject, see Dorey's (2012) 'Fantastic Mr. Filmmaker: Paratexts and the Positioning of Wes Anderson as Roald Dahl's Cinematic Heir'.
7. As note in Chapter 5, Naremore (1988: 26) uses the term 'performative sentence'

to describe those notably long lines that have to be kept 'in play' by the reader or speaker.

8. This 'story' is discussed in more detail in relation to lying in Chapter 5.

9. Hartley, for instance, has spoken of his strong preference for words over action, particularly in early films: 'I was more interested in what happens when people talk about something that happened in the past[,] or something that will happen in the future[,] or is simply happening somewhere else' (see Hartley in Wyatt 2011 [1998]: 72).

10. Writing on *Flirt*, Perkins (2012: 39) also identifies how Hartley's dialogue that directly discusses the maker of *Flirt*'s film within a film is 'a tongue-in-cheek rebuttal' to critics.

11. Hartley received a fellowship from the American Academy of Berlin (Avila 2007: 85).

12. An informative comparison can be made between double-voicing and Naremore's discussion of 'doubling' in terms of actors and roles. Discussing instances in which the actor plays a role that overlaps substantially with their real-life identity, Naremore (1988: 270) describes such doubling as allusions for the well-informed audience members, whom he refers to as 'the cognoscenti'.

CONCLUSION:
VERBAL EXTREMES AND EXCESS

In order to thoroughly consider engaging dialogue in American independent cinema, this book has analysed the design and execution of the work of six contemporary writer-directors from a variety of perspectives. By coining and developing the term 'cinematic verbalism', I underscore how dialogue can be central to the working and effect of independent cinema, without necessarily overshadowing the more medium-specific components (such as the sound and image tracks), as tends to be assumed when dialogue is classified as a 'literary' device. Instead, Wes Anderson, Noah Baumbach, Hal Hartley, Jim Jarmusch, Richard Linklater and Whit Stillman use speech in such ways that it gains impact through the specifics of the medium.

Focusing on the relationship between their dialogue and other components of their work (and areas of film studies more generally) has established the importance of dialogue analysis to studies of: the soundtrack, visual style, character, performance, gender and adaptation, as well as reception and auteur studies. Taking an audience-focused approach has then allowed for an exploration of the ways each cinematic verbalist's dialogue can perceptually and cognitively engage us. Their speech is generally written, performed, recorded and integrated in such ways that audiences construct meaning by joining the dialogue dots, or filling the dialogue blanks. Individual lines are rarely memorable in a way that would earn them a place on the American Film Institute's '100 Movie Quotes' (2005), a list compiled by a jury of filmmakers, critics and historians on the basis of cultural impact (measured by a line of dialogue's quotability) and legacy (its ability to evoke memories of the film).[1] This is not a weakness of such independent film dialogue, but the outcome of speech that is carefully entwined with their films' various components. The remembering and repetition of specific lines by audioviewers is uncommon in these cases precisely because the language accumulates meaning through its execution in the finished film. Instead, their dialogue operates on complex levels that allows for alternative forms of audience pleasure. Overall, their dialogue can be characterised by: (1) alternations between verbal efficiency and excess; (2) 'gaps' in verbal meaning; and (3) the reflexive, exaggerated treatment of mainstream dialogue norms. In various ways, the cinematic verbalists' dialogue is both more stylised and more naturalistic than that of generic dialogue. As a result, it draws attention to ways that generic dialogue is also stylised, but in less overt ways.

By establishing links between independent American cinema, film dialogue and reception and auteur studies, the book has opened up discourse between these areas of film studies. In addition to revealing how dialogue plays a significant role in American independent cinema, this study establishes the general value of the grouping of filmmakers on the basis of a distinctive verbal style. Through the development and use of the label 'cinematic verbalists', it subverts the historical tendency for auteur studies to focus on recognisable *visual* styles and/or recurring thematic concerns. In these ways, this research contributes to the growing body of literature in film studies that identifies and analyses filmmakers' uses of dialogue. Excluding Jaeckle's (2013a) comparison of Anderson's and Preston Sturges's verbal style, each existing study focuses on a single filmmaker. By comparing six writer-directors from approximately the same time period (1984–present) and location (the United States, specifically New York and Texas), we can see that a shared cinematic tendency or movement can be established on the basis of dialogue, even if there are notable differences among other dimensions of their work: on first impression, Jarmusch's films appear to have little in common with those of Anderson or Stillman, for instance, but on closer inspection each designs dialogue to similar effect.

Alternations of Verbal Extremes

The engaging dialogue considered in this study is marked by alternations between contrasting dialogue extremes, in particular between elements that are excessive or efficient. Such verbal efficiency indicates an unwillingness (intentional or otherwise) to use speech redundantly. Instead, the cinematic verbalists apportion meaning among the various channels of signification so that verbal cues are important yet minimal; the words may be few, but they are carefully chosen. But their dialogue also includes clear moments of excess, as when characters engage in lengthy miscommunications and extensive monologues.

By extending Kristin Thompson's concept of 'cinematic excess' from visual to verbal aesthetics, we can see the suitability of the term to the ways that verbal norms can be playfully manipulated to engage audiences. This manipulation often occurs through exaggeration, as when attention is drawn to language's sound properties, or when close relationships are developed between spoken words and text embedded in the mise en scène. Other excessive verbal techniques include the stream-of-conscious listing of words, and characters who vocalise a noise that would normally be a sound effect. Excessive dialogue can thus provide the kind of 'perceptual play' that Thompson (1977: 56) describes as accompanying excessive devices that encourage the audience 'to linger over devices longer than their structured function would seem to warrant'.

Verbal repetition is one of the principal techniques uniting American independent cinema's excessive and efficient speech. In keeping with Joseph Anderson's discussion of the active, meaning-seeking human mind, part of the effectiveness of their dialogue is due to speech being designed around formal patterns. Although the repetition can be strictly verbal, it can also be verbal-visual or even audio-verbal – when a relationship is developed between the rhythms of sound and speech. In the six writer-directors' work, repetition reveals their dialogue integration to be more complex than in Jean Mitry's 'image-text' model (1997 [1963]: 234–8). According to Mitry, audience members are expected only to connect A' to A (a line of dialogue to the image that precedes it), or B' to A' (a line of dialogue to the line that precedes it). But the cinematic verbalists script and integrate dialogue so that we are required to connect lines or words of dialogue to verbal and visual cues at *various* points down the chain. This may seem like an over-simplistic claim – since individuals are accustomed to making non-sequential verbal connections in everyday exchanges – but it is worth mentioning given the prominence of such connections in the films under discussion.

Other alternations in the cinematic verbalists' dialogue design include the contrast between characters who are markedly articulate and characters who are markedly inarticulate, and the contrast between characters who are verbose or close to mute. Characters' communication styles also alternate between the repressed withholding of feelings and overblown verbal rants. In her study of 'hyper-dialogue', Wilkins (2013) draws a historical distinction between 'incessant talking' that suggests deferred anxiety in selected contemporary cinema and the use of silence and naturalistic dialogue to represent anxiety in New Hollywood cinema. But both extremes seem to be present in the cinematic verbalists' work.

In addition to these alternations in characters' speech, this independent cinema uses dialogue to partly exclude the audioviewer *or* to verbally address them more overtly. Although audience members tend to be treated as 'overhearers', as when speech is difficult to hear (either due to performance, recording or soundtrack mixing), there are clear exceptions in the form of 'double voicing' and instances in which we hear things that the characters cannot. And yet, since double-voiced discourse directs two levels of meaning at the audio-viewer (and one at the character addressee(s) in the film), it still departs from the audience as 'side-participant' model that Gerrig and Prentice (1996) argue is the norm in cinema. Because although 'side-participation' involves designing utterances to inform those who can hear a conversation, even when they are not personally being addressed, these writer-directors can formulate utterances for their characters that have an additional level of meaning for us.

These rather extreme shifts in dialogue style explain how verbal communication serves as an entertaining substitute for (and form of) action in this work. Although drawing on a body of roughly seventy films, the findings from the preceding chapters also have broader relevance, in terms of our understanding of how dialogue tends to function in independent cinema, and non-mainstream cinema more broadly.

Cinematic Verbalism in the Context of Independent and 'Art' Cinema

Since independent cinema's lower budgets can restrict narrative complexity and visual aesthetics, it is unsurprising that verbal experiments are often used as a substitute – as already considered by Berliner in relation to the work of Cassavetes. Writing on independent productions, Geoff King (2005: 62) explains how they tend to deliberately subvert classical narrative conventions, such as being: (1) omniscient, by 'displaying a wide range of knowledge about the narrative situation'; (2) highly communicative, by 'giving rather than withholding relevant information'; and (3) unselfconscious, by 'not laying bare the process of narrative address'. While King was not writing in relation to dialogue, this study has helped reveal how design and execution of speech can be a crucial way that indie filmmakers who came after Cassavetes also work against these classical norms. The pleasure of the cinematic verbalists' unconventional dialogue also aligns with his discussion of formal experimentation in independent cinema as 'a source of affirmative pleasure' for those who are 'suitably attuned' (149).

King's description of indie cinema's minor departures from dominant conventions is in line with the kind of schemata stretching that Joseph Anderson explains as key to individuals' optimum mental stimulation. Thus, many of the cinematic verbalists' dialogue techniques can be considered examples of what Anderson (1998: 119) refers to as cognitive 'pacers'. He explains how the human mind finds pleasure in novelty that connects to, but stretches, existing schemata (117–18). Reapplying this model to dialogue has revealed how didactic or overly familiar film speech can fail to provide this kind of stimulation.

Instead, when the writer-directors create dialogue that alternates between being more realistic, and more overtly stylised, they stretch Hollywood's verbal schemata in *both* directions. The same can be said of notably efficient or notably excessive dialogue. So, rather than assuming that well-written film dialogue is either (1) extractable and repeatable, or (2) evokes memories of the film (the criteria used by the American Film Institute survey), dialogue can be lauded for its ability to engage and surprise the audience based on its overall design. This underscores the superficiality of praising individual lines of speech, without requisite attention to the overall verbal design and execution. It is impossible to determine whether the cinematic verbalists intentionally or intuitively move between excess and naturalism as a matter of course. But, given their cinephilia and various explicit references to dialogue both in interviews and characters' own references to clichéd speech and stock dialogue, it seems that an underlying desire to subvert dialogue norms has led to their incorporation of dialogue at both endpoints of the naturalistic-stylised spectrum.

Writing on cinema in general, Joseph Anderson (1998: 156) asserts that by inviting the audience to suspend belief and embrace imaginary worlds, cinema involves 'vigorous mental play'. In a variety of ways, American independent cinema uses dialogue to heighten such play. Aside from incorporating actual wordplay, they play with audience expectations of how dialogue typically functions. So while Berliner (2010: 213–14) argues that New Hollywood speech that delays forward momentum is indifferent to the spectator's needs, an important distinction can be made in relation to the cinematic verbalists' dialogue design. They are not indifferent to audioviewers' needs, but instead show awareness of the ways dialogue is usually channelled to meet these needs. This allows them to partly subvert these conventions, but in a way that is not so radical as to remove pleasure. In contrast, when dialogue is designed to transfer meaning directly – the kind of patronising didactic speech to which Boon refers in his study of active dialogue in *Glengarry Glen Ross* – it disregards not only audiences' ability to determine meaning from limited data or to selectively perceive patterns, but the rewards inherent in these processes.

This study also expands upon Sconce's and Perkins's writing on the American 'smart' film – a sub-category of indie cinema – to show dialogue's central role in creating the kind of interpersonal alienation and irony associated with smart cinema. Sconce identifies the importance of synchronicity to smart cinema, something that has been addressed in relation to dialogue by considering how the cinematic verbalists' synchronise speech with other visual, verbal and aural cues to create 'closed worlds'. Indeed dialogue such as the cinematic verbalists', which encourages audioviewers to 'fill in the blanks', is another way in which such cinema can be classified as 'smart'. The same could be said for dialogue that expresses less narrative information than is typical in generic cinema, with characters failing to say things for our benefit if they are redundant in the diegetic world.

In terms of the implications of this study to dialogue in art cinema (as another kind of non-mainstream cinema), it is worth briefly visiting Elsaesser's (1994) argument that audiences accept art films as an unspoken challenge. He explains how 'the tasks of the art film are intuitively recognized by the spectator and either avoided as a chore or sought as a challenge' (24). Challenging dialogue seems fundamental to audiences classifying certain films as 'independent' or 'art', regardless of whether they are strictly independent (from a production perspective) or art-house (from a distribution perspective). As has been shown, certain *Nouvelle Vague* auteurs, and certain New Hollywood auteurs, have had a strong influence on the dialogue in contemporary American independent cinema. These earlier filmmakers can be regarded as pioneers of certain components of cinematic verbalism, but they incorporate these elements less consistently, and in a less encompassing way.

All three groupings can include declamatory characters who engage in talk for its own sake, or whose speech is made intentionally digressive and, at points, inaudible. Of the *Nouvelle Vague* filmmakers, Godard aligns most fully with the criteria laid out for cinematic verbalism. Although carefully integrating speech with the soundtrack, embedded texts and intertitles, he tends to use these techniques to alienate through distanciation rather than to provide audioviewers with the pleasure of feeling 'smart' when recognising the norms of film dialogue that are playfully being subverted. The performance of Rohmer's dialogue is cinematic from the perspective of actors' performances that indicate interiority and suggest that the speech is being improvised. Yet Rohmer does not design intricate relationships between the dialogue and the rest of the soundtrack, nor between the dialogue and intertitles or words embedded in the mise en scène. The same could be said for Truffaut and Malle, who foreground spoken words but are less concerned than the cinematic verbalists with combining the words with the sound and image tracks in order to create 'closed' worlds – ones marked by patterns between speech and image, or speech and sound or rhythm.

Like New Hollywood filmmakers such as Robert Altman, who pioneered the use of radio microphones that could provide atmospheric realism over dialogue audibility, the cinematic verbalists do not always prioritise dialogue on the sound mix. They are also indebted to Woody Allen's unashamed wordiness and to Cassavetes' experiments with digressive, naturalistic dialogue, as well as his willingness to embrace an air of improvisation – even when that was not strictly the case. At the same time, one cannot discount the impact of Hollywood verbal conventions – both as a baseline to playfully subvert and as a genuine inspiration. Just as Jaeckle (2013a) identifies similarities between the verbal stylistics of Preston Sturges and Wes Anderson, we can identify similarities between Wilson's (2013) discussion of the dialogue of Howard Hawks and those of the cinematic verbalists – since both include speech that is both naturalistic and highly stylised.

FUTURE RESEARCH DIRECTIONS

Since the cinematic verbalists typically write and direct their screenplays, points about verbal style have been made here without much ambiguity about who scripted or determined the execution of a given line. Furthermore, as explored in Chapter 7, audiences can derive additional pleasure from the dialogue when they pick up on overlaps between the words of a character and those of the filmmaker in extra-textual interviews and commentaries. This kind of authorial 'double voicing' could likely be identified and analysed elsewhere, to reveal how other filmmakers, especially other writer-directors, can use one or more character(s) as a kind of mouthpiece. But elements of this study's framework could also be applied to other *screenwriters*, in terms of identifying the components of their scripted verbal style, including screenplay references to sound and performance. Other elements could be applied to *directors*, by identifying how they integrate dialogue – written by another party or parties – with the sound and image tracks. Thus, although not a central focus of this research, the particularities of the three groupings (writers, directors and writer-directors) suggest the value of consulting screenplays during analyses of dialogue in the finished films.

Written descriptions of the dialogue's eventual execution can help distinguish between elements that reflect the writer's or director's input, or, in the case of dialogue embodiment, the input of the performer. Although naturally involving a degree of subjectivity on the part of the scholar, comparisons of the screenplay and the finished film are preferable to an absence of critical reflection on (1) the potential imprint of the screenwriter on the final film and (2) the potential of a director to leave an imprint on dialogue that (s)he did not write. Since these independent filmmakers' considerable control over each stage of the dialogue process has been shown as crucial to their dialogue's overall effect, such control appears to be a necessary (but not sufficient) condition for categorising a filmmaker as a cinematic verbalist. As such, while a screenwriter or a director who is partly responsible for the dialogue may incorporate elements of cinematic verbalism, the label of 'cinematic verbalist' is unlikely to fit if elements of the dialogue's evolution are outside of their control.

Some of the dialogue forms and functions identified here can be applied to other contemporary writer-directors. For illustrative purposes, it is worth providing some examples that indicate the value of further research into other auteurial verbal styles. As briefly discussed in Chapter 3, Tarantino is another writer-director who carefully integrates his dialogue with music and sound effects (cf. Coulthard 2012). Although the design of Tarantino's dialogue is distinctive and complex, it departs from the concept of cinematic verbalism in its extractability. Unlike the cinematic verbalists whose individual lines are generally not memorable, Tarantino's exclamatory one-liners are frequently circulated by fans.[2] Additionally, unlike the cinematic verbalists' alternation between dialogue that is more naturalistic or more stylised than that of Hollywood, Tarantino's speech tends to lack elements that channel realism. Nonetheless, given the distinctiveness of his dialogue, there is considerable scope for considering the ways in which Tarantino combines speech with the other components of his films.

Preceding Tarantino's experiments with dialogue, however, are those of Terrence Malick, Stanley Kubrick, Ingmar Bergman, Peter Greenaway and David Lynch.[3] When Malick's verbal style receives attention, scholarship tends to focus somewhat myopically on his use of voice-over.[4] In a departure from this, Patterson (2007: 37) has outlined the significance to *Badlands'* narrative of characters' distinctive communication and she notes that the audience is required to fill in gaps between what is said and what is meant. With further study, greater insights could be gained into Malick's characterisation via dialogue, as well as his use of dialogue to actively engage the audience (as inferred by Patterson's identification of 'gaps'). As with Malick, analyses of Kubrick's dialogue typically focus on the voice-over, despite Kubrick's broader appreciation for what he described as 'the magic of words'.[5] In *The Kubrick Facade: Faces and Voices in the Films of Stanley Kubrick* (2006), Jason Sperb argues that Kubrick's early films 'organize the content and meaning of diegetic experiences through the power of nondiegetic language' (2). But despite voice-overs typically being associated with a 'literary' style of dialogue – the aural authority to which Sperb refers – a case could be made for Kubrick's dialogue as cinematic and execution dependent. Consider, for example, the significance to *The Shining* (1980) of the word 'REDRUM' on the mirror; the written text is used to clarify the significance of words that had, until that point, only been spoken. Scholars of Kubrick's work have also identified the importance of vocal performance to individual dialogue scenes, as when Naremore (2007: 93) provides details of the instructions Kubrick wrote for dubbing actors working on *Paths of Glory* (1957).[6] Like with Malick, Kubrick's dialogue could benefit from further consideration of more than just his use of voice-over.

Cinematic verbalism is not necessarily limited to independent and art cinema produced in the United States, or in the English language. Marc Gervais (1999: 203) entitles a section of his Ingmar Bergman study 'Words, Dialogue, Ideas' and explains how the role of speech is 'immensely important, essential' in Bergman's work. Gervais commends Bergman for tailoring speech in *The Seventh Seal* (1957) to each character's 'essential' nature (ibid.).[7] Furthermore, he identifies the 'cinematic' nature of Bergman's dialogue, stressing that although essentially theatrical, the words are fully adapted to cinema as a medium, in part due to regular pauses and ellipses (ibid.). British writer-director Peter Greenaway is another filmmaker who appears to integrate dialogue in ways that are notably creative and medium-specific. Indeed, Greenaway is one of the filmmakers referenced by Noël Carroll (2008: 49) when he asserts that speech can be juxtaposed with imagery in stimulating ways. In his monograph on Greenaway, David Pascoe (1997) draws attention to the filmmaker's complex and experimental use of dialogue. As noted of the cinematic verbalists' use of definitions and labels, Pascoe (1997: 50–1) explains how *H is for House* (Greenaway 1973) is a study of the process of naming, including 'the bafflingly arbitrary and confusing means by which words and objects are ascribed with meaning'. Like the cinematic verbalists' use of free association, alliteration and rhyme, *H is for House*'s voice-over of words beginning with 'H' similarly makes a feature of the language's aesthetic and poetic qualities. Similarly, David Lynch's early short film *The Alphabet* (1968) features animated images accompanied by the chanting of the alphabet rhyme.

Lynch's experimental sound design receives considerable attention, but generally with a focus on his use of music and sound effects.[8] Colin Odell and Michelle Le Blanc (2007: 22) identify how Lynch uses sound to create unease, showing an understanding of the way that 'vision and sound can be deliberately dissonant or mood provoking'. They introduce their book on Lynch with a quote by Jeffrey Beaumont (Kyle MacLachlan) in *Blue Velvet* (1986): 'See that clock on the wall? In five minutes you are not going to believe what I just told you ...' (11). Like Hartley's dialogue, Lynch's dialogue often takes a riddle-like format, but Lynch typically uses circular phrasing to contribute to the mystery of his narratives, rather than to obfuscate meaning for its own sake (as Hartley is inclined to). Lynch's cinematic uses of speech could also be extended to characters revealed to be miming in *Blue Velvet* and *Mulholland Drive* (2001), and the way speech is de-familiarised when run backwards in *Twin Peaks* (1990–1). Identifying Dale Cooper's (Kyle MacLachlan) 'propensity to name' in relation to the television series, Sheli Ayers (2004: 94) insightful discussion of how 'names divide and multiply in the [show's] linguistically volatile spaces' indicates the value of considering Lynch's verbal style in further detail.

There are also overlaps between certain tendencies identified in the cinematic verbalists' dialogue and the verbal style of later filmmakers like Harmony Korine, Shane Carruth and those associated with the 'Mumblecore' movement, including Andrew Bujalski, Mark Duplass and Joe Swanberg. In J. J. Murphy's (2007: 226) analysis of Korine's screenplays, he identifies *Gummo*'s (1997) oral collage in the form of spoken songs and narrated essays. Murphy describes the 'dreamy free association' of Tummler's (Nick Sutton) dialogue (229; 234), a poetic verbal trait Korine shares with the cinematic verbalists.

More recently, *Spring Breakers* (Korine 2012) takes repeated dialogue that serves as a musical hook to the extreme, to blur the line between music and dialogue on the soundtrack (something also noted of the cinematic verbalists).

Elements of Korine's, Greenaway's and Lynch's dialogue are exaggerated in a hyper-stylised way. However, as touched on as part of Chapter 5's analysis of Greta Gerwig, filmmakers grouped under the label of 'Mumblecore' instead channel (as the name would suggest) the kind of inarticulate, realistic speech exemplified by that of Linklater and Jarmusch. Noting Gerwig's ascent from Mumblecore to Baumbach's and Stillman's films, James Lyons (2013: 164) asserts that *Greenberg* draws on Mumblecore's 'everyday emotional dysfunctionalism'. But this chain of influence seems to move in the opposite direction: Mumblecore films take the kind of dialogue-rich films driven by miscommunication that Baumbach and Linklater have been producing to a more naturalistic extreme. Although not a Mumblecore film, in analysing the sound design of the low budget sci-fi film *Primer* (Carruth 2004), Nessa Johnston (2012: 6) details how the dialogue 'strives towards a type of realism', with actors speaking over one another and leaving sentences unfinished.[9]

These points of contact between the verbal style of the cinematic verbalists and that of selected other writer-directors provides further evidence that nuanced dialogue design is important to a significant sub-section of non-mainstream cinema. Although more thorough research would be required in order to definitively rule out the suitability of the label 'cinematic verbalists' to the filmmakers briefly considered here, I would estimate that, like with the *Nouvelle Vague* auteurs, they incorporate elements of cinematic verbalism less consistently. Furthermore, the authorial verbal styles briefly outlined here are no doubt idiosyncratic and deserving of more thorough examinations. For although the cinematic verbalists generally integrate dialogue in ways that are alternatively excessive or efficient, other models of design and integration could be identified in relation to other filmmakers.

Although this book focuses on consistencies in verbal style across the cinematic verbalists' bodies of work, its approach can also provide insights into the dialogue of *individual* films. The resistance that the cinematic verbalists face when trying to obscure dialogue on the soundtrack is recalled in Claire Denis's struggle to maintain this effect in *Vendredi Soir*'s (*Friday Night*'s) (2002) subtitles. Denis asked that words or letters be omitted from the subtitles for a scene in which a conversation behind glass is largely inaudible (cited in Egoyan and Balfour 2004: 26). Denis's request was refused and, as a result, the subtitles present the dialogue with more clarity than she intended. The changes made to Denis's dialogue neatly captures the distinction made throughout this book between audience members being positioned as a 'side-participant' or 'overhearer'. In the original French version, Denis's unclear dialogue is designed to partly exclude the audioviewer, but the subtitles fully inform the audience and thus shift their position from one of 'overhearing' to one of 'side-participation'. Denis's situation also demonstrates the importance of a writer-director being in control of their dialogue at each stage in the process, thus highlighting the significance to the cinematic verbalists' dialogue of their rare control over the speech.

As revealed in Chapter 6, the gendering of speech in cinema is another topic that deserves more attention, particularly since most analysis of this nature has been carried out in relation to classical Hollywood. Such a focus fails to acknowledge subsequent developments in male and female speech. By questioning the applicability to contemporary cinema of findings on female film dialogue by DiBattista, Lawrence and Silverman this book has begun to address historic developments in cinema's verbal gender dynamics and provides an impetus for more comprehensive research on the subject. Although a tendency for performers like Julie Delpy and Anjelica Huston to play outspoken roles in these films was identified, it is worth considering the verbally 'unruly' female in contemporary cinema and television more generally, as well as broader trends in women's verbal and vocal (dis)empowerment – a topic I have since begun to research.[10]

Closing Remarks

Discussing film music, Chion (2007: 95) writes that '[i]n a way, the cinema gives us the ability to rediscover what we call music, what we have heard thousands of times, in conditions that approximate the first time by virtue of creating its own new context'. The independent film dialogue considered here reveals why the same can be said for words. When characters argue over pronunciation or provide one another with definitions, for example, they capture the sense of what it is like to hear or understand a word for the first time. Speech is not a feature unique to the medium of cinema, but this does not prevent speech from being incorporated in unique, medium-specific ways. The cinematic verbalists' awareness of this is suggested both by their dialogue's design and its execution.

Although their speech is designed for an audience's benefit, it can bear less obvious signs than generic dialogue that this is the case. Conversations do not necessarily have a clear narrative function and, rather than relationships and situations being summed up for the audience, they must piece together verbal information over time. At other points, we are reminded of the artifice of film dialogue when the cinematic verbalists' dialogue is used stylistically, as a means to engage the audioviewer through formal patterns, or to subvert mainstream dialogue norms. The distinctiveness of the cinematic verbalists' dialogue can result from choices made during the writing stage, but also from choices made at the level of performance (low volume, poor enunciation), recording (maintaining sound and image scale), or soundtrack post-production (failing to privilege dialogue above music and effects). At each stage, then, the design and execution of the cinematic verbalists' dialogue can distinguish it from more mainstream dialogue conventions.

The complex dynamics of dialogue integration prevent film speech from being reduced to the semantic content of the words. Fully capturing the way that the cinematic verbalists' dialogue works, and what their words 'tell us', is more complicated than quoting the lines. Isolating what meaning is conveyed by dialogue versus other filmic channels requires close attention to be paid. Appreciation of the ways in which dialogue is threaded throughout a given film or films also requires engagement with various sub-fields of film theory. Such efforts are as rewarding as they are complex. Examining the cinematic verbalists' dialogue not only illuminates their films, but informs our general understanding of dialogue's relationship with American independent cinema, and with film studies.

Notes

1. The full list can be viewed on the website of the American Film Institute: http://www.afi.com/100years/quotes.aspx (last accessed 18 January 2017).
2. According to Toby McShane (2013) who compiled a list of the '50 Most Memorable Quentin Tarantino Movie Quotes' for the website *whatculture.com*, debates on Tarantino's work require 'holding off from quoting the memorable lines long enough to discuss anything else'.
3. References to other early pioneers of experimental dialogue such as Woody Allen, Robert Altman, Howard Hawks, Preston Sturges and Orson Welles have also been incorporated at various points in this book.
4. For example, in Anne Latto's (2007) 'Innocents Abroad: The Young Woman's Voice in *Badlands* and *Days of Heaven*, with an Afterword on *The New World*'. See also Steven Rybin's (2012) 'Voicing Meaning: On Terrence Malick's Characters', in *Terrence Malick and the Thought of Film*.
5. Discussing *Dr. Strangelove, or: How I Learned to Stop Worrying and Love the Bomb* (1964), Kubrick referred to the 'magic of words' as the impression that 'if you can talk brilliantly about a problem, it can create the consoling illusion that it has been mastered' (cited in Sperb 2006: 63).
6. Randy Rasmussen (2005: 81) also explains the revelatory narrative details signalled by changes to HAL's voice in *2001: A Space Odyssey* (1968).
7. As Gervais (1999: 203) explains, the Knight (Sten Ardenstam) speaks philosophically and sententiously, the Squire (Sten Ardenstam) is instead 'abrupt, cynical, witty', and Jof's dialogue alternates between playful and ingratiating and lyrical solemnity.
8. Writing on Lynch's sound includes: John Richardson's (2004) 'Laura and *Twin Peaks*: Postmodern Parody and the Musical Reconstruction of the Absent Femme Fatale'; Annette Davison's (2004) '"Up in Flames": Love, Control and Collaboration in the Soundtrack to Wild at Heart'; and Robert Miklitsch's (2008) 'Real Fantasies: Connie Stevens, Silencio, and Other Sonic Phenomena in *Mulholland Drive*'.
9. Like my discussion of the cinematic verbalists' dialogue as actively engaging the audioviewer by, at times, confusing meaning, Johnston (2012: 7) also explains

how *Primer*'s dialogue is difficult to follow, with the speech instead contributing to a 'sense of bewilderment in the auditor/spectator'. See also 'Theorizing "Bad" Sound: What Puts the "Mumble" into Mumblecore?' (Johnston 2014).

10. See 'What "The Bechdel Test" Doesn't Tell Us: Examining Women's Verbal and Vocal (Dis)Empowerment in Cinema' (O'Meara 2016a).

FILMOGRAPHY

2 Days in New York, directed by Julie Delpy, France; Germany; Belgium: Polaris Film Production & Finance; Tempête Sous un Crâne; Senator Film Produktion, 2012.

2 Days in Paris, directed by Julie Delpy, France; Germany: Polaris Film Production & Finance; Tempête Sous un Crâne; 3L Filmproduktion, 2007.

2001: A Space Odyssey, directed by Stanley Kubrick, UK; USA: Metro-Goldwyn-Mayer; Stanley Kubrick Productions, 1968.

À bout de souffle/Breathless, directed by Jean-Luc Godard, France: Les Films Impéria; Les Productions Georges de Beauregard; Société Nouvelle de Cinématographie, 1960.

A Scanner Darkly, directed by Richard Linklater, USA: Warner Independent Pictures; Thousand Words; Section Eight; Detour Filmproduction; 3 Arts Entertainment, 2006.

About a Boy, directed by Nick Weitz and Paul Weitz, UK; USA: Universal Pictures, 2002.

All About Eve, directed by Joseph L. Mankiewicz, USA: Twentieth Century Fox, 1950.

Alphabet, The, directed by David Lynch, USA: Pensylvania Academy of Fine Arts, 1968.

Amateur, directed by Hal Hartley, UK; US; France: American Playhouse; Channel Four Films; La Sept Cinéma; True Fiction Pictures, 1994.

An Angel at My Table, directed by Jane Campion, New Zealand; Australia; UK: Hibiscus Films, 1990.

Annie Hall, directed by Woody Allen, USA: Rollins-Joffe Productions, 1977.

Badlands, directed by Terrence Malick, USA: Warner Bros; Pressman-Williams; Jill Jakes Production, 1973.

Bad News Bears, directed by Richard Linklater, USA: Paramount Pictures; Media Talent Group; Detour Filmproduction, 2005.

Bande à parte/Band of Outsiders, directed by Jean-Luc Godard, France: Columbia Films; Anouchka Films; Orsay Films, 1964.

Barcelona, directed by Whit Stillman, USA: Barcelona Films; Castle Rock Entertainment; Fine Line Features; Westerly Films, 1994.

Before Midnight, directed by Richard Linklater, USA; Greece: Faliro House Productions; Venture Forth; Castle Rock Entertainment; Detour Filmproduction, 2013.

Before Sunrise, directed by Richard Linklater, USA; Austria; Switzerland: Castle Rock Entertainment; Detour Filmproduction; Filmhaus Wien Universa Filmproduktios; Sunrise Production; Columbia Pictures Corporation, 1995.

Before Sunset, directed by Richard Linklater, Warner Independent Pictures; Castle Rock Entertainment; Detour Filmproduction, 2004.

Bernie, directed by Richard Linklater, USA: Mandalay Vision; Wind Dancer Productions; Detour Filmproduction; Castle Rock Entertainment; Collins House Productions; Horsethief Pictures, 2011.

Blackmail, directed by Alfred Hitchcock, UK: British International Pictures, 1929.

Blade Runner, directed by Ridley Scott, USA; Hong Kong; UK: The Ladd Company; Shaw Brothers; Warner Bros; Blade Runner Partnership, 1982.

Blue Velvet, directed by David Lynch, USA: De Laurentiis Entertainment Group, 1986.

Book of Life, The, directed by Hal Hartley, France; USA: Haut et Court; La Sept-Arte; True Fiction Pictures, 1998.

Bottle Rocket, directed by Wes Anderson, USA: Columbia Pictures Corporation; Gracie Films, 1996.

Boyhood, directed by Richard Linklater, USA: IFC Productions; Detour Filmproduction, 2014.

Broken Flowers, directed by Jim Jarmusch, USA; France: Focus Features; Five Roses; Bac Films, 2005.

Charlotte et Véronique, ou Tous les garçons s'appellent Patrick/All the Boys are Called Patrick, directed by Jean-Luc Godard, France: Les Films de la Pléiade, 1959.

Chinatown, directed by Roman Polanski, USA: Paramount Pictures; Penthouse; Long Road Productions; Robert Evans Company, 1974.

Citizen Kane, directed by Orson Welles, USA: RKO Productions; Mercury Productions, 1941.

Clerks, directed by Kevin Smith, USA: View Askew Productions; Miramax, 1994.

Clueless, directed by Amy Heckerling, USA: Paramount Pictures, 1995.

Coffee and Cigarettes, directed by Jim Jarmusch, USA; Japan; Italy: Asmik Ace Entertainment; BIM Distribuzione; Smokescreen Inc., 2003.

Conversation, The, directed by Francis Ford Coppola, USA: The Directors Company; The Coppola Company, 1974.

Damsels in Distress, directed by Whit Stillman, USA: Westerly Films, 2011.

Darjeeling Limited, The, directed by Wes Anderson, USA: Fox Searchlight Pictures; Collage Cinemagraphique; American Empirical; Dune Entertainment, 2007.

Dazed and Confused, directed by Richard Linklater, USA: Gramercy Pictures, Alphaville Films, Detour Filmproduction, 1993.

Dead Man, directed by Jim Jarmusch, USA; Germany; Japan: Pandora Filmproduktion; JVC Entertainment Networks; Newmarket Capital Group; 12 Gauge Productions: 1995.

Die Hard, directed by John McTiernan, USA: Twentieth Century Fox Film Corporation; Gordon Company; Silver Pictures, 1988.

Down by Law, directed by Jim Jarmusch, USA; West Germany: Black Snake; Grokenberger Film Produktion; Island Pictures, 1986.

Dr. Strangelove, or: How I Learned to Stop Worrying and Love the Bomb, directed by Stanley Kubrick, USA; UK: Columbia Pictures Corporation; Hawk Films, 1964.

Election, directed by Alexander Payne, USA: Bona Fide Productions; MTV Films; Paramount Pictures: 1999.

Entourage, created by Doug Ellin, USA: HBO, 2004–11.

Everybody Wants Some!!, directed by Richard Linklater, USA: Annapurna Pictures; Detour Filmproduction; Paramount Pictures, 2016.

Fantastic Mr. Fox, directed by Wes Anderson, USA: Twentieth Century Fox; Indian Paintbrush; Regency Enterprises; American Empirical Pictures, 2009.

Fast Food Nation, directed by Richard Linklater, UK; USA: Fox Searchlight; Participant Productions; HanWay Films; BBC Films; Recorded Picture Company, 2006.

Father of the Bride, directed by Vincente Minnelli, USA: MGM, 1950.

Fay Grim, directed by Hal Hartley, USA; Germany; France: HDNet Films; Neon Productions; Possible Films; This is That Productions; Zero Fiction Film, 2007.

Fight Club, directed by David Fincher, USA; Germany: Fox 2000 Pictures; Regency Enterprises; Linson Films, 1999.

Flirt, directed by Hal Hartley, USA; Germany; Japan: Neue Deutsche Filmgesellschaft; Olive Films; Pandora Filmproduktion; True Fiction Pictures, 1995.

Frances Ha, directed by Noah Baumbach, USA; Brazil: RT Features; Pine District Pictures; Scott Rudin Productions, 2012.

Frozen, directed by Chris Buck and Jennifer Lee, USA: Walt Disney Animation Studios; Walt Disney Pictures, 2013.

Garage, directed by Lenny Abrahamson, Ireland: Element Pictures; Broadcasting Commission of Ireland; Bórd Scannán na hÉireann, 2007.

Gas, Food, Lodging, directed by Allison Anders, USA: Cineville, 1992.

Ghost Dog: The Way of the Samurai, directed by Jim Jarmusch, France; Germany; USA; Japan: Pandora Filmproduktion; Arbeitsgemeinschaft der öffentlich-rechtlichen Rundfunkanstalten der Bundesrepublik Deutschland; Degeto Films; Plyfood Productions, Bac Films, Canal+, 1999.

Gilmore Girls, created by Amy Sherman-Palladino, USA: Warner Bros, 2000–7.

Girl from Monday, The, directed by Hal Hartley, USA: Possible Films; The Monday Company, 2005.

Girl, Interrupted, directed by James Mangold, USA; Germany: Columbia Pictures Corporation; Red Wagon Entertainment, 1999.

Glengarry Glen Ross, directed by James Foley, USA: GGR; New Line Cinema; Zupnik Cinema Group, 1992.

Greenberg, directed by Noah Baumbach, USA: Scott Rudin Productions; Twins Financing, 2010.

Guardians of the Galaxy, directed by James Gunn, USA; UK: Marvel Studios; Marvel Enterprises; Moving Picture Company, 2014.

Gummo, directed by Harmony Korine, USA: First Line Features; Independent Pictures, 1997.

H is for House, directed by Peter Greenaway, UK: British Film Institute, 1973.

Hannah Takes the Stairs, directed by Joe Swanberg, USA: Film Science, 2007.

Heathers, directed by Michael Lehmann, USA: New World Pictures; Cinemarque Entertainment, 1988.

Heavy, directed by James Mangold, USA: Available Light Productions, 1995.

Henry Fool, directed by Hal Hartley, USA: Shooting Gallery; True Fiction Pictures, 1997.

High Fidelity, directed by Stephen Frears, UK; USA: Touchstone Pictures; Working Title Films; Dogstar Films; New Crime Productions, 2000.

Highball, directed by Noah Baumbach, USA: Shoreline Entertainment, 1997.

His Girl Friday, directed by Howard Hawks, USA: Columbia Pictures Corporation, 1940.

Hotel Chevalier, directed by Wes Anderson, USA: France: Fox Searchlight; American Empirical Pictures, 2007.
Hours, The, directed by Stephen Daldry, USA; UK: Paramount Pictures; Miramax, 2002.
In a World, directed by Lake Bell, USA: 3311 Productions; In A World; Team G, 2013.
In Bruges, Martin McDonagh, UK; USA: Blueprint Pictures; Focus Features; Scion Films, 2008.
Intermission, directed by John Crowley, Ireland; UK: Brown Sauce Film Productions; Bórd Scannán na hÉireann, Company of Wolves, 2003.
Jack Reacher, directed by Christopher McQuarrie, USA: Paramount Pictures; Skydance Media, 2012.
Jennifer's Body, directed by Karyn Kusama, USA: Fox Atomic; Dune Entertainment, 2009.
Jules et Jim/Jules and Jim, directed by François Truffaut, France: Les Film du Carrosse; Sédif Productions, 1962.
Kicking and Screaming, directed by Noah Baumbach, USA: Trimark Pictures; Castleberg Productions; Sandollar Productions, 1995.
La Collectionneuse/The Collector, directed by Éric Rohmer, France: Les Films du Losange; Rome Paris Films, 1967.
La Maman et la Putain/The Mother and the Whore, directed by Jean Eustache, France: Elite Films; Ciné Qua Non; Les Films du Losange, 1973.
L'année dernière à Marienbad/Last Year at Marienbad, directed by Alain Resnais, France; Italy: Cocinor; Terra Film; Cormoran Films; Precitel, 1961.
Last Days of Disco, The, directed by Whit Stillman, USA: Castle Rock Entertainment; Polygram Filmed Entertainment; Westerly Films, 1998.
Laura, directed by Otto Preminger, USA: Twentieth Century Fox, 1944.
Le Feu Follet/The Fire Within, directed by Louis Malle, France: Nouvelles Éditions de Films, 1963.
Life Aquatic with Steve Zissou, The, directed by Wes Anderson, USA: Touchstone Pictures; American Empirical Pictures; Scott Rudin Productions, 2004.
Limits of Control, The, directed by Jim Jarmusch, USA; Japan: Focus Features; Entertainment Farm; PointBlank Film, 2009.
LOL, directed by Joe Swanberg, USA: IFC, 2006.
Love & Friendship, directed by Whit Stillman, Ireland; France; the Netherlands: Westerly Films; Blinder Films; Centre National de la Cinématographie et de l'Image Animée; Chic Films; Protagonist Pictures; Revolver Amsterdam, 2016.
Ma nuit chez Maud/My Night at Maud's, directed by Éric Rohmer, France: FFD; Les Films de la Pléiade; Les Films des deux mondes; Les Films du Carrosse, 1969.
Made in U.S.A., directed by Jean-Luc Godard, France: Anouchka Films; Rome Paris Films; S.E.P.I.C., 1966.
Magnolia, directed by Paul Thomas Anderson, USA: Ghoulardi Film Company; New Line Cinema; The Magnolia Project, 1999.
Man Who Knew Too Much, The, directed by Alfred Hitchcock, USA: Paramount Pictures, 1956.
Manhattan, directed by Woody Allen, USA: Jack Rollins & Charles H. Joffe Productions, 1979.
Margot at the Wedding, directed by Noah Baumbach, USA: Scott Rudin Productions, 2007.
Mean Girls, directed by Mark Waters, USA; Canada: Paramount Pictures; M.G. Films; Broadway Video, 2004.
Mean Streets, directed by Martin Scorsese, USA: Warner Brothers; Taplin – Perry – Scorsese Productions, 1973.

Metropolitan, directed by Whit Stillman, USA: Westerly Films; Allagash Films, 1990.

Midnight in Paris, directed by Woody Allen, Spain; USA; France: Mediapro; Versátil Cinema; Gravier Productions; Pontchartrain Productions, 2011.

Mistress America, directed by Noah Baumbach, USA: Brazil: Fox Searchlight Pictures; RT Features, 2015.

Moonrise Kingdom, directed by Wes Anderson, USA: Indian Paintbrush; American Empirical Pictures, 2012.

Mr. Jealousy, directed by Noah Baumbach, USA: Joel Castleberg Productions, 1997.

Mrs. Parker and the Vicious Circle, directed by Alan Parker, USA; Canada: Fine Line Features; Mayfair Entertainment; Miramax; Odyssey Entertainment; Park Bench Productions, 1994.

Mulholland Drive, directed by David Lynch, France; USA: Les Films Alain Sarde; Asymmetrical Productions; Babbo Inc.; Canal+; The Picture Factory, 2001.

My Dinner with André, directed by Louis Malle, USA: Saga Productions, Inc.; The Andre Company, 1981.

Mystery Train, directed by Jim Jarmusch, USA; Japan: JVC Entertainment Networks; Mystery Train, 1989.

Ned Rifle, directed by Hal Hartley, USA: Possible Films, 2014.

Night on Earth, directed by Jim Jarmusch, France; UK; Germany; USA; Japan: Victor Company of Japan; Victor Musical Industries; Pyramide Productions; Canal+; Pandora Cinema, 1991.

Nights and Weekends, directed by Greta Gerwig and Joe Swanberg, USA: Film Science, 2008.

Notorious, directed by Alfred Hitchcock, USA: RKO Radio Pictures, 1946.

Notting Hill, Roger Mitchell, UK; USA: Polygram Filmed Entertainment; Working Title Films; Bookshop Productions, 1999.

Oleanna, directed by David Mamet, UK; USA: Bay Kinescope; Channel Four Films; The Samuel Goldwyn Company, 1994.

Only Lovers Left Alive, directed by Jim Jarmusch, Germany; UK; France; Greece; USA; Cyprus: Recorded Picture Company; Pandora Filmproduktion; Snow Wolf Produktion; Faliro House Productions, 2013.

Paterson, directed by Jim Jarmusch, USA; France; Germany: Amazon Studios, Animal Kingdom; Inkjet Productions; K5 Film; Le Pacte, 2016.

Paths of Glory, directed by Stanley Kubrick, USA: Bryna Productions, 1957.

Pierrot le Fou, directed by Jean-Luc Godard, France; Italy: Films Georges De Beauregard; Rome Paris Films; Société Nouvelle de Cinématographie, 1965.

Possessed, directed by Curtis Bernhardt, USA: Warner Brothers, 1947.

Primer, directed by Shane Carruth, USA: ERBP, 2004.

Private Life of Don Juan, The, directed by Alexander Korda, UK: London Film Productions, 1934.

Psycho, directed by Alfred Hitchcock, USA: Shamley Productions, 1960.

Quick and the Dead, The, directed by Sam Raimi, USA; Japan: TriStar Pictures; Japan Satellite Broadcasting, 1995.

Reservoir Dogs, directed by Quentin Tarantino, USA: Live Entertainment; Dog Eat Dog Productions, 1992.

Rich are Always with Us, The, directed by Alfred E. Green, USA: First National Pictures, 1932.

Rocky Horror Picture Show, The, directed by Jim Sharman, UK; USA: Twentieth Century Fox; Michael White Productions, 1975.

Royal Tenenbaums, The, directed by Wes Anderson, USA: Touchstone Pictures; American Empirical Pictures, 2001.

Rushmore, directed by Wes Anderson, USA: American Empirical Pictures; Touchstone Pictures, 1998.

School of Rock, directed by Richard Linklater, USA; Germany, Paramount Pictures; Scott Rudin Productions; MFP Munich Film Partners GmbH & Company I Produktions KG; New Century, 2003.

Seventh Seal, The, directed by Ingmar Bergman, Sweden: Svensk Filmindustri, 1957.

sex, lies and videotape, directed by Steven Soderbergh, USA: Outlaw Productions, Virgin, 1989.

Shadows, directed by John Cassavetes, USA: Lion International, 1959.

Shining, The, directed by Stanley Kubrick, UK; USA: Warner Bros; Hawk Films; Pregrine, 1980.

Sideways, directed by Alexander Payne, USA; Hungary: Fox Searchlight Pictures; Michael London Productions, 2004.

Simple Men, directed by Hal Hartley, Italy; UK; USA: American Playhouse; Channel Four Films; Fine Line Features; True Fiction Pictures; Zenith Entertainment, 1992.

Slacker, directed by Richard Linklater, USA: Detour Filmproduction, 1991.

Snatch, directed by Guy Ritchie, UK; USA, Columbia Pictures Corporation; SKA Films, 2000.

Social Network, The, directed by David Fincher, USA: Columbia Pictures; Relativity Media; Scott Rudin Productions; Michael De Luca Productions, 2010.

Soltane Ghalbha, directed by Mohammad Ali Fardin, Iran: Misaghieh, 1968.

Sopranos, The, created by David Chase, USA: HBO, 1999–2007.

Spiral Staircase, The, directed by Robert Siodmak, USA: RKO Radio Pictures; Dore Schary Productions, 1945.

Spring Breakers, directed by Harmony Korine, USA: Muse Productions; Division Films; O' Salvation; Iconoclast; MJZ; RabbitBandini Productions, 2012.

Squid and the Whale, The, directed by Noah Baumbach, USA: American Empirical Pictures; Peter Newman Productions; InterAL; Samuel Goldwyn Films; Sony Pictures International, 2005.

Storytelling, directed by Todd Solonz, New Line Cinema, USA; Killer Films; Good Machine, 2001.

Stranger Than Paradise, directed by Jim Jarmusch, USA; West Germany: Cinesthesia Productions; Grokenberger Film Produktion; Zweites Deutsches Fernsehen, 1984.

subUrbia, directed by Richard Linklater, USA: Castle Rock Entertainment; Detour Filmproduction, 1996.

Surviving Desire, directed by Hal Hartley, USA: American Playhouse; True Fiction Pictures, 1991.

Sylvia, directed by Christine Jeffs, UK: Focus Features, 2003.

Tape, directed by Richard Linklater, USA: Detour Filmproduction; IFC Productions; Independent Digital Entertainment; The Independent Film Channel Productions, 2001.

Taxi Driver, directed by Martin Scorsese, USA: Columbia Pictures; A Bill/Phillips Production; Italo/Judeo Productions, 1976.

Things Behind the Sun, directed by Allison Anders, USA: Echo Lake Entertainment; Sidekick Entertainment, 2001.

Trainspotting, directed by Danny Boyle, UK: Channel Four Films; Figment Films; The Noel Gay Motion Picture Company, 1996.

True Heart Susie, directed by D. W. Griffith, USA: D. W. Griffith Productions, 1919.

Trust, Hal Hartley, UK; USA: Channel Four Films; Republic Pictures; True Fiction Pictures; Zenith Entertainment, 1990.

Twin Peaks, created by Mark Frost and David Lynch, USA: Lynch/Frost Productions; Propaganda Films; Spelling Entertainment, 1990–1.

Unbelievable Truth, The, directed by Hal Hartley, USA: Action Features, 1989.

Une femme est une femme/A Woman is a Woman, directed by Jean-Luc Godard, France; Italy: Euro International Film; Rome Paris Films, 1961.

Vendredi Soir/Friday Night, directed by Claire Denis, France: Arena Films; Canal+; Centre National de la Cinématographie; France 2 Cinéma, 2002.

Waking Life, directed by Richard Linklater, USA: Fox Searchlight Pictures; Independent Film Channel; Thousand Words; Flat Black Films; Detour Filmproduction, 2001.

West Wing, The, created by Aaron Sorkin, USA: John Wells Productions; Warner Bros Television, 1999–2006.

What's Your Number?, directed by Mark Mylod, USA: Regency Enterprises; New Regency Pictures, 2011.

Wire, The, created by David Simon, USA: Blown Deadline Productions; Home Box Office, 2002–8.

Witness, directed by Peter Weir, USA: Paramount Pictures; Edward S. Feldman Production, 1985.

Zazie Dans Le Métro, directed by Louis Malle, France: Nouvelles Éditions de Films, 1960.

BIBLIOGRAPHY

Aisenberg, J. (2008), 'Wes's World: Riding Wes Anderson's Vision Limited', *Bright Lights Film Journal*, No. 59, February, <http://www.brightlightsfilm.com/59/59wesanderson.php> (last accessed 28 January 2017).

Alexander Child, D. (2010), *Charlie Kaufman: Confessions of an Original Mind*, Santa Barbara: Praeger.

Altman, R. (1980), 'Moving Lips: Cinema as Ventriloquism', *Yale French Studies*, No. 60, pp. 67–79.

____ (1992), *Sound Theory, Sound Practice*, London: Routledge.

American Film Institute (2005), 'AFI's 100 Greatest Movie Quotes of All Time', 21 June, <http://www.afi.com/100years/quotes.aspx> (last accessed 28 January 2017).

Anderson, J. D. (1998), *The Reality of Illusion: An Ecological Approach to Cognitive Film Theory*, Carbondale: Southern Illinois University Press.

Anderson, J. M. (2007), 'Pie in the Sky', *Combustible Celluloid*, 11 May, <http://www.combustiblecelluloid.com/2007/waitress.shtml> (last accessed 28 January 2017).

Anderson, M. J. (2009), 'Face & Form in Rohmer: From *Ma nuit chez Maud's* Talking Cinema to the Denial of Eloquence in *Le Rayon vert*', *Tativille – A Place for Cinema & the Visual Arts*, 9 August, <http://tativille.blogspot.ie/2009/08/face-form-in-rohmer-from-ma-nuit-chez.html> (last accessed 28 January 2017).

Anderson, W. and Baumbach, N. (2009), *Fantastic Mr. Fox*, Screenplay dated 1 June 2009, <http://rushmoreacademy.com/wp-content/uploads/2007/06/fmf.pdf> (last accessed 28 January 2017).

Anderson, W. and Wilson, O. (2001), *The Royal Tenenbaums*, London: Faber & Faber.

Arnheim, R. (1967 [1932]), *Film as Art*, 4th printing, Berkeley/Los Angeles: University of California Press.

Arons, B. (1992), 'A Review of The Cocktail Party Effect', *Journal of the American Voice I/O Society,* Volume 12, No. 7, pp. 35–50.

Ascarelli, M. (2004), 'A Feminist Connection: Jane Austen and Mary Wollstonecraft', *Persuasions Online*, Vol. 25, No. 1, <http://www.jasna.org/persuasions/on-line/vol25 no1/ascarelli.html> (last accessed 25 June 2017).

Austen, J. (2005 [1805]), *Lady Susan*, Mineola: Dover Publications, Inc.

Auster, P. (2007), '*Night on Earth*: New York – Jim Jarmusch, Poet', *Criterion*, 3 September, <http://www.criterion.com/current/posts/571-night-on-earth-new-york-jim-jarmusch-poet> (last accessed 28 January 2017).

Avila, R. (2007), 'Hal Hartley, Not So Simple', originally published on *SF360.org*, reprinted in Berrettini, M. (2011), *Hal Hartley (Contemporary Film Directors)*, Champaign: University of Illinois, pp. 77–94.

Axelrod, M. (2014), *Constructing Dialogue: From* Citizen Kane *to* Midnight in Paris, New York: Bloomsbury.

Ayers, S. (2004), '*Twin Peaks*, Weak Language and the Resurrection of Affect', in E. Sheen and A. Davison (eds) *The Cinema of David Lynch: American Dreams, Nightmare Visions*, London: Wallflower Press, pp. 93–106.

Bakhtin, M. (1984), *Problems of Dostoevsky's Poetics*, edited and translated from Russian by Caryl Emerson, Minneapolis: University of Minnesota Press.

Balázs, B. (1970), *Theory of the Film: Character and Growth of a New Art*, trans. Edith Bone, New York: Dover.

Barthes, R. (1977), 'The Grain of the Voice', in S. Heath (ed.) *Image-Music-Text*, London: Fontana Press, pp. 179–89.

Basinger, J. (1993), *A Woman's View: How Hollywood Spoke to Women, 1930–1960*, New York: Knopf.

Baumann, S. (2007), *Hollywood Highbrow: From Entertainment to Art*, Princeton/ Woodstock: Princeton University Press.

Baumbach, N. (2005), The Squid and the Whale: *The Shooting Script (Newmarket Shooting Script)*, New York: Newmarket Press.

_____ (2007), Margot at the Wedding: *The Shooting Script (Newmarket Shooting Script)*, New York: Newmarket Press.

Baumbach, N. and Gerwig, G. (n.d.), *Mistress America* screenplay, *LA-screenwriter.com*, <http://la-screenwriter.com/wp-content/uploads/2015/12/Mistress-America.pdf> (last accessed 25 June 2017).

Beach, C. (2002), *Class, Language, and American Film Comedy*, Cambridge: Cambridge University Press.

Bechdel, A. (1986), 'The Rule', *in Dykes to Watch Out For*, first published in comic-strip format, Ann Arbor: Firebrand Books, p. 22.

Beckett, S. (1954), *Waiting for Godot*, New York: Grove Press.

Belber, S. (2000), '*Tape*', in M. Bigelow Dixon and A. Wegener (eds) *Humana Festival 2000: The Complete Plays*, Hanover: Smith and Kraus, pp. 1–45.

Bellow, S. (1964), *Herzog*, New York: Viking Press.

Berger, J. (1972), *Ways of Seeing*, London: BBC Publishing.

Berliner, T. (1999), 'Hollywood Movie Dialogue and the "Real Realism" of John Cassavetes', *Film Quarterly*, Vol. 52, No. 3, pp. 2–16.

_____ (2010), *Hollywood Incoherent: Narration in Seventies Cinema*, Austin: University of Texas Press.

Berrettini, M. L. (2011), *Hal Hartley (Contemporary Film Directors)*, Champaign: University of Illinois Press.

Betts, J. (n.d.), 'Movie Review: Margot at the Wedding (2007)', *therighteousremnant.com*, <http://www.therighteousremnant.com/moviereviews/margotatthewedding.asp> (last accessed 4 August 2014).

Biskind, P. (2004), *Down and Dirty Pictures: Miramax, Sundance, and the Rise of Independent Film*, New York: Simon & Schuster.

Bogosian, E. (1994), *subUrbia*, 'Festival of New American Plays', Lincoln Center Theater, New York, May.

Boon, K. A. (2008), 'Dialogue as Action: Discourse, Dialectics, and the Rhetoric of Capitalism in David Mamet's *Glengarry Glen Ross*', in *Script Culture and the American Screenplay*, Detroit: Wayne State University Press, pp. 89-113.

Bordwell, D. (1979), 'The Art Cinema as a Mode of Film Practice', *Film Criticism*, Vol. 4, Issue 1, Fall, pp. 56–64.

____ (1985), *Narration in the Fiction Film*, Madison: University of Wisconsin Press.

____ (1989a), *Making Meaning: Inference and Rhetoric in the Interpretation of Cinema*, Cambridge, MA/London: Harvard University Press.

____ (1989b), 'A Case for Cognitivism', *IRIS*, No. 9, spring, pp. 11–40.

____ (2005), 'Up Close and Impersonal: Hal Hartley and the Persistence of Tradition', *16:9*, Volume 3, No. 12, June, <http://www.16-9.dk/2005-06/side11_inenglish. htm#_ednref14> (last accessed 28 January 2017).

____ (2008), 'The Hook: Scene Transitions in Classical Cinema', *Davidbordwell.net*, January, <http://www.davidbordwell.net/essays/hook.php> (last accessed 28 January 2017).

Bordwell, D. and Carroll, N. (eds) (1996), *Post-Theory: Reconstructing Film Studies*, Madison: University of Wisconsin Press.

Bordwell, D. and Thompson, K. (1997), *Film Art: An Introduction,* 5th edition, New York/London: McGraw Hill.

Bordwell, D., Thompson, K. and Staiger, J. (1985), *The Classical Hollywood Cinema: Film Style and Mode of Production to 1960*, New York: Columbia University Press.

Boschi, E. and McNelis, T. (2012), '"Same Old Song": On Audio-visual Style in the Films of Wes Anderson', *New Review of Film and Television Studies*, Volume 10, No. 1, March, pp. 28–45.

Bourdieu, P. (1984), *Distinction: A Social Critique of the Judgement of Taste*, translated from French by Richard Nice, Cambridge, MA: Harvard University Press.

Brandon, T. J. (1956), 'Foreign Film Distribution in the U.S.', *Film Culture*, No. 2, pp. 15–17.

Brereton, P. (2012), *Smart Cinema, DVD Add-ons and New Audience Pleasures*, Basingstoke: Palgrave Macmillan.

Brooks, B. (2012), 'Greta Gerwig Goes Lovably Awkward in Frances Ha', *Movieline. com*, 21 September, <http://movieline.com/2012/09/21/greta-gerwig-frances-ha/> (last accessed 28 January 2017).

Brooks, P. (1985), *The Melodramatic Imagination: Balzac, Henry James, Melodrama and the Mode of Excess*, New York: Columbia University Press.

Brown, C. (2012), 'Whit Stillman and the Song of the Preppy', *The New York Times*, 18 March, <http://www.nytimes.com/2012/03/18/magazine/whit-stillman-and-the-wasps.html> (last accessed 28 January 2017).

Brown, E. (2012), 'The Soul of Whit', *Interview Magazine,* 5 April, <http://www. interviewmagazine.com/film/whit-stillman-damsels-in-distress/#> (last accessed 28 January 2017).

Brown, R. S. (1994), *Overtones and Undertones: Reading Film Music*, Berkeley/Los Angeles: University of California Press.

Browning, M. (2011), *Wes Anderson: Why His Movies Matter*, Santa Barbara: Praeger, ABC-CLIO.

Burrell, I. (2014), 'Jamaica Inn: BBC Sound Technicians Deny Fault for Mumbled Dialogue', *The Independent*, 23 April, <http://www.independent.co.uk/arts-enter tainment/tv/news/jamaica-inn-bbc-sound-technicians-deny-fault-for-mumbled-dia logue-9277665.html> (last accessed 28 January 2017).

Butler, J. (1997), *Excitable Speech: A Politics of the Performative*, New York/London: Routledge.

Butler, M. (1975), *Jane Austen and the War of Ideas*, Oxford: Clarendon Press.

Caley, M. and Lannin, S. (eds) (2005), *Pop Fiction: The Song in Cinema*, Bristol: Intellect.

Carney, R. (1994), *The Films of John Cassavetes: Pragmatism, Modernism and the Movies*, Cambridge: Cambridge University Press.

Carnicke, S. M. (1999), 'Lee Strasberg's Paradox of the Actor', in P. Krämer and A. Lovell (eds) *Screen Acting*, London/New York: Routledge, pp. 75–87.

Carringer, R. L. (1996), *The Making of Citizen Kane*, Berkeley/Los Angeles: University of California Press.

Carroll, N. (1988), *Mystifying Movies: Fads and Fallacies in Contemporary Film Theory*, New York: Columbia University Press.

_____ (1992), 'Cognitivism, Contemporary Film Theory and Method: A Response to Warren Buckland', *Journal of Dramatic Theory and Criticism*, Vol. 6, Issue 2, spring, pp. 199–219.

_____ (1996), 'Language and Cinema: Preliminary Notes for a Theory of Verbal Images', in *Theorizing the Moving Image*, Cambridge: Cambridge University Press, pp. 187–211.

_____ (1998), 'Interpreting Citizen Kane', in *Interpreting the Moving Image*, Cambridge/New York: Cambridge University Press, pp. 153–65.

_____ (2008), *The Philosophy of Motion Pictures,* Oxford/Malden: Blackwell.

Carson, D. (1994), 'To Be Seen but Not Heard: *The Awful Truth*', in D. Carson, L. Dittmar and J. Welsch (eds) *Multiple Voices in Feminist Film Criticism*, Minneapolis: University of Minnesota Press, pp. 213–25.

Cettl, R. (2010), *Film Talk*, Adelaide: Wider Screenings TM.

Chaudhuri, S. (2006), *Feminist Film Theorists: Laura Mulvey, Kaja Silverman, Teresa de Lauretis, Barbara Creed*, London: Routledge.

Chen, J. (n.d.), 'The Realistic Human Monster', *ReelTalkReviews.com*, <http://www.reeltalkreviews.com/browse/viewitem.asp?type=review&id=2412> (last accessed 28 January 2017).

Chion, M. (1994), *Audio-Vision: Sound on Screen,* translated from French by C. Gorbman, New York/Chichester: Columbia University Press.

_____ (1999), *The Voice in Cinema*, translated from French by C. Gorbman, New York: Columbia University Press.

_____ (2007), 'Mute Music: Polanski's *The Pianist* and Campion's *The Piano*', in D. Goldmark, L. Krämer and R. Leppert (eds), *Beyond the Soundtrack: Representing Music in Cinema*, Berkeley: University of California Press, pp. 86–96.

_____ (2009), *Film, A Sound Art*, translated from French by C. Gorbman, New York/Chichester: Columbia University Press.

Clark, H. H. and Carlson, T. B. (1982), 'Hearers and Speech Acts', *Language,* Issue 58, pp. 332–73.

'CLR Search' (2012), 'Paterson, New Jersey Demographics – Population by Race and Ethnicity', <http://www.clrsearch.com/Paterson-Demographics/NJ/Population-by-Race-and-Ethnicity> (last accessed 25 June 2017).

Coates, J. (2003), *Men Talk – Stories in the Making of Masculinities,* Malden/Oxford: Blackwell Publishing.

Cohan, S. (1997), 'Why Boys Are Not Men', in *Masked Men – Masculinity and the Movies in the Fifties,* Bloomington and Indianapolis: Indiana University Press, pp. 201–64.

Conley, T. (2006), *Film Hieroglyphs: Ruptures in Classical Cinema*, Minneapolis: University of Minnesota Press.

Connell, R. W. (2005), *Masculinities*, Cambridge: Polity.

Corliss, R. (1973), 'Notes on a Screenwriter's Theory, 1973', in B. K. Grant (ed.) *Auteurs and Authorship: A Film Reader*, Malden/Oxford: Blackwell, 2008, pp. 140–7.

____ (1974), *Talking Pictures: Screenwriters in the American Cinema, 1927–1973*, Woodstock: Overlook Press.

Corrigan, T. (1990), 'The Commerce of Auteurism: A Voice without Authority', *New German Critique*, No. 49, winter, pp. 43–57.

Coughlin, P. (2005), 'Language Aesthetics in Three Films by Joel and Ethan Coen', *The Film Journal*, Issue 12, April, <http://www.thefilmjournal.com/issue12/coens.html> (last accessed 12 July 2014).

____ (2008), 'Acting for Real: Performing Characters in Miller's Crossing and Fargo', *Journal of Popular Culture*, Vol. 41, No. 2, pp. 224–44.

Coulthard, L. (2012), 'The Attractions of Repetition – Tarantino's Sonic Style', in J. Wierzbicki (ed.) *Music, Sound and Filmmakers: Sonic Style in Cinema*, New York: Routledge, pp. 165–75.

Coyle, J. (2006), 'Robert Downey Jr. and the Art of the Chatterbox', *Canadian Press*, 16 July, <http://abclocal.go.com/wpvi/story?section=news/entertainment&id=4365160> (last accessed 15 November 2013).

Crafton, D. (1999), *The Talkies: American Cinema's Transition to Sound, 1926–1931*, Berkeley/Los Angeles/London: University of California Press.

Craw, B. and Noble, O. (2013), 'Every Woody Allen Stammer', *The Huffington Post*, 26 April, <http://www.huffingtonpost.com/2013/03/26/every-woody-allen-stammer_ n_2936067.html> (last accessed 28 January 2017).

Crisell, A. (1986), *Understanding Radio*, London: Methuen.

Cunha, T. (1998), 'Play That Funky Music Whit Boy: The Last Days of Disco', *indieWIRE*, 1 June, <http://www.indiewire.com/article/play_that_funky_music_whit _boy_the_last_days_of_discos_stillman> (last accessed 28 January 2017).

Currie, G. (2004), *Arts and Minds*, Oxford: Clarendon Press.

Dahl, R. (1988 [1970]), *Fantastic Mr. Fox*, New York: Puffin Books.

Dancyger, K. (2007), *The Technique of Film and Video Editing*, 4th edition, Burlington/ Oxford: Focal Press.

Davis, D. (2013), 'Environmental Health Trust: Beware of Digital Zombies', *newswise. com*, 29 July, <http://www.newswise.com/articles/beware-of-the-digital-zombies> (last accessed 25 June 2017).

Davison, A. (2004), '"Up in Flames": Love, Control and Collaboration in the Soundtrack to *Wild at Heart*', in E. Sheen and A. Davison (eds) *The Cinema of David Lynch: American Dreams, Nightmare Visions*, London: Wallflower Press, pp. 119–35.

Deevy, D. (2010), 'Ben Stiller Interview for Greenberg', *The Cinema Source*, 29 March, <http://www.thecinemasource.com/blog/interviews/ben-stiller-interview-for-green berg/> (last accessed 22 September 2017).

De Jonge, P. (1996), 'The Jean-Luc Godard of Long Island', *The New York Times Magazine*, 4 August, pp. 18–21.

Denby, D. (2010), 'Image Problems – "Greenberg" and "Vincere"', *The New Yorker*, 22 March, <http://www.newyorker.com/arts/critics/cinema/2010/03/22/100322crci_ cinema_denby> (last accessed 16 November 2013).

DiBattista, M. (2001), *Fast-Talking Dames*, New Haven/London: Yale University Press.

Dick, P. K. (1977), *A Scanner Darkly*, New York: Ballantine Books.

Disher, C. (2008), 'Margot at the Wedding', *dvdizzy.com*, 19 February, <http://www. dvdizzy.com/margotatthewedding.html> (last accessed 28 January 2017).

Doane, M. A. (1980), 'The Voice in the Cinema: The Articulation of Body and Space', *Yale French Studies*, No. 60, pp. 33–50.

Dorey, T. (2012), 'Fantastic Mr. Filmmaker: Paratexts and the Positioning of Wes Anderson as Roald Dahl's Cinematic Heir', *New Review of Film and Television Studies*, Volume 10, Issue 1, pp. 169–85.

Dostoevsky, F. (1864), 'Notes from Underground', *Epoch*, Issues 1–2, p. 4.

____ (1866), *The Gambler*, original publisher unknown.

Dovere, M. (2013), 'Robert Menendez, New Senate Foreign Relations Committee Chair: "No Daylight Between US, Israel On My Watch"', *Algemeiner.com*, 13 March, <http://www.algemeiner.com/2013/03/13/robert-menendez-new-senate-foreign-relations-committee-chair-no-daylight-between-us-israel-on-my-watch/> (last accessed 25 June 2017).

Dwyer, T. (2005), 'Universally Speaking: *Lost in Translation* and Polyglot Cinema', *Linguistica Antverpiensia*, Vol. 4, special issue 'Fictionalising Translation and Multilingualism', pp. 295–310.

Dyer, R. (1998 [1979]), *Stars,* revised edition, London: BFI.

____ (1982), 'Don't Look Now: The Male Pin-Up', *Screen*, Vol. 23, Nos 3–4, pp. 61–73.

Eaves, H. (2005), 'Free to Investigate: Hal Hartley', *GreenCine*, 24 April, <http://www.greencine.com/article?action=view&articleID=206> (last accessed 27 July 2014).

Eggert, B. (2007), 'The Definitives – *A Scanner Darkly*', *Deepfocusreview.com*, 6 May, <http://www.deepfocusreview.com/reviews/scannerdarkly.asp> (last accessed 24 August 2014).

Egoyan, A. and Balfour, I. (2004), 'Introduction' to *SUBTITLES – on the Foreignness of Film,* Cambridge, MA: MIT Press/Alphabet City, pp. 21–30.

Ellis, M. J. (1973), *Why People Play*, Englewood Cliffs: Prentice-Hall.

Elsaesser, T. (1985), 'Tales of Sound and Fury: Observations on the Family Melodrama', in B. Nichols (ed.) *Movies and Methods, Volume 2*, Berkeley/Los Angeles: University of California Press, pp. 165–90.

____ (1994), 'Putting on a Show: The European Art Movie', *Sight and Sound*, Vol. 4, No. 4, April, pp. 22–7.

____ (2005), *European Cinema: Face to Face with Hollywood*, Amsterdam: Amsterdam University Press.

____ (2013), 'ImpersoNations: National Cinema, Historical Imaginaries and New Cinema Europe', *Mise au point*, Issue 5, <http://map.revues.org/1480> (last accessed 23 August 2014).

Everett, C. (2012), 'Whit Stillman & Chris Eigeman Discuss Their Indie Classic "The Last Days of Disco" With Lena Dunham at BAM', *indieWIRE*, 6 April, <http://blogs.indiewire.com/theplaylist/whit-stillman-chris-eigeman-discuss-their-indie-classic-the-last-days-of-disco-with-lena-dunham-at-bam-20120406> (last accessed 20 August 2014).

Fawell, J. (1989), 'The Musicality of the Filmscript', *Literature/Film Quarterly*, Vol. 17, No. 1, pp. 44–9.

Felando, C. (2012), 'A Certain Age: Wes Anderson, Anjelica Huston and Modern Femininity', *New Review of Film and Television Studies*, Volume 10, No. 1, March, pp. 68–82.

Feld, R. (2007), 'Noah Baumbach – Home Entertainment', *Directors Guild of America Quarterly,* fall, <http://www.dga.org/Craft/DGAQ/All-Articles/0703-Fall-22007/Independent-Voice-Noah-Baumbach.aspx> (last accessed 4 August 2014).

Fellowes, J. (2012), *Downton Abbey: The Complete Scripts, Season 1*, New York: HarperCollins.

____ (2013), *Downton Abbey: The Complete Scripts, Season 2*, New York: HarperCollins.

Ferenz, V. (2008), *Don't Believe His Lies: The Unreliable Narrator in Contemporary American Cinema*, Trier: Wissenschaftlicher Verlag Trier.

Fleeger, J. (2014), *Mismatched Women: The Siren's Song through the Machine*, New York/Oxford: Oxford University Press.

Focus Features (n.d.), 'Production Notes – Broken Flowers', *Hollywood Jesus*, 25 June 2005, <http://hollywoodjesus.com/movie/broken_flowers/notes.pdf> (last accessed 12 January 2016).

Fradley, M. (2013), '"Hell is a Teenage Girl"?: Postfeminism and Contemporary Teen Horror', in J. Gwynne and N. Muller (eds) *Postfeminism and Contemporary Hollywood Cinema*, Basingstoke: Palgrave Macmillan, pp. 204–22.

Fuller, G. (1992), 'Finding the Essential: Hal Hartley an Interview by Graham Fuller', in H. Hartley, *Simple Men and Trust*, London: Faber & Faber, pp. vi–xli.

Füredi, F. (2004), *Therapy Culture: Cultivating Vulnerability in an Uncertain Age*, London/New York: Routledge.

Ganz, A. (2011), '"Let the Audience Add Up Two Plus Two. They'll Love You Forever": The Screenplay as a Self-teaching System', in J. Nelmes (ed.) *Analysing the Screenplay*, London: Routledge, pp. 127–41.

Gerrig, R. and Prentice, D. (1996), 'Notes on Audience Response', in D. Bordwell and N. Carroll (eds) *Post-Theory: Reconstructing Film Studies*, Madison: University of Wisconsin Press, pp. 388–403.

Gervais, M. (1999), *Ingmar Bergman: Magician and Prophet*, Montreal: McGill-Queen's University Press.

Ging, D. (2012), *Men and Masculinities in Irish Cinema*, Basingstoke: Palgrave Macmillan.

Goffman, E. (1959), *The Presentation of Self in Everyday Life*, New York: Anchor Books.

____ (1961), *Encounters: Two Studies in the Sociology of Interaction*, Indianapolis: Bobbs-Merrill.

Goldman, W. (1983), *Adventures in the Screen Trade: A Personal View of Hollywood and Screenwriting*, New York: Warner Books.

Gorbman, C. (1987), *Unheard Melodies: Narrative Film Music*, London: BFI.

____ (2007), 'Auteur Music', in D. Goldmark, L Krämer and R. Leppert (eds) *Beyond the Soundtrack: Representing Music in Cinema*, Berkeley: University of California Press, pp. 149–63.

Grant, C. (2000), 'auteur.com?', *Screen*, Vol. 41, No. 1, pp. 101–8.

Greene, L. (2009), 'Speaking, Singing, Screaming: Controlling the Female Voice in American Cinema', *The Soundtrack*, Vol. 2, No. 1, pp. 63–76.

Greene, L. and Kulezic-Wilson, D. (eds) (2016), *The Palgrave Handbook of Sound Design and Music in Screen Media: Integrated Soundtracks*. London: Palgrave Macmillan.

Gritten, D. (2012), 'Whit Stillman on Damsels in Distress', *The Telegraph*, 26 April, <http://www.telegraph.co.uk/culture/film/filmmakersonfilm/9228759/Whit-Stillman-on-Damsels-in-Distress.html> (last accessed 16 August 2014).

Gritten, D. (2013), 'Before Midnight: The Lovers Return', *The Telegraph*, 21 June, < http://www.telegraph.co.uk/culture/film/starsandstories/10131966/Before-Midnight-the-lovers-return.html> (last accessed 25 July 2016).

Gustafsson, H. (2013), 'A Wet Emptiness: The Phenomenology of Film Noir', in A. Spicer and H. Hanson (eds) *A Companion to Film Noir*, Malden/Oxford: John Wiley & Sons, pp. 50–67.

Hansen, M. (1991), *Babel and Babylon*, Cambridge, MA: Harvard University Press.

Harris, M. (2010), 'The Vulture Transcript: An In-depth Chat with David Fincher about *The Social Network*', *Vulture*, 21 September, <http://www.vulture.com/2010/09/vulture_transcript_david_finch.html> (last accessed 26 July 2016).

Hartley, H. (1992), *Simple Men and Trust*, London: Faber & Faber.

____ (1996), *Flirt*, London: Faber & Faber.

Hartley, H. and Kaleta, K. (2008), *True Fiction Pictures & Possible Films*, Berkeley: Soft Skull Press.

Henrie, M. C. (ed.) (2001), *Doomed Bourgeois in Love: Essays on the Films of Whit Stillman*, Wilmington:: Intercollegiate Studies Institute.

Hill, D. (2008), *Charlie Kaufman and Hollywood's Merry Band of Pranksters, Fabulists and Dreamers: An Excursion into the American New Wave*, Harpenden: Kamera Books.

Hirschberg, L. (2005), 'The Last of the Indies', *The New York Times*, 31 July, <http://www.nytimes.com/2005/07/31/magazine/31JARMUSCH.html?pagewanted=all&_r=> (last accessed 5 August 2014)

Hogan, R. (2000), 'Interview: Whit Stillman', *Beatrice*, <http://www.beatrice.com/interviews/stillman/> (last accessed 7 August 2014).

Holquist, M. (ed.) (1981), *The Dialogic Imagination – Four Essays by M. M. Bakhtin*, trans C. Emerson and M. Holquist, Austin: University of Texas Press.

Horton, J. (2013), 'The Unheard Voice in the Sound Film', *Cinema Journal*, Vol. 52, No. 4, summer, pp. 3–24.

Hrycaj, L. (2013), 'What Is This Music? Auteur Music in The Films of Wes Anderson', Wayne State University Dissertations, Thesis 662, <http://digitalcommons.wayne.edu/oa_dissertations/662> (last accessed 6 August 2014).

Hutcheon, L. (2013 [2006]), *A Theory of Adaptation*, 2nd edition, New York: Routledge.

Insdorf, A. (2005), 'Ordinary People, European-style – Or How to Spot and Independent Feature', in C. Holmlund and J. Wyatt (eds) *Contemporary American Independent Film: From the Margins to the Mainstream*, New York and Oxfordshire: Routledge, pp. 27–33.

Jacobson, H. (1985), 'The 1984 Movie Revue [*sic*]: I: Three Guys in Three Directions', *Film Comment*, January/February, pp. 54–61.

Jaeckle, J. (2013a), 'The Verbal Stylistics of Preston Sturges and Wes Anderson', *New Review of Film and Television Studies*, Vol. 11, Issue 2, pp. 154–70.

____ (2013b), 'Introduction: A Brief Primer for Film Dialogue Study', in J. Jaeckle (ed.) *Film Dialogue*, New York/Chichester: Wallflower Press, pp. 1–16.

Johnson, C. L. (1990), *Jane Austen: Women, Politics, and the Novel*, Chicago/London: University of Chicago Press.

Johnson, D. T. (2012), *Richard Linklater* (*Contemporary Film Directors*), Champaign: University of Illinois Press.

Johnston, N. (2012), 'Beneath Sci-Fi Sound: Primer, Science Fiction Sound Design, and American Independent Cinema', *Alphaville Journal of Film and Screen Media*, No. 3, summer, <http://www.alphavillejournal.com/Issue%203/HTML/ArticleJohnston.html> (last accessed 22 September 2017).

____ (2014), 'Theorizing "Bad" Sound: What Puts the "Mumble" into Mumblecore?' *The Velvet Light Trap*, No. 74, fall, pp. 67–79.

Joyce, J. (1922), *Ulysses*, Paris: Sylvia Beach.

Kael, P. (1971), 'Onwards and Upwards with the Arts: Raising Kane', *The New Yorker*, 20 February and 27 February, reprinted in Kael, P. (1994), *For Keeps: 30 Years at the Movies*, New York: Dutton.

____ (1993), *5001 Nights at the Movies: Shorter Reviews from the Silents to the '90s*, New York/London: Boyars.

Kafka, F. (1915), *The Metamorphosis*, originally published in German as *Die Verwandlung*, Leipzig: Kurt Wolff Verlag.

Kawin, B. (1972), *Telling It Again and Again: Repetition in Literature and Film*, Ithaca: Cornell University Press.

Keogh, P. (2008), 'The Conversation (1974)', in D. Sterritt and J. Anderson (eds) *The B List: The National Society of Film Critics on the Low-budget Beauties, Genre-bending Mavericks, and Cult Classics We Love*, Cambridge, MA: Da Capo Press, pp. 63–7.

Kertzer, A. (2011), 'Fidelity, Felicity, and Playing around in Wes Anderson's *The Fantastic Mr. Fox*', *Children's Literature Association Quarterly*, Vol. 36, No. 1, spring, pp. 4–24.

King, B. (1985), 'Articulating Stardom', *Screen*, Vol. 26, Issue 5, pp. 27–50.

King, G. (2002), *New Hollywood Cinema – An Introduction*, London/New York: I. B. Tauris.

____ (2005), *American Independent Cinema*, London: I. B. Tauris.

____ (2009), *Indiewood, USA: Where Hollywood Meets Independent Cinema*, London: I. B. Tauris.

Kord, S. and Krimmer, E. (2005), 'Hidden Alternatives: Judi Dench, Kathy Bates, Parker Posey, Whoopi Goldberg, and Frances McDormand', in *Hollywood Divas, Indie Queens, and TV Heroines: Contemporary Screen Images of Women*, Lanham/Oxford: Rowman & Littlefield, pp. 115–41.

Koresky, M. and Reichert, J. (2004), 'A Conversation with Richard Linklater', *Reverse Shot*, 2 July, <http://reverseshot.org/interviews/entry/204/richard-linklater> (last accessed 12 January 2017).

Kozloff, S. (1989), *Invisible Storytellers: Voice-Over Narration in American Fiction Film*, Berkeley/Los Angeles/London: University of California Press.

____ (2000), *Overhearing Film Dialogue*, Berkeley/Los Angeles/London: University of California Press.

____ (2012), 'About a Clueless Boy and Girl: Voice-Over in Romantic Comedy Today', *Cinephile*, Vol. 8, No. 1, spring, pp. 5–13.

Kracauer, S. (1997 [1960]), 'Dialogue and Sound', in *Theory of Film: The Redemption of Physical Reality*, Princeton: Princeton University Press, pp. 102–33.

Krutnik, F. (2006 [1991]), *In a Lonely Street: Film Noir, Genre, Masculinity*, London: Routledge.

Kunze, P. C. (ed.) (2014), *The Films of Wes Anderson: Critical Essays on an Indiewood Icon*, New York: Palgrave Macmillan.

Latto, A. (2007), 'Innocents Abroad: The Young Woman's Voice in *Badlands* and *Days of Heaven*, with an Afterword on *The New World*', in H. Patterson (ed.) *The Cinema of Terrence Malick: Poetic Visions of America*, London/New York: Wallflower Press/Columbia University Press, pp. 88–103.

Lawrence, A. (1991), *Echo and Narcissus: Women's Voices in Classical Hollywood Cinema*, Berkeley/Los Angeles: University of California Press.

____ (1994), 'Staring the Camera Down: Direct Address and Women's Voices' in L. C. Dunn and N. A. Jones (eds) *Embodied Voices: Representing Female Vocality in Western Culture*, Cambridge: Cambridge University Press, pp. 166–79.

Lee, N. (2010), '"Let's Hug It Out, Bitch!" The Negotiation of Hegemony and Homosociality through Speech in HBO's Entourage', *Culture, Society and Masculinity*, Vol. 2, No. 2, pp. 181–98.

Leibowitz, F. (1988), 'Neither Hollywood nor Godard: The Strange Case of Stranger than Paradise', *Persistence of Vision*, Issue 6, pp. 20–5.

Levy, E. (1999), *Cinema of Outsiders: The Rise of American Independent Film*, New York/London: NYU Press.

_____ (2005), 'Squid and Whale: Baumbach on his Best Film', *Emanuel Levy: Cinema 24/7*, 14 September, <www.emanuellevy.com/interview/baumbachs-squid-and-whale-6> (last accessed 7 June 2014).

Linklater, R. and Krizan, K. (2005), Before Sunrise *and* Before Sunset: *Two Screenplays*, New York/Toronto: Vintage Books.

Lyon, D. (2001), 'Places in the Heart', in M. C. Henrie (ed.) *Doomed Bourgeois in Love: Essays on the Films of Whit Stillman*, Wilmington: Intercollegiate Studies Institute, pp. 154–60.

Lyons, J. (2013), 'Low-Flying Stars; Cult Stardom in Mumblecore', in K. Egan and S. Thomas (eds) *Cult Film Stardom: Offbeat Attractions and Processes of Cultification*, Basingstoke: Palgrave Macmillan, pp. 163–78.

McBane, B. (2016), 'Walking, Talking, Singing, Exploding ... and Silence: Chantal Akerman's Soundtracks', *Film Quarterly*, Vol. 70, No. 1, <http://www.filmquarterly.org/2016/09/walking-talking-singing-exploding/> (last accessed 20 January 2017).

MacDowell, J. (2012), 'Wes Anderson, Tone and the Quirky Sensibility', *New Review of Film and Television Studies*, Vol. 10, Issue 1, pp. 6–27.

McElhaney, J. (2006), 'Fast Talk: Preston Sturges and the Speed of Language', in M. Pomerance (ed.) *Cinema and Modernity*, New Brunswick, NJ: Rutgers University Press, pp. 273–96.

McShane, T. (2013), '50 Most Memorable Quentin Tarantino Movie Quotes', *What Culture*, February, <http://whatculture.com/film/50-most-memorable-quentin-tarantino-movie-quotes.php> (last accessed 27 August 2014).

Malcolm, P. (2005), 'Family Matters', *LA Weekly*, 13 October, <http://www.laweekly.com/2005-10-13/film-tv/family matters> (last accessed 6 September 2014).

Malinowski, B. (1923) 'Supplement 1: The Problem of Meaning in Primitive Languages', in C. Ogden and I. Richards (eds) *The Meaning of Meaning*, London: Routledge & Keegan Paul, pp. 296–336.

Manley, S. (2013), *The Cinema of Hal Hartley*, New York/London: Bloomsbury.

Marcello, S. A. (2006), 'Performance Design: An Analysis of Film Acting and Sound Design', *Journal of Film & Video*, Vol. 58, Issue 1/2, spring/summer, pp. 59–70.

Marie, M. (2003), *The French New Wave: An Artistic School*, translated from French by R. Neupert, Malden/Oxford: Blackwell.

Martens, T. (2010), 'Greenberg's Noah Baumbach on his Music-obsessed Films: "There are the People who Overthink Making Mix CDs"', *The L. A. Times Music Blog*, 2 April, <http://latimesblogs.latimes.com/music_blog/2010/04/noah-baumbach-greenberg-lcd-soundsystem-.html> (last accessed 5 August 2014).

Martin, A. (2004), 'Possessory Credit', *Framework: The Journal of Cinema and Media*, Vol. 45, Issue 1, spring, pp. 95–99.

_____ (2008), 'Secret Agents: Film Performance: From Achievement to Appreciation (Andrew Klevan)', *Undercurrent*, Issue 4, October, <http://www.fipresci.org/undercurrent/issue_0407/martin_secret.htm> (last accessed 5 August 2014).

Mathijs, E. (2012), 'From Being to Acting: Performance in Cult Cinema', in A. Taylor (ed.) *Theorizing Film Acting*, London: Routledge, pp. 135–51.

Mekas, J. (1959), 'Shoot the Screenwriters', *Village Voice*, 25 November, reprinted in J. Mekas, J. (1972), *Movie Journal: The Rise of a New American Cinema, 1959–1971*, New York: Collier Books, pp. 6–7.

Merry, S. (2015), 'Female Characters Tell it Like it is in "Mistress America"', *The Washington Post*, 13 August, <http://wapo.st/1LaKfNH?tid=ss_tw&utm_term=.c6834f7c0c83> (last accessed 25 June 2017).

Michaels, L. (1998), *The Phantom of the Cinema: Character in Modern Film*, Albany: SUNY Press.

Miklitsch, R. (2008), 'Real Fantasies: Connie Stevens, Silencio, and Other Sonic Phenomena in *Mulholland Drive*', in J. Beck and T. Grajeda (eds) *Lowering the Boom: Critical Studies in Film Sound*, Urbana and Chicago: University of Illinois Press, pp. 233–47.

Mio, T. (1994), *Simone de Beauvoir: The Making of an Intellectual Woman*, Oxford: Blackwell.

Mitry, J. (1997 [1963]), *The Aesthetics and Psychology of the Cinema*, trans. C. King, Bloomington: Indiana University Press.

Molière (1882 [1664]), *Le Tartuffe Comédie, 1664*, Cambridge, MA: Harvard University Press.

____ (1958 [1666]), *The Misanthrope: Comedy in Five Acts, 1666*, translated into English by R. Wilbur, London: Faber & Faber.

Morson, G. S. (1989), 'Parody, History, and Metaparody', in G. S. Morson and C. Emerson (eds) *Rethinking Bakhtin: Extensions and Challenges*, Evanston: Northwestern University Press, pp. 63–86.

Morson, G. S. and Emerson, C. (1990), *Mikhail Bakhtin: Creation of a Prosaics*, Stanford: Stanford University Press.

Mottram, J. (2006), *The Sundance Kids: How the Mavericks Took Back Hollywood*, London: Faber & Faber.

Murphy, J. J. (2007), *Me and You and Memento and Fargo: How Independent Screenplays Work*, New York/London: Continuum.

Nannicelli, T. and Taberham, P. (2014), 'Introduction' to *Cognitive Media Theory*, New York/London: Routledge, pp. 1–25.

Naremore, J. (1988), *Acting in the Cinema*, Berkeley/London: University of California Press.

____ (2007), *On Kubrick*, London: BFI.

Nayman, A. (2009), 'The Limits of Control', *Cineaste*, Vol. 34, Issue 4, fall, pp. 48–50.

Neale, S. (1983), 'Masculinity as Spectacle – Reflections on Men and Mainstream Cinema', *Screen*, Vol. 24, No. 6, pp. 2–17.

Negra, D. (2005), '"Queen of the Indies": Parker Posey's Niche Stardom and the Taste Cultures of Independent Film', in C. Holmlund and J. Wyatt (eds) *Contemporary American Independent Film: From the Margins to the Mainstream*, New York/Abingdon: Routledge, pp. 71–88.

Nelmes, J. (2011), 'Realism and Screenplay Dialogue', in *Analysing the Screenplay*, London: Routledge, pp. 217–36.

Nelson, E. (2002), 'A Laugh a Minute? In TV Today, That's Not Nearly Fast Enough', *Wall Street Journal*, 12 November, <http://online.wsj.com/article/SB1037053554251611508.html> (last accessed 20 August 2014).

Newman, M. Z. (2011), *Indie: An American Film Culture*, New York/Chichester: Columbia University Press.

Odell, C. and Le Blanc, M. (2007), *David Lynch*, Harpenden: Kamera Books.

O'Meara, J. (2013), 'Poetic Dialogue: Lyrical Speech in the Work of Hal Hartley and Jim Jarmusch', in M. Santos (ed.) *Verse, Voice and Vision: Poetry and the Cinema*, Lanham: Scarecrow Press, pp. 165–78.

____ (2014a), 'A Shared Approach to Familial Dysfunction and Sound Design: Wes Anderson's Influence on the Films of Noah Baumbach', in P. C. Kunze (ed.) *The Films of Wes Anderson: Critical Essays on an Indiewood Icon*, New York: Palgrave Macmillan, pp. 109–24.

____ (2014b), 'Cate Blanchett's Deconstruction of Performance through Performance', *The Cine-files: A Scholarly Journal of Cinema Studies*, Issue 6, spring, <http://www.thecine-files.com/cate-blanchetts-deconstruction-of-performance-through-performance/> (last accessed 17 August 2016).

____ (2014c), 'Inside the Outsider's Ear – Hyperacousia and Marginalized Character Identification', *The Soundtrack*, Vol. 5, Issue 2, pp. 121–9.

____ (2015), 'Character as DJ: Melomania and Diegetically Controlled Music', *The New Soundtrack*, Vol. 5, No. 2, pp. 133–51.

____ (2016a) 'What "The Bechdel Test" Doesn't Tell Us: Examining Women's Verbal and Vocal (Dis)Empowerment in Cinema', *Feminist Media Studies*, Commentary and Criticism section on 'Feminism and Sound', Vol. 16, Issue 6, pp. 120–3.

____ (2016b), 'Parker Posey as Hal Hartley's "Captive Actress"', in S. Rybin (ed.) *The Cinema of Hal Hartley: Flirting with Formalism* (Directors' Cuts Series), Chichester: Wallflower Press, pp. 144–58.

____ (forthcoming), 'The Actor-Writer as Author in the *Before Sunrise* Trilogy', *Mediascape*, special edition on The Question of Authorship in Cinema and Media.

Olsen, M. (1999), 'If I Can Dream: The Everlasting Boyhoods of Wes Anderson', *Film Comment*, January/February, pp. 12–17.

Orgeron, D. (2007), 'La Camera-Crayola: Authorship Comes of Age in the Cinema of Wes Anderson', *Cinema Journal*, Vol. 46, No. 2, winter, pp. 40–65.

Orpen, V. (2003), *Film Editing: The Art of the Expressive*, London: Wallflower Press.

O'Sullivan, C. (2008), 'Multilingualism at the Multiplex: A New Audience for Screen Translation?', *Linguistica Antverpiensia*, Vol. 6, pp. 81–95.

'PageSix.com staff', (2012) 'She Swears by It', *NY Post*, 12 March, <http://pagesix.com/2012/03/12/she-swears-by-it/> (last accessed 16 August 2014).

Pascoe, D. (1997) *Peter Greenaway: Museums and Moving Images*, London: Reaktion Books.

Patterson, H. (2007), 'Two Characters in Search of a Direction: Motivation and the Construction of Identity in Badlands', in H. Patterson (ed.) *The Cinema of Terrence Malick: Poetic Visions of America*, 2nd edition, New York/Chichester: Columbia University Press, pp. 27–39.

Paul, L. (2007), *Tales from the Cult Film Trenches: Interviews with 36 Actors from Horror, Science Fiction and Exploitation*, Jefferson: McFarland.

Peberdy, D. (2007), 'Tongue-Tied: Film and Theatre Voices in David Mamet's Oleanna', *Screening the Past*, No. 21, Special Issue: Cinema/Theatre: Beyond Adaptation, No. 21, summer, <http://tlweb.latrobe.edu.au/humanities/screeningthepast/21/david-mamet-oleanna.html> (last accessed 27 June 2014).

____ (2011), *Masculinity and Film Performance: Male Angst in Contemporary American Cinema*, Basingstoke: Palgrave Macmillan.

____ (2012), '"I'm Just a Character in Your Film": Acting and Performance from Autism to Zissou", *New Review of Film and Television Studies*, Vol. 10, Issue 1, pp. 46–67.

____ (2013a), 'Acting and Performance in Film Noir', in A. Spicer and H. Hanson (eds) *A Companion to Film Noir*, Malden/Oxford: John Wiley & Sons, pp. 318–35.

____ (2013b), 'Male Sounds and Speech Affectations: Voicing Masculinity', in J. Jaeckle (ed.) *Film Dialogue*, New York/Chichester: Wallflower Press, pp. 206–19.

Pecknold, D. (2016), '"These Stupid Little Sounds in Her Voice": Valuing and Vilifying the New Girl Voice', in J. Warwick and A. Adrian (eds) *Voicing Girlhood in Popular Music: Performance, Authority, Authenticity*, New York/London: Routledge, pp. 77–98.

Perkins, C. (2008), 'Remaking and the Film Trilogy: Whit Stillman's Authorial Triptych', *Velvet Light Trap*, Issue 61, spring, pp. 14–25.

____ (2012), *American Smart Cinema*, Edinburgh: Edinburgh University Press.

Persson, P. (2003), *Understanding Cinema: A Psychological Theory of Moving Imagery*, Cambridge, MA: Cambridge University Press.

Piazza, R., Bednarek, M. and Rossi, F. (eds) (2011) *Telecinematic Discourse: Approaches to the Language of Films and Television Series*, Amsterdam/Philadelphia: John Benjamins Publishing.

Piechota, C. L. (2006), 'Give Me a Second Grace: Music as Absolution in The Royal Tenenbaums', *Senses of Cinema*, Issue 38, February, <http://sensesofcinema.com/2006/38/music_tenenbaums/> (last accessed 26 June 2014).

Pinkerton, N. (2009), 'Whit Stillman Speaks Eleven Years After His Last Film', *The Village Voice*, 25 August, <http://www.villagevoice.com/2009-08-25/film/whit-still man-speaks-eleven-years-after-his-last-film/> (last accessed 15 August 2014).

Plantinga, C. (2009), *Moving Audioviewers: American Film and the Spectator's Experience*, Berkeley/Los Angeles/London: University of California Press.

Pomerance, M. (ed.) (2008), *A Family Affair: Cinema Comes Home*, London: Wallflower Press.

Pudovkin, V. I., Eisenstein, S. M. and Alexandrov, G. V. (1985 [1928]) 'A Statement', in J. Belton and E. Weis (eds) *Film Sound: Theory and Practice*, New York: Columbia University Press, pp. 83–5.

Rabin, S. (2009), 'Avoid a Weak Link in Screenplays', *Writer Magazine*, Vol. 122, Issue 3, March, pp. 36–8.

Rangan, P. (2015), 'In Defense of Voicelessness: The Matter of the Voice and the Films of Leslie Thornton', *Feminist Media Histories*, Vol. 1, No. 3, summer, pp. 95–126.

Raskin, R. (2002), 'Coffee and Cigarettes' in *The Art of the Short Fiction Film: A Shot by Shot Study of Nine Modern Classics*, Jefferson: McFarland, pp. 36–51.

Rasmussen, R. (2005), *Stanley Kubrick: Seven Films Analyzed*, Jefferson: McFarland.

Rawle, S. (2009), 'Hal Hartley and the Re-Presentation of Repetition', *Film Criticism*, Vol. 34, No. 1, September, pp. 58–75.

____ (2011), *Performance in the Cinema of Hal Hartley*, Amherst: Cambria Press.

____ (2013), 'Hal Hartley's "Look-out-Martin-Donovan's-in-the-House!" Shot: The Transformative Cult Indie Star–Director Relationship and Performance "Idiolect"', in K. Egan and S. Thomas (eds) *Cult Film Stardom: Offbeat Attractions and Processes of Cultification*, Basingstoke: Palgrave Macmillan, pp. 126–43.

Rea, S. (1990), 'Two Outcasts Meet in a Low-cost Comedy', *Philadelphia Inquirer*, 5 December, <http://articles.philly.com/1990-12-05/news/25920889_1_hartley-unbe lievable-truth-adrienne-shelly/2> (last accessed 10 August 2014).

____ (2012), 'Gerwig Sees 'Damsels in Distress' as Relevant Comment on Campus Life', *philly.com*, 22 April, <http://articles.philly.com/2012-04-22/news/31382736_1_ whit-stillman-distress-campus-life> (last accessed 5 August 2014).

Reay, P. (2004), *Music in Film: Soundtracks and Synergy*, London: Wallflower Press.

Richardson, J. (2004), 'Laura and *Twin Peaks*: Postmodern Parody and the Musical Reconstruction of the Absent Femme Fatale', in E. Sheen and A. Davison (eds) *The Cinema of David Lynch: American Dreams, Nightmare Visions*, London: Wallflower Press, pp. 77–92.

____ (2011), 'Neosurrealist Tendencies in Recent Films: *Waking Life* and *Be Kind Rewind*', in *An Eye for Music – Popular Music and the Audiovisual Surreal*, New York: Oxford University Press, pp. 54–108.

Richardson, J., Gorbman, C. and Vernallis, C. (2013), *The Oxford Handbook of New Audiovisual Aesthetics*, Oxford/New York: Oxford University Press.

Richardson, K. (2010), *Television Dramatic Dialogue: A Sociolinguistic Study*, New York: Oxford University Press.

Rickman, J. (2014), 'Lola Kirke (Yes, Jemima's Sis) is on the Verge of Breaking Out', *Papermag.com*, 20 May, <http://www.papermag.com/lola-kirke-yes-jemimas-sis-is-on-the-verge-of-breaking-out-1427303715.html> (last accessed 25 June 2017).

Robertson Wojcik, P. (2006), 'The Sound of Film Acting', *Journal of Film & Video*, Vol. 58, Issue 1/2, spring/summer, pp. 71–83.

Rosenbaum, J. (1996), 'A Gun Up Your Ass', *Cineaste*, Vol. 22, No. 2, June, pp. 20–3. Reprinted in Hertzberg, L. (ed.) (2001) *Jim Jarmusch: Interviews*, Jackson: University Press of Mississippi, pp. 154–65.

Roud, R. (2010 [1970]), *Jean-Luc Godard*, 3rd edition, London: BFI.

Rowe, K. (1995), *The Unruly Woman: Gender and the Genres of Laughter*, Austin: University of Texas Press.

Russell, C. (1995), *Narrative Mortality: Death, Closure, and New Wave Cinemas*, Minneapolis: University of Minnesota Press.

Rybin, S. (2012), 'Voicing Meaning: On Terrence Malick's Characters', in *Terrence Malick and the Thought of Film,* Lanham: Lexington Books, pp. 1–35.

____ (2014), 'Parker Posey: New York Flight', *The Cine-files: A Scholarly Journal of Cinema Studies,* Issue 6, spring, <http://www.thecine-files.com/parker-posey-new-york-flight/> (last accessed 10 August 2015).

Sante, L. (1989), 'Mystery Man', *Interview Magazine*, November. Reprinted in Hertzberg, L. (ed.) (2001) *Jim Jarmusch: Interviews*, Jackson: University Press of Mississippi, pp. 87–98.

Santos, M. (ed.) (2013), *Verse, Voice, and Vision: Poetry and the Cinema*, Lanham: Scarecrow Press.

Sarris, A. (1968), *The American Cinema: Directors and Directions, 1929–1968*, Chicago: University of Chicago Press.

Sconce, J. (2002), 'Irony, Nihilism and the New American 'Smart' Film', *Screen*, Vol. 43, No. 4, pp. 349–69.

Scott, A. O. (2007), 'Margot at the Wedding: Dearly Beloved, We Are Gathered Here Today to Rend One Another Apart', *The New York Times*, 16 November, <http://www.nytimes.com/2007/11/16/movies/16marg.html?_r=0> (last accessed 10 August 2014).

Segrave, K. (1997), *American Films Abroad: Hollywood's Domination of the World's Movie Screens*, Jefferson: McFarland.

Sella, M. (2001), 'Wes Anderson, Boyish Wonder', *The New York Times*, 2 December, <http://www.nytimes.com/2001/12/02/magazine/02ANDERSON.html?pagewanted=1> (last accessed 27 March 2014).

Sellors, C. P. (2010), *Film Authorship: Auteurs and Other Myths*, London: Wallflower Press.

Sergi, G. (1999), 'Actors and the Sound Gang', in P. Krämer and A. Lovell (eds) *Screen Acting*, London: Routledge, pp. 126–37.

____ (2001), 'The Sonic Playground: Hollywood Cinema and its Listeners', in M. Stokes and R. Maltby (eds) *Hollywood Spectatorship: Changing Perceptions of Cinema Audiences,* London: BFI, pp. 121–31.

Shadoian, J. (1981), 'Writing for the Screen ... Some thoughts on Dialogue', *Literature/Film Quarterly*, Vol. 9, Issue 2, pp. 85–91.

Shary, T. (2002), *Generation Multiplex: The Image of Youth in Contemporary American Cinema*, Austin: University of Texas Press.

Shingler, M. (2006a) 'Breathtaking: Bette Davis's Performance at the End of *Now, Voyager'*, *Journal of Film & Video*, Vol. 58, No. 1/2, spring/summer, pp. 46–58.

____ (2006b), 'Fasten Your Seatbelts and Prick Up Your Ears: The Dramatic Human Voice in Film', *Scope*, Issue 5, June, <http://www.nottingham.ac.uk/scope/documents/2006/june-2006/shingler.pdf> (last accessed 17 January 2016).

_____ (2010), 'Rich Voices in Talky Talkies: The Rich Are Always with Us', *The Soundtrack*, Vol. 3, Issue 2, December, pp. 109–15.

Silverman, K. (1988), *The Acoustic Mirror: The Female Voice in Psychoanalysis and Cinema*, Bloomington: Indiana University Press.

_____ (1990), 'Dis-Embodying the Female Voice', in P. Erens (ed.) *Issues in Feminist Film Criticism*. Bloomington: Indiana University Press, pp. 309–30.

Simmon, S. (2003), *The Invention of the Western Film: A Cultural History of the Genre's First Half Century*, Cambridge/New York: Cambridge University Press.

Sinha, A. (2004), 'The Use and Abuse of Subtitles', in A. Egoyan and I. Balfour (eds) *SUBTITLES – on the Foreignness of Film*, Cambridge, MA: MIT Press/Alphabet City, pp. 171–92.

Sjogren, B. (2006), *Into the Vortex: Female Voice and Paradox in Film*, Champaign: University of Illinois Press.

Skolsky, S. (1957), 'The New Look in Hollywood Men', *Photoplay*, Vol. 52, No. 1, July, pp. 41–3 and 111–12.

Smith, Jacob (2008), *Vocal Tracks: Performance and Sound Media*, Berkeley/London: University of California Press.

Smith, Jeff (1998), *The Sounds of Commerce: Marketing Popular Film Music*, New York/Chichester: Columbia University Press.

Smith, M. (1995), *Engaging Characters: Fiction, Emotion and the Cinema*, Oxford: Clarendon Press.

Smith, S. (2007), 'Voices in Film', in D. Pye and J. Gibbs (eds) *Close-Up 02*, London: Wallflower Press, pp. 159–238.

Solis, G. (2007), '"Workin' Hard, Hardly Workin'/Hey Man, You Know Me": Tom Waits, Sound, and the Theatrics of Masculinity', *Journal of Popular Music Studies*, Vol. 19, Issue 1, April, pp. 26–58.

Sonnenschein, D. (2001), *Sound Design: The Expressive Power of Music, Voice, and Sound Effects in Cinema*, Studio City: Michael Wiese Productions.

Speed, L. (2007), 'The Possibilities of Roads Not Taken: Intellect and Utopia in the Films of Richard Linklater', *Journal of Popular Film & Television*, Vol. 35, Issue 3, pp. 98–106.

Sperb, J. (2006), *The Kubrick Facade: Faces and Voices in the Films of Stanley Kubrick*, Lanham/Oxford: Scarecrow Press.

Staiger, J. (2000), 'Writing the History of American Film Reception', in *Perverse Spectators: The Practices of Film Reception*, New York/London: NYU Press, pp. 43–61.

Stillman, W. (1995), Barcelona & Metropolitan – *Tale of Two Cities*, Boston/London: Faber & Faber.

_____ (2000a), *The Last Days of Disco, With Cocktails at Petrossian Afterwards*, New York: Farrar, Straus, and Giroux.

_____ (2000b), 'An Excerpt from the Novel *The Last Days of Disco, With Cocktails at Petrossian Afterwards* by Whit Stillman', *January Magazine*, August, <http://www.januarymagazine.com/features/discoexcerpt.html> (last accessed 27 January 2017).

Stone, R. (2013), *The Cinema of Richard Linklater: Walk, Don't Run*, New York/Chichester: Columbia University Press.

Suárez, J. A. (2007), *Jim Jarmusch (Contemporary Film Directors)*, Champaign: University of Illinois Press.

Sussler, B. (1991), 'Whit Stillman', *BOMB*, Issue 34, winter, <http://bombsite.com/issues/34/articles/1392> (last accessed 14 August 2015).

Tandon, B. (2003), *Jane Austen and the Morality of Conversation*, London: Anthem Press.

Tasker, Y. (1993), *Spectacular Bodies: Gender, Genre, and the Action Cinema*, London/New York: Routledge.

____ (2002), *Working Girls: Gender and Sexuality in Popular Cinema*, 2nd edition, London: Routledge.

Tavella, D. (2007), 'Foreword', in J. Purcell, *Dialogue Editing for Motion Pictures: A Guide to the Invisible Art,* Oxford: Focal Press, pp. ix–xi.

Testa, B. (1990), 'Un Certain Regard; Characterization in the First Years of the French New Wave', in C. Zucker (ed.) *Making Visible the Invisible: An Anthology of Original Essays on Film Acting*, Metuchen/London: Scarecrow Press, pp. 92–142.

Théberge, P. (2008), 'Almost Silent: The Interplay of Sound and Silence in Contemporary Cinema and Television', in J. Beck and T. Grajeda (eds) *Lowering the Boom: Critical Studies in Film Sound*, Champaign: University of Illinois Press, pp. 51–68.

Thomas, F. (2013), 'Orson Welles' Overlapping Film Dialogue' in J. Jaeckle (ed.) *Film Dialogue*, New York/Chichester: Wallflower Press, pp. 126–39.

Thomas, S. (2013), '"Marginal Moments of Spectacle": Character Actors, Cult Stardom and Hollywood Cinema', in K. Egan and S. Thomas (eds) *Cult Film Stardom: Offbeat Attractions and Processes of Cultification*, Basingstoke: Palgrave Macmillan, pp. 37–54.

Thompson, K. (1977), 'The Concept of Cinematic Excess', *Ciné-Tracts*, Vol. 1, No. 2, summer, pp. 54–63.

____ (1999), *Storytelling in the New Hollywood: Understanding Classical Narrative Technique*, Cambridge, MA/London: Harvard University Press.

Thompson, P. (2000), "Notes on Subtitles and Superimpositions", *Chicago Media Works*, Vol. 1, No. 18, <http:/ /www.chicagomediaworks.com/2instructworks/3instruct_writings/wrsubtit.doc> (last accessed 5 August 2014).

Thoreau, H. D. (1854), *Walden*, Boston: Ticnknor and Fields.

Tobias, S. (2007), 'Margot at the Wedding', *The AV Club*, 16 November, <http://www.avclub.com/review/margot-at-the-wedding-3195> (last accessed 14 January 2017).

Tompkins, J. (2010) 'Pop Goes the Horror Score: Left Alone in *The Last House on the Left*', in Lerner, N. (ed.) *Music in the Horror Film: Listening to Fear*, New York: Routledge, pp. 98–113.

Toolan, M. (2011), '"I Don't Know What They're Saying Half the Time, but I'm Hooked on the Series" – Incomprehensible Dialogue and Integrated Multimodal Characterisation in *The Wire*', in R. Piazza, M. Bednarek and F. Rossi (eds) *Telecinematic Discourse: Approaches to the Language of Films and Television Series*, Amsterdam/Philadelphia: John Benjamins Publishing, pp. 161–84.

Tracz, T. (2003), 'Éric Rohmer – Great Directors', *Senses of Cinema*, Issue 24, January, <http://sensesofcinema.com/2003/great-directors/rohmer/> (last accessed 6 August 2014).

Troy, T. (2012), 'William Blake and *Dead Man*', *Adaptation*, Vol. 5, No. 1, pp. 57–87.

Truffaut, F. (2009), *The Films in My Life*, New York: Da Capo Press.

Truffaut, F. and Scott, H. G. (1984), *Hitchcock*, New York: Simon and Schuster.

Tzioumakis, Y. (2006), *American Independent Cinema: An Introduction*, Edinburgh: Edinburgh University Press.

____ (2012), *Hollywood's Indies: Classics Divisions, Specialty Labels and the American Film Market*, Edinburgh: Edinburgh University Press.

Vest, J. P. (2009), *Future Imperfect: Philip K. Dick at the Movies*, Lincoln, NE: University of Nebraska Press.

Von Bagh, P. and Kaurismäki, M. (1987), 'In Between Things', originally published in Finnish as 'Asioiden välissä', *Filmihullu* 5-6. Reprinted in Hertzberg, L. (ed.) (2001) *Jim Jarmusch: Interviews*, Jackson: University Press of Mississippi, pp. 71–81.

Waldron, M. (1999), *Jane Austen and the Fiction of her Time*, Cambridge/New York: Cambridge University Press.

Warner, J. (1926), 'Talking Movies', *Associated Press*, 3 September, <http://www.widescreenmuseum.com/sound/sound01.htm> (last accessed 10 August 2014).

Weiner, J. (2007), 'Unbearable Whiteness', *Slate*, 27 September, <http://www.slate.com/articles/arts/culturebox/2007/09/unbearable_whiteness.html> (last accessed 21 September 2017).

Weiner, L. (2001), 'Whit Stillman's Restorative Irony', in M. C. Henrie (ed.) *Doomed Bourgeois in Love: Essays on the Films of Whit Stillman*, Wilmington: Intercollegiate Studies Institute, pp. 19–39.

Weinstock, J. (2007) *The Rocky Horror Picture Show (Cultographies)*, London/New York: Wallflower Press.

Weis, E. (1999), 'Eavesdropping: An Aural Analogue of Voyeurism?', in P. Brophy (ed.) *Cinesonic: The World of Sound in Film*, Sydney: Southwood Press, pp. 79–107.

Weston, J. (2003), *The Film Director's Intuition: Script Analysis and Rehearsal Techniques*, Studio City: Michael Wiese Productions.

Whalen, D. (2001), 'The Apotheosis of Disco', in M. C. Henrie (ed.) *Doomed Bourgeois in Love: Essays on the Films of Whit Stillman,* Wilmington: Intercollegiate Studies Institute, pp. 119–32.

Widawski, M. (2015), *African American Slang: A Linguistic Description*, Cambridge: Cambridge University Press.

Wiegand, C. (2012), *French New Wave*, 4th edition, Harpenden: Oldcastle Books Ltd.

Wilinsky, B. (2001), *Sure Seaters: The Emergence of Art-house Cinema*, Minneapolis/London: University of Minnesota Press.

Wilkins, K. (2013), 'The Sounds of Silence: Hyper-dialogue and American Eccentricity', *New Review of Film and Television Studies*, Vol. 11, Issue 4, pp. 403–23.

Williams, A. (1980), 'Is Sound Recording Like a Language?', *Yale French Studies*, No. 60, pp. 51–66.

Wilson, B. (2013), 'The Film Dialogue of Howard Hawks', in J. Jaeckle (ed.) *Film Dialogue*, New York/Chichester: Wallflower Press, pp. 116–25.

Winters, B. (2012), '"It's All Really Happening": Sonic Shaping in the Films of Wes Anderson', in J. Wierzbicki (ed.) *Music, Sound, and Filmmakers: Sonic Style in Cinema*, Abingdon: Routledge, pp. 45–60.

'WNYC' (2013), 'Greta Gerwig Wants "Frances Ha" to Feel Like a Pop Song', WYNC podcast, 19 June, <http://www.wnyc.org/story/300309-greta-gerwig-pick-three/> (last accessed 11 January 2017).

Wood, R. (1986), *Hollywood from Vietnam to Reagan*, New York/Chichester: Columbia University Press.

Wyatt, J. (2011 [1998]), 'The Particularity and Peculiarity of Hal Hartley: An Interview', originally published in *Film Quarterly*, Vol. 52, No. 1, fall. Reprinted in Berrettini, M. (2011) *Hal Hartley (Contemporary Directors Series)*, Champaign: University of Illinois Press, pp. 71–7.

INDEX